Parental Choice
and
Educational Policy

Michael Adler
Alison Petch
Jack Tweedie

EDINBURGH UNIVERSITY PRESS

© Michael Adler, Alison Petch
and Jack Tweedie 1989

Edinburgh University Press
22 George Square, Edinburgh

Set in Linotron Palatino and
printed in Great Britain by
The Redwood Press Limited,
Trowbridge, Wilts

British Library Cataloguing
    in Publication Data
Adler, M.
Parental choice and
    educational policy.
1. School, Choice of—Scotland
I. Title   II. Petch, A.   III. Tweedie, J.
371'.009411   LB1027.9

ISBN 0 85224 555 6
      0 85224 656 0 (pbk)

CONTENTS

ACKNOWLEDGEMENTS

This book and the programme of research on which it is based could not have been completed without the support and co-operation of a large number of people and organisations. First of all, we should like to acknowledge our gratitude to the Economic and Social Research Council for awarding the grant (Grant No. E00360023) which made it possible for us to embark on the research; to the Scottish Education Department for commissioning some further work from us which enabled us to continue with our research; and to the Centre for Educational Sociology, the Research Centre for Social Sciences and the Faculty of Social Sciences at Edinburgh University which jointly provided us with some further resources when these were most needed. In addition, Jack Tweedie wishes to acknowledge the support of the Department of Political Science at the State University of New York at Binghamton.

We should, secondly, like to record our thanks to the many people who contributed to the project and, without whom, we could not possibly have completed it. We include among them Jack Brand and Peida Associates of Edinburgh for administering the survey; Jim Carnie, Susan Hutchison and Pat Sharkey for coding the questionnaires; and Howard Davis and Helen Williams for their help with the statistical analysis of school admissions. In this connection we should also like to acknowledge our very considerable indebtedness to Gillian Raab who designed and carried out the statistical analysis which is to be found in Chapter 6. Whatever merits this may have are largely attributable to her.

Thirdly, there are those who have given us help and encouragement. At a fairly early stage in the project, we organised a small seminar at which we presented early drafts of some of the material which has subsequently found its way into this book. We are grateful to Tony Bradley, David Bridges, David Bull, Tyrrell Burgess, John Gray, Chris Himsworth, Daphne Johnson, Maurice Kogan, Alastair Macbeth, Andrew McPherson, Angus Mitchell, Charles Raab, Andy Stillman and Doug Willms for their helpful comments and the general encouragement we received from them. We are also very indebted to Liz Bondi, Neil MacCormick, Andrew McPherson, Richard Parry and Charles Raab who commented on later versions of some of this material. In each case their comments prevented us from making errors and led to substantial improvements. Andrew McPherson really deserves a special mention – he has not only given us every possible encouragement, but was also largely responsible for enabling us to get further funding from the SED and for negotiating the small but nevertheless invaluable grant we obtained from Edinburgh University. We are also very grateful to the Centre for Educational Sociology for giving us access to data from their School-Leavers Surveys.

Fourthly, we should like to thank those who were the subjects of our research. We should like to record our indebtedness to all the parents who took part in our survey and to everyone we interviewed in connection with the making and implementation of policy. The names of those we interviewed in connection with the passage of the English and Scottish legislation are listed at the end of Chapter 2. Since we were committed to respecting the anonymity of the authorities concerned, those we interviewed in connection with the implementation of the legislation cannot be identified in the same way. However, their offices are listed at the end of Chapter 2. We are particularly grateful to the Directors of Education in Burns, Maxton and Watt Regions for granting us virtually unrestricted access to documents, records, meetings and members of staff, and to officials for answering our numerous questions and responding to our many requests. We should also like to record our thanks to officials in McDiarmid Region for providing us with information about appeals and to the Association of County Councils (ACC), the Association of Metropolitan Authorities (AMA), the Convention of Scottish Local Authorities (COSLA) and the Scottish Consumer Council (SCC) for granting us access to their extensive files.

We should, fifthly, record our thanks to those who have helped with the production of this book: to Valerie Chuter who was associated with the project from beginning to end and was a tremendous source of help and encouragement throughout, for typing and retyping successive versions of each chapter with such skill and for dealing with our seemingly endless amendments to the text with such good humour; to Elizabeth Clark for preparing the original figures and to the staff of Edinburgh University Press for being so patient and understanding.

Finally, we should like to thank our partners, Ruth, David and Susan who have had to live with this project and know only too well how difficult it has sometimes been.

PREFACE

This book represents the culmination of a period of collaboration which began in 1983 when Michael Adler was awarded a fairly substantial research grant to carry out a programme of research on the socio-legal and policy implications of parental choice legislation in Scotland and was joined by Alison Petch and Jack Tweedie.

The promise of collaborative research is that the whole will prove to be more than the sum of its parts, that the several participants can together produce something better than the sum of what they could each produce on their own. The danger is that the research will represent an unsatisfactory compromise between what each of the participants would separately have liked to produce. We do not wish to give the impression that the process of collaboration has always been an easy one – indeed there have been occasions when each of us has been tempted to abandon the enterprise. But we have persisted and hope that this book, which is the product of our collaboration, justifies our decision to persevere.

Although strategic decisions were taken collectively, the scope of the project and our different backgrounds and interests called for a division of labour. The project itself was in five parts which covered the events that led up to parental choice legislation in England and Wales, as well as in Scotland in the early 1980s; the implementation of the Scottish legislation in three local authorities; a survey of parents designed to ascertain their responses to the legislation and whether, and how, they took advantage of it; a detailed study of case-level decision making and the operation of the appeals machinery; and, finally, a study of the impact of the legislation on admissions to primary and secondary schools. Jack Tweedie had primary responsibility for the English legislation, for implementation in Burns Region and for the appeals process; Alison Petch was primarily responsible for the surveys of parents and for implementation in Watt Region, and took a special interest in under-age admissions; while Michael Adler took responsibility for the Scottish legislation, for implementation in Maxton Region and for the statistical analysis of school admissions. However, most of the research was jointly planned and much of it jointly carried out.

The theoretical concerns which inform this book are also, to a large extent, a product of our respective backgrounds and preoccupations. Alison Petch has a background in social work and social policy research, and was particularly interested in research from a consumer perspective; Jack Tweedie has a background in political science and in law, and had a particular interest in the place of rights in social welfare programmes; while Michael Adler, whose background is in social policy and in socio-legal research, was likewise especially interested in the relationship between legal rights and social policy. Jack Tweedie brought a North American perspective to bear on these issues, while Michael Adler and Alison Petch approached them on the basis of their British backgrounds and experience. Our approaches were inevitably somewhat different and, although they were frequently complementary, this was not always the case. In spite of this, we have tried to create a true symbiosis of our respective concerns. Whether we have succeeded is really for others to judge.

Although each of us has had some input into every chapter, we have agreed to identify our particular contributions to the book. Michael Adler and Jack Tweedie were primarily responsible for Chapter 1; Jack Tweedie (England and Wales) and Michael Adler (Scotland) were the primary authors of Chapter 2; Jack Tweedie wrote the major part of Chapter 3 dealing with Burns Region, while Alison Petch wrote the section on Watt Region and Michael Adler the section on Maxton Region; Alison Petch wrote Chapter 4; Jack Tweedie wrote most of Chapter 5 with an input from Alison Petch on under-age appeals; while Michael Adler was the primary author of Chapters 6 and 7. In addition, Michael Adler prepared the manuscript for publication.

LIST OF TABLES

LIST OF FIGURES

1

INDIVIDUAL RIGHTS AND COLLECTIVE POLICY GOALS IN EDUCATION

Parental choice of school has become one of the major concerns of educational policy in Britain. However, its importance extends far beyond its impact on schools in that it also raises a number of key issues for social policy, in particular, the place of the individual within what are often referred to as the social services; the implications of a focus on individual choice for the pursuit of collective policy goals; and where, as in the case of parental choice of school in Britain, statutory rights are enacted, the effects of individual rights on the nature and pattern of case-level decision making. It is with such issues, which are equally important outside Britain, that this book is primarily concerned. In this introductory chapter, we first discuss these three issues in a general way and then consider them in the light of recent legislation which provided stronger rights of school choice for British parents.

SOCIAL WELFARE AND THE INDIVIDUAL

Social welfare programmes typically provide benefits and services to clients in ways that are intended to promote collective welfare.[1] In deciding what benefits and services an individual client should receive, that individual's circumstances are only one of several considerations that are taken into account. Social welfare programmes have to operate within the resources that are available to them and are expected to do so in an efficient manner (Glennerster, 1975 and 1985; Walker, 1984). Moreover, they must have regard to their substantive goals, which may be expressed in distributional as well as aggregative terms. In addition to enhancing aggregate levels of well-being, the programme may be enjoined to promote the fair or equitable treatment of particular client groups or to achieve fairer or more equitable outcomes. It follows that social welfare agencies need to devise ways of balancing the claims of an individual client vis à vis those of other clients against a background of limited resources and in such a way as to promote the achievement of policy goals in an efficient manner.

The dependence of clients on social welfare programmes, coupled with those considerations that can lead programmes to disregard a particular client's circumstances, raises central questions about how social welfare programmes balance the claims of individual clients against these other concerns. In the fields of education, health, housing, social security and the personal social services, the characteristic post-war British approach has been much the same: the statutory framework and a set of general aims and objectives were laid down in brief enabling legislation, while the necessary resources were provided out of public expenditure. With the notable exception of national insurance,[2] welfare legislation did not establish rights for individual clients or the means by which such rights to welfare might be enforced. Rather, legislation imposed general duties on those who ran the services in question to promote the welfare of all their clients (Adler, 1986a). Conflicts between the individual concerns of particular clients and the collective concerns of the programme were frequently not recognised but were instead resolved by the agency in the course of case-level decision making (Parker, 1967; Foster, 1983). Clients were not seen as being entitled to particular levels of benefits or services, or to having their claims dealt with in a particular way. Rather, subject to the availability of resources, the manner in which their claims were dealt with and the level of benefits or services they received were seen to fall within the discretion of those vested with responsibility for administering the benefits or providing the service. One result of this was that the distribution of benefits and services frequently reflected the moral judgments of officials and the presence of situational constraints on decision makers as well as the collective concerns of the agency (Hill, 1969 and 1972; Lipsky, 1980; Foster, 1983; Howe, 1985).

The way in which British social welfare programmes dealt with the claims of individual clients was increasingly called into question during the 1970s. Coupled with the failure to make progress against a number of long-standing social problems such as poverty, multiple deprivation or inequalities in health and education, it led to a general loss of confidence in social policy and a withdrawal of trust from officials who staffed the services in question. This loss of confidence was, of course, fuelled by public expenditure cuts which imposed severe expenditure constraints on many social welfare programmes. One result of this was to fuel demands for greater accountability and to encourage the search for attempts to promote welfare in ways other than through the public provision of additional benefits and services.[3] Thus, governments of both political parties came to place increasing emphasis on public regulation of the private sector. Regulation has been important in some policy fields, e.g. in public health, in the private rented housing market, and in relation to minimum wages, for a long time (Cranston, 1985) but, more recently, there has been a spate of legislation covering, for example, redundancy, unfair dismissal, health and safety at work, race discrimination and sex discrimination (Baldwin and McCrudden, 1987). As far as governments were concerned, the great advantage of regulation over public provision was that it cost relatively little.

Another approach, which was particularly favoured by the Conservative Party while it was in opposition between 1974 and 1979 and, most evidently, since it was returned to government in 1979, has been to impose constraints on the discretion of those who administer the public services by granting rights to the consumers of those services. What had been regarded, by almost everyone, as unthinkable became, for many people, a necessary and desirable development. When the Conservatives were returned to government in 1979, this led to a number of important pieces of legislation. In addition to legislation enacting the Parents' Charter (which is the concern of this book and which, among other things, gave parents the right to choose schools for their children and limited the circumstances in which education authorities could refuse to go along with parental preferences), other important examples were legislation reforming the supplementary benefits scheme (in which the extension of rights was matched to a more restrictive formulation of the rules governing entitlement in an attempt to cut back on administrative costs and on overall expenditure) (Prosser, 1981; Donnison, 1982); and legislation implementing the Tenants' Charter (which extended security of tenure to public sector tenants and gave them the right to buy their homes) (for England and Wales, see Forrest and Murie, 1985; for Scotland, see Alexander, 1984).

The enactment of the Education Act 1980, which gave statutory effect in England and Wales to ideas which were first outlined in the Parents' Charter and, more particularly, the passage of the Education (Scotland) Act 1981 which, in a somewhat different and rather stronger form, gave statutory effect to these ideas in Scotland, provide a particularly good illustration of the problems inherent in the attempt to balance the claims of particular individuals against the general concerns of collective policy.

TWO ORIENTATIONS TO CASE-LEVEL DECISION MAKING

Conflicts between the claims of particular individuals and the broader concerns of social welfare programmes are resolved in case-level decision making. Two ideal-type approaches to case-level decision making can be constructed and provide a framework for analysing parental rights of school choice (Tweedie, 1989a).[4] In the first of these, case-level decision making is primarily orientated towards the achievement of collective ends, using bureaucratic standards and procedures to guide it towards the desired balance among the various ends the policy seeks to achieve. This orientation, known as the *collective welfare orientation*, emphasises the programme's responsibilities for promoting the well-being of all its clients. It can be described in terms of four characteristics. First, it focuses on the achievement of collective ends, i.e. on the socially defined goals of the programme. Secondly, it is primarily concerned with the overall pattern of case-level decisions and with the ways in which this relates to the programme's goals, rather than with the particular decisions in individual cases. Thirdly, it exercises control over case-level decisions through the development and application of bureaucratic standards and procedures. Policy makers exercise control over lower-level officials by requiring them to apply the appropriate standards and follow the recommended procedures in deciding individual cases. By altering the standards and adjusting the procedures, they attempt to produce a satisfactory pattern of outcomes (Ham and Hill, 1984). Fourthly, it recognises that resource constraints make it necessary to make trade-offs between the various ends the policy seeks to achieve. Taken together, these four characteristics entail the subordination of case-level decision making to the achievement of collective policy goals. This is, in part, because the programmes seldom have the resources to satisfy the claims of every client and, in part, because the programmes often have distributive goals.

In the second ideal-type, case-level decision making is primarily orientated to the achievement of individual ends, either through the mobilisation of individual claims or through the mediation of professional assessment, in order to ensure that case-level decision making is responsive to the particular circumstances of individual clients. This orientation, known as the *individual client orientation*, is rooted in two sets of ideals – the client's autonomy as an individual and the professional judgment of case-level workers. These two versions of the individual client orientation share many premises but also conflict in several ways. Both versions reject the subordination of case-level decision making to the achievement of collective policy goals, but differ in the emphasis they place on client autonomy and expert judgment (Mashaw, 1983; Simon, 1983). The client autonomy version can also be described in terms of four characteristics. First, it focuses on each client's case. This precludes a consideration of other factors, such as the claims of other clients or the resources of the programme. Secondly, it regards clients as autonomous individuals who are capable of deciding and acting for themselves. Thus, case-level decision making is largely responsive to clients' preferences and does not involve the application of bureaucratic standards and procedures which would impose constraints on decision makers. Thirdly, clients are encouraged to participate in the consideration of their own cases, and are entitled to challenge unfavourable decisions. Fourthly, focus on each client's case, respect for client autonomy and case-level discretion combine to preclude trade-offs between different clients.[5] Thus policy is determined by case-level decision making and the claims of clients effectively determine what the programme provides (Weale, 1983; Simon, 1985).

The expert judgment version of the individual client orientation is similar, in that it shares the first and third of these characteristics. However, it assumes that individuals are not necessarily the best judges of what is in their interests and that case-level decision making calls for the application of professional judgment. Moreover, although policy is still, in effect, determined by case-level decision making, expert judgment does enable one individual's circumstances to be compared with another's (Wilding, 1983).

Conflicts between these ideal-type orientations underlie case-level decision making in social welfare programmes. The two orientations influence the enactment of a statutory framework, the ways in which agencies structure case-level decision making, and the manner in which case-level decision makers deal with individual clients. Neither orientation entirely dominates, but social welfare programmes in Britain have clearly tended to emphasise a collective welfare orientation (Foster, 1983; Cranston, 1986; Hill and Bramley, 1986).

RIGHTS AND DISCRETION IN CASE-LEVEL DECISION MAKING

Normative discussions about the place of individual clients in social welfare programmes involve, at their core, key questions about rights. How should the circumstances of particular individuals be taken into account in case-level decision making? Different theories of rights suggest different answers (Adler, 1985). According to the 'choice theory' of rights, rights are devices which give effect to clients' choices. Within the scope of the rights in question, clients' preferences are therefore paramount and their wishes, whatever they may be, should prevail. According to the 'interest theory' of rights, rights are devices for protecting clients' interests. Although clients' rights include the interests which they have in ensuring that their wishes prevail, they include other interests as well. Case-level decisions should therefore involve a system of weighing and balancing in which clients' preferences are merely one of the factors which fall to be considered in determining how the client should be treated. MacCormick (1977) has highlighted the difference between the two theories by asking the following question:

> Are [rights] to be conceived primarily in terms of giving a special status to the choice of one individual over others in relation to a given subject matter or primarily in terms of the protection of the interests of individuals against possible forms of intrusion (or the advancement in other ways of individuals' interests)? (p.192)

Although the two theories have rather different implications for case-level decision making (to which we shall return in Chapter 7), the key point to emphasise at this stage is that, on either theory, rights impose constraints on the discretion of case-level decision makers. An agency has discretion to the extent that its officials are authorised to exercise choice in determining how it carries out its duties (Davis, 1971). Discretion can be exercised by policy makers who formulate rules, guidelines, procedures and standards to govern case-level decision making and by lower level administrators who routinely decide cases (Bull 1980a; Goodin, 1986). Having rights means that clients can invoke the duties of the agency which require it to act in certain ways. The rights that clients have correspond to those duties of the agency that they can invoke (Hohfeld, 1919; Wellman, 1980). Thus, an understanding of rights in social welfare programmes requires a detailed analysis of the duties that clients can invoke, that is, precisely what measure of control they have over the consideration and determination of their claims (Campbell, 1983).

That clients have rights does not, of course, mean that, in practice, they actually have control over the agency's actions. The extent to which they do so is an empirical question (Baldwin and Hawkins, 1984). The effects of clients' rights raise another, and more difficult, set of empirical questions. These questions address both how rights shape decisions and how they affect the programme's overall operation. Answering these questions calls for a careful empirical examination of case-level decision making.

PARENTAL RIGHTS UNDER THE 1944 AND 1945 EDUCATION ACTS

The statutory framework for post-war education was laid down in the Education Act 1944 (for England and Wales) and the Education (Scotland) Act 1945 (for Scotland).[6] Although there are many significant differences between these two pieces of legislation, their structure was very similar.

The 1944 Act laid down the statutory framework for the development of public education in England and Wales in the post-war era. Under section 36, a duty was imposed on the parent of every child of 'compulsory school age'[7] to cause him or her to receive 'efficient full-time education suitable to his age, ability and aptitude', by attending school regularly or by some other means. Section 6 required that the educational system was to be locally administered and, under section 7, a duty was imposed on local education authorities (LEAs) to ensure that 'efficient education . . . shall be available to meet the needs of the population of their area'. Section 7 also required education to be provided in three progressive stages (primary education, secondary education and further education) while section 8 required, *inter alia*, that education authorities should 'have regard to the need for securing that primary and secondary education were to be provided in separate schools'. Also under section 8, every education authority had to ensure that sufficient schools were available for its area[8] and, under section 11, to prepare and submit for the Minister of Education's approval a development plan setting out how it proposed to achieve this. Under section 61, LEAs were prohibited from charging fees at any school maintained by them, but the Act contained no further statutory restrictions on the system of schooling an authority could choose to operate.

Just as the 1944 Act laid down a statutory framework for England and Wales, so the 1945 Act performed the same function for Scotland. Under section 22, an analogous duty was imposed on the parents of school-age children to provide education for their children. Education was to be administered locally (by education authorities) and under section 1, a duty was imposed on these authorities 'to secure that adequate and efficient provision is made throughout their area of all forms of primary, secondary and further education'. Primary and secondary education were to be offered in separate schools or departments but, although it was envisaged that education would normally be free, education authorities were given the power (under section 11) to charge fees 'in a limited number of primary and secondary schools, provided it could be done . . . without prejudice to the adequate provision of free education' in other primary and secondary schools. With these general provisos, section 2 provided that the functions of an education authority were to be exercised in accordance with schemes prepared and approved by the Secretary of State for Scotland: an education authority was under a duty to prepare and submit for the Secretary of State's approval a scheme or schemes for the exercise of their powers and duties, and if so required by the Secretary of State, to submit a revised or modified scheme. More specifically, under section 21, an education authority was also under a duty to prepare and submit for the Secretary of State's approval, a 'promotion scheme' (later known as a 'transfer scheme') showing the method by which pupils were to be promoted from primary schools to secondary schools. This could also be modified or revised by the Secretary of State.

It will be seen that the 1944 and the 1945 Acts made numerous references to powers and duties. They also laid down procedures which were available to enforce those duties. As we have already noted, both pieces of legislation imposed a duty on parents to provide 'efficient education' for their children. Where a parent was in default of this duty, section 37 of the 1944 Act and section 26 of the 1945 Act imposed a further duty on the authority to impose an 'attendance order' and, if the order was not complied with, the legislation specified that the parent would be guilty of a criminal offence. Thus, parents' duties could be enforced in the courts. By contrast, the duties of education authorities could be enforced by the Minister. Under section 1 of the 1944 Act, the Minister was under a duty 'to secure the effective execution by local authorities . . . of the national policy for providing a varied and comprehensive educational service in every area' while under section 68, 'where the Minister was satisfied that any local education authority . . . [has] acted or [is] proposing to act unreasonably with respect to the exercise of any power conferred or the performance of any duty imposed . . . he may give such directions as to the exercise of the power or the performance of the duty as may appear to him to be expedient'. Similarly in Scotland, where education authorities were under a duty 'to prepare and submit for the Secretary of State a scheme or schemes for the exercise of their powers and duties', under section 59 of the 1945 Act, the Secretary of State could require any modifications or amendments he thought proper. Moreover, under section 60, he had the power to declare any authority which had failed to discharge any of the duties imposed on it by the Act to be in default of that duty and require the authority to discharge that duty.

The corollary of this emphasis in both pieces of legislation on powers and duties was a corresponding absence of any overt reference to individual rights. One can search the 1944 and 1945 Acts in vain for any reference to the rights of parents, or indeed of pupils or teachers. Of course, the absence of any overt reference to the rights of the various parties does not necessarily imply that they had no rights, and it can certainly be argued that one or two of the more prescriptive statutory duties, did create, if only by implication, a set of correlative rights. Thus, the fact that the legislation gave statutory force to the principle of free, compulsory schooling for everyone of school age implies (at least on the interest theory of rights) that children of school age had a right to free schooling. While such rights are certainly of great importance, so much so that, along with similar rights in other areas of social welfare, they have been deemed to constitute an important dimension of citizenship (Marshall, 1983; Plant, 1988), they exerted very little influence over educational decision making. In relation to choice of school, the topic with which this book is primarily concerned, section 76 of the 1944 Act, and likewise section 20 of the 1945 Act, laid down that education authorities were 'to have regard to the general principle that, so far as is compatible with the provision of suitable instruction and training and the avoidance of unreasonable public expenditure, pupils are to be educated in accordance with the wishes of their parents'. This provision was included in the legislation to provide a guarantee that education authorities would, wherever possible, continue to provide denominational schools and was clearly not intended to mean that individual pupils would necessarily and in all cases be educated in accordance with the wishes of their parents. As Lord Denning said in *Watt* v *Kesteven County Council* [1955] 1 Q.B.408, one of the leading English cases:

> [the Act] only lays down a general principle to which [the authority] must have regard. This leaves it open to [the authority] to have regard to other things as well and also to make exceptions to the general principle if it thinks fit to do so. It cannot be said that [an authority] is at fault simply because it does not see fit to comply with the parents' wishes.

Lord Denning's opinion is generally accepted as the correct interpretation of section 76 of the English Act and attempts to secure judicial backing for an interpretation of section 76 which would have required a closer adherence to parental choice were largely unsuccessful (Meredith 1981). Likewise, attempts to persuade the Minister to intervene (under section 68) on the grounds that an LEA has been 'unreasonable' in not complying with parents' wishes were also largely unsuccessful (see Chapter 2). The position in Scotland was not dissimilar and a number of Scottish decisions (most recently *Keeney* v *Strathclyde Regional Council* (1986)) have likewise made it clear that section 20 of the Scottish Act placed Scottish education authorities under a similar duty to take parents' wishes into account, but did not necessarily require authorities to give effect to them. Thus, on no occasion did ministers ever attempt to use their powers (under section 60) to declare an authority in default of its duty, or require an authority to give effect to parental wishes.

Both pieces of legislation, however, contained a small 'loophole' which parents who were really insistent and were prepared to make (and to get their children to make) a not inconsiderable sacrifice, could exploit. Any parent who kept a school-age child off school would (eventually) be served with an attendance order (under section 37(1) of the 1944 Act and section 26(1) of the 1945 Act). The detailed provisions were slightly different under the two Acts. In England, parents were given an opportunity, under section 37(4) of the 1944 Act, to request that another school be substituted for the one named in the order, and if the authority refused to comply with this request, the parents could apply to the Minister for direction as to which school should be named in the order. In Scotland, the authority was merely required (under section 26(2) of the 1945 Act) to consider 'any views expressed by the parent as to the school which he desires his child to attend'. However, under section 26(4) of the 1945 Act, parents who were aggrieved by the terms of the order could appeal to the sheriff who was empowered to 'confirm, vary or annul the order'.

Although procedures did exist for determined parents to pursue their claims and, although both the minister (in England and Wales) (Meredith, 1981) and the local sheriff (in Scotland) (Himsworth, 1980) usually decided in favour of the parent, the personal sacrifices (to parents and their children) were quite substantial and ensured that the procedures were used rather sparingly. Moreover, although a few determined parents were able to use them to secure the admission of their children to the schools of their choice, the provisions were not introduced with this end in mind, but rather to ensure that children of school age attended school.

The idea that parents, not to mention children, might have been given explicit statutory rights (over and above the implied right of school-age children to receive free primary or secondary schooling) was quite foreign to the spirit of the legislation and to the spirit of the times. A legal right is, after all, a legally enforceable claim which is made against some person (or institution) who might attempt to deny its enactment. In the case of education, a parental right would, in practice, have been enforceable against an education authority or, conceivably, against the Minister (or the Secretary of State). However, the legislation entrusted education authorities to promote the educational well-being of all the pupils and, in the event of an authority failing to do so, enabled the government to prevent an authority from exercising its powers unreasonably (under section 68 of the English Act) or to require an authority to discharge its statutory duties (under section 60 of the Scottish Act). It would not have occurred to those who framed the legislation to give rights to individual parents to use against education authorities when those same authorities had been entrusted to promote the educational well-being of all children through the progressive expansion of educational opportunities for all. Government trusted the education authorities and could itself be trusted to bring them into line if they erred by exercising their powers unreasonably or defaulted in discharging their duties. Thus the education system was, in effect, built on mutual trust and political accountability: parents were to place their trust in their local education authority to discharge its powers and duties in such a manner as to enhance their collective well-being and in the Government to restrain an unreasonable authority or require it to discharge its duties when it failed to do so. Government could likewise trust the local authorities and would therefore only be called upon to exercise its default powers very infrequently. Moreover, local and central government were accountable to the electorate and, if the electorate lost confidence in them, they could be removed from office at the next election.

SCHOOL ORGANISATION UNDER THE 1944 AND 1945 ACTS

Under the 1944 and 1945 Education Acts, English and Scottish education authorities had considerable discretion to formulate and implement educational policies as they saw fit.

Throughout the post-war period, equality of opportunity has been one of the central goals of educational policy. In the aftermath of the 1944 and 1945 Acts, equality of opportunity meant 'equality of access'. Moreover, in the context of a selective system of secondary education, equality of access meant equality of access to selective schools. Except at a handful of selective schools in Scotland, fees were abolished and thus any financial obstacle to entry was removed. Moreover, a great deal of effort was put into developing tests for identifying those who could benefit from an academic education. In this way, it was thought that bias could be eliminated, the social barriers to entry for working class children would be lowered, and selection would be on grounds of ability and aptitude alone. Professional experts devised and administered selection tests, and claimed that these tests were both objective and scientific, while education authorities based their allocation decisions on the pupils' test scores. At first, the testers' claims to objectivity were widely believed but, later on, even when this was no longer so, it was very hard for parents to argue against allocation decisions when the authority claimed that these were based on scientific evidence.

The educational system responded to increasing public expectations in a number of ways. First, the number of selective secondary school places was increased. Secondly, the examination system was reformed and non-selective secondary schools were allowed to prepare pupils for the new examinations. Thirdly, increased resources were allocated to education. However, these three responses were insufficient in themselves to prevent a growing loss of confidence in selection or its eventual demise.[9] Evidence of a large and seemingly irreducible number of errors in the selection process led to a loss of confidence in its scientific basis, while evidence of a strong and continuing relationship between social class and allocation to selective schools led to a loss of confidence in the objectivity of selection. Selection lost its credibility and, as a result, the comprehensive school gained in popularity.

The changeover from a selective to a comprehensive system of secondary education reflected a change in the goals of education policy, and a change in the meaning of equality of opportunity from 'equality of access' to 'equality of attainment'. In this sense, society could only be said to afford equality of educational opportunity 'if the proportion of people from different social, economic or ethnic categories at all levels and in all types of education was more or less the same as the proportion of these people in the population at large' (Halsey, 1972). Taking its lead from the USA (Coleman et al. 1966), governments (in particular the 1964–1970 Labour Government) experimented with the idea of positive discrimination in education (Banting, 1979). The 1964–1970 Labour Government also championed the cause of the comprehensive school which was not only seen as a more efficient but also as a fairer means of promoting equality of opportunity in education. As a result, the nature of school admissions changed. Selection was no longer the key issue and parents' attention focused instead on which school their child would attend. However, authorities could no longer rely on intelligence tests devised by educational experts to justify their admission decisions.

Although there was substantial opposition from some authorities to the abolition of selective schools (Benn and Simon, 1972; Gray, McPherson and Raffe, 1983; McPherson and Raab, 1988), there was initially a good deal of enthusiasm for reorganisation. This opposition was more successful in England and Wales, where a number of authorities have succeeded in retaining selective schools, than in Scotland, where selection has been completely abolished. But, in both cases, the replacement of selective secondary schools by non-selective secondary schools was typically presented as an extension to all of opportunities that had previously only been available to some, i.e. as a positive sum change from which some people would certainly benefit but none would lose. And, to dilute the impact of this change, many authorities devised arrangements which maintained a degree of social segregation (reflecting the considerable residential segregation characteristic of most cities and urban areas).

After a while, cracks began to appear in the new edifice. It soon became clear that, although secondary schools now enjoyed the same formal status, there were still substantial differences between them. During the 1970s, there was a growing concern (at least in England) with declining standards (see Chapter 2). Although the concern with standards was general, schools which were performing less well than others were inevitably the focus of particular attention. Leaving aside the question of whether or not governments could have done so, governments were no longer willing to buy their way out of the crisis by spending more on education.

Further problems were created by the decline in the birth rate. Primary school admissions fell by 30 per cent in the early 1970s and this effected secondary school admissions some seven years later (Central Policy Review Staff, 1977). While secondary school numbers were buoyant, there was relatively little scope for parents to challenge the administrative allocation of children to particular schools. But with falling school rolls the situation changed. Local authorities responded in a variety of ways. Some were prepared to admit pupils to 'popular' schools as long as places were available, even if this led to marked disparities in school intakes while others countenanced few exceptions to their determination of school intakes. In order to prevent a general fall in school intakes and school rolls and in the expectation that this would also produce financial savings, some authorities sought to 'rationalise' the provision of school places and embarked on programmes of school closures (Briault and Smith, 1980; Dennison, 1983; Meredith, 1984). These were frequently very contentious and produced a great deal of acrimony (Adler and Bondi, 1988). But, as far as parental choice of school was concerned, parents were increasingly prepared to challenge local authority decisions. Parents who found themselves in dispute with local authorities were not necessarily critical of comprehensive schooling or advocates of open-enrolment, their pursuit of their own preferences brought them into conflict with an important element of the collective welfare orientation. Moreover, the growing antipathy of the Conservative Party to the collective goals of the (mainly Labour-controlled) local authorities and the increasing support within the Conservative Party for policies which aimed to enhance individual freedom of choice, led the Conservatives not only to support individual challenges to local authority decisions, but also to advocate policies designed to enhance the rights of individual parents against the collective concerns of educational policy makers in local government.

SCHOOL ADMISSIONS UNDER THE 1944 AND 1945 ACTS

Under a system of selective secondary schooling which prevailed in most parts of the country (north and south of the border) until the early to mid-1970s, education authorities could determine how many selective secondary school places there were to be. However, the selection of pupils to fill those places was deemed to be a matter for 'expert judgment', i.e. for educational psychologists who devised tests of intelligence and ability and selected those tests which the authority used, and for teachers who prepared children for the tests and, in some authorities, submitted their own assessments of the children concerned. Officially there was 'parity of esteem' between selective and non-selective schools, in practice there was not and selective schools enjoyed a considerably higher status in the community. Thus, few parents whose children were offered a place at a selective school turned it down.

Most authorities gave parents an opportunity to state which selective school or schools they wished their children to be considered for. Little is known about the ways in which authorities allocated children among their selective schools. Nevertheless, it is clear that, as far as selective schools were concerned, parental preferences were routinely taken into consideration along with the child's performance in the selection tests. By contrast, few authorities gave parents any opportunity to state which non-selective school they preferred and allocation to non-selective schools was usually to the secondary school which served the area in which the child lived or which took children from the primary school which the child attended. Thus there was a degree of choice, albeit mediated by the child's performance in the selection tests, for children who attended selective schools but little, if any, for those who attended non-selective schools.

Under a system of comprehensive secondary schooling, which has prevailed throughout Scotland and over most of England and Wales since the early to mid-1970s, local authorities have had to devise a different set of procedures for allocating pupils to secondary schools. Due to local government reorganisation (which took place in England and Wales in 1974 and in Scotland in 1975), the issue was frequently decided on more than one occasion: first by the pre-reorganisation authorities and subsequently by the post-reorganisation authorities which were often faced with the task of adopting a common set of procedures in place of the disparate arrangements which had been adopted by their predecessors.

Among the transfer procedures for allocating pupils to comprehensive secondary schools were the following:

(i) *Catchment Areas*: This was already the most common means of allocating children to primary schools. Secondary schools (like primary schools) were each given a catchment area and every child who

lived in the catchment area was expected to attend the school serving
that area. Catchment areas often served identifiable local communities
but were sometimes constructed to achieve a balanced social mix.

(ii) *Feeder Primary Schools*: Each secondary school was linked to a set of
'feeder' primary schools and every child who attended a given primary school was subsequently offered a place at the associated secondary school.

(iii) *Banding*: In order to equalise the intakes to comprehensive secondary schools, some authorities operated a 'banding' system and imposed limits on intakes to ensure that no school had too many (or too
few) pupils from each ability band.

(iv) *Free Choice*: Parents could be given a free choice between all, or at
least some secondary schools. However, particularly while secondary
school numbers were buoyant, it was inevitable that some limits on
free choice would have to be imposed. In a free choice system, when a
school was over-subscribed, priority might be determined by the date
of application, distance from the school, connections with the school,
affinity for the school, the need to ensure a balanced educational mix
or some combination of these factors.

Local authorities had discretion to adopt whichever set of transfer
arrangements they deemed most appropriate. Moreover, having selected one or other of these four general approaches, they had discretion
to devise whatever detailed schemes they wished. For example, local
authorities were free to draw up catchment areas as they pleased. Authorities which chose to preserve the high status of formerly selective
schools gave them predominantly middle-class catchment areas while
authorities which sought to eliminate their erstwhile advantage had
several options open to them: previously selective schools could be
closed, or be transformed into sixth form colleges (in England and Wales
only since no such schools were established in Scotland), or have their
names changed or be allocated catchment areas which did not confer any
advantages on them. Authorities which emphasised the links between
school and community created a system of neighbourhood schools. As a
result, in the larger cities, school intakes often reflected substantial
differences in the socio-economic characteristics of the communities they
served. On the other hand, authorities which sought to establish schools
with balanced intakes sometimes devised catchment areas which resembled patchwork quilts and bore little relationship to any identifiable
community.

In Scotland, all education authorities adopted transfer schemes based
either on catchment areas or on feeder primary schools. In England and
Wales, on the other hand, the range of variation was wider and examples
of all four sets of transfer arrangements could be found (Stillman and
Maychell, 1986). As far as catchment area, feeder primary and banding
schemes were concerned, such schemes could be operated flexibly (in

which case the authority would be prepared to grant some exceptions to its general policy) or rigidly (in which case few, if any, exceptions would be accepted by the authority). However, there were invariably limits on the number of exceptions an authority was prepared to make, just as there were limits on the operation of free choice schemes, and some parents were inevitably disappointed. Many local authorities set up procedures for considering appeals from dissatisfied parents (Lewis and Birkenshaw, 1979a and 1979b) and, to a greater or lesser extent, these provided some means of weighing individual considerations against collective policy concerns.

TWO PERSPECTIVES ON SCHOOL ADMISSIONS

Parents and education authorities frequently have different perspectives on school admissions. For the authority, whether a particular child attends a given school is generally quite immaterial. Its main concern will be to ensure that pupils are distributed among schools in such a way as to facilitate good educational practices and the efficient use of resources. For parents, their child will usually be the focus of their concern. They will want to ensure that their child receives a good education and may care a great deal about which school their child attends. Parents are only concerned with one child – their child – while the authority is concerned with children collectively and cannot really focus on any one of them. From these two perspectives, two ideal type approaches to school admissions can again be constructed. These two approaches highlight the central issues involved in school admissions. While no authority would adopt either of these alternatives to the exclusion of the other, they contribute to our understanding of the conflict between the particular concerns of individual parents and the general (collective) concerns of educational policy.

The statutory duties of education authorities under the 1944 Act (in England and Wales) and the 1945 Act (in Scotland) have already been described in some detail. Their collective goals are to promote the educational well-being of all pupils in their area by providing education suited to their 'age, ability and aptitude', and, by so doing, to bring about equality of educational opportunity. Since resources are invariably limited, authorities may have to operate under quite severe resource constraints (Hewton, 1986). As far as admissions to comprehensive secondary schools and, to a lesser extent, to primary schools are concerned, we can characterise an *authority-wide approach to school admissions* in the following way. First, each school should contain a sufficient number of pupils to offer a broad set of curricular options in an efficient manner. Since small schools and/or small classes require higher spending per pupil, a decline in pupil numbers may lead either to increased costs or to a cut in the curriculum. The effects of small decreases in enrolment can be relatively minor, e.g. where there are one or two fewer pupils in each class, but, below a certain number, the effects of under-enrolment on costs per pupil or on curricular breadth (particularly at secondary school) can be crucial (Briault and Smith, 1980; McFadyen and McMillan, 1984; Dennison, 1985; Audit Commission, 1986). Secondly, each school should have a balanced academic and social mix of pupils. A balanced academic mix allows a broad curriculum to be sustained with a smaller number of pupils. However, if the academic mix is unbalanced, it will become harder and more expensive to maintain courses aimed at the under-represented group. More controversially, it is argued that children benefit socially from contact with children from diverse social backgrounds (Benn and Simon, 1972) and that levels of attainment are higher in schools with intakes that are balanced in terms of measured ability and socio-economic status (Rutter, Maughan, Mortimore, Ouston and Smith, 1979; Willms, 1986). Thirdly, no school should contain so many pupils that its facilities and/or teaching staff are over-burdened. Admitting pupils in excess of the school's capacity may require expensive extensions to the school buildings or the use of temporary accommodation if it is not to lead to overcrowding. The effects of small increases in enrolment can be relatively minor, e.g. if there are one or two extra pupils in the class, but, as over-enrolment increases, the effects can become critical, e.g. with over-sized classes, the establishment of additional classes, the use of composite classes at primary school (although this may equally be a consequence of under-enrolment), the displacement of special facilities, and pupils having to move to and from distant annexes. In addition, some authorities may adopt neighbourhood school policies which seek to promote links between schools and the communities they serve. The central principle is that all the children who are resident in the school's catchment area attend the school for that area. Although neighbourhood schools can have balanced enrolments, if schools are linked to 'natural communities' rather than to arbitrary geographical areas there may be and, particularly in the larger cities, there often are significant trade-offs between a commitment to the neighbourhood school principle and a concern for balanced school enrolments.

The importance of controlling school admissions depends on the amount of slack in the system. If schools are well resourced, the problems which would otherwise be caused by minor imbalances in enrolments can often be resolved by additional spending. But, where schools are not well resourced, this option will not be available. The consequences of falling school rolls (referred to above) make the problem particularly acute in that surplus school places are expensive while school closures are often politically damaging. Schools which had turned away pupils when rolls were high could now accept more pupils. However, where this led to an exodus from an already under-enrolled school, the effect was to amplify the problems faced by that school. The paradox of falling school rolls is that they create places which can be filled through parental choice but that, at the same time, they make it more important for authorities to control admissions in order to avoid the consequences of under-enrolment.

In spite of these dilemmas, many education authorities viewed parental choice positively. From their point of view, parental choice can serve several purposes. To the extent that schools differ and to the extent that parents know what is best for their children, parental choice may help to ensure that pupils attend appropriate schools. Parents may become more involved with their child's education if their child attends a school that they have chosen and, for this reason, children may even do better at school.[10] A large number of requests by parents away from a particular school may point to widespread dissatisfaction with the school and help the authority to identify and remedy problems faced by the school (Hirschman, 1970). Most fundamentally, however, education authorities generally acknowledge that the principle of parental responsibility for children's education implies some receptiveness on their part to parental preferences (Saran, 1973; Ribbins and Brown, 1979; Petch, 1988). As a result, most authorities are willing to admit children to schools requested by their parents as long as this does not interfere with their other concerns.

Apart from the factors already mentioned, the authority's concerns also include the costs of admission procedures. Simple allocation of pupils to schools on the basis of catchment areas is inexpensive. Allowing for some measure of parental choice requires a procedure for parents to register requests and for officials to process them. Unless there are no circumstances in which requests can be refused, the authority will have to formulate rules and guidelines to structure official decision making.[11] If some requests are refused, the authority will also have to decide whether the parents can appeal against the authority's decision and devise procedures for hearing appeals. Thus, parental choice can generate significant administrative costs which authorities may wish to take into account in formulating a policy for parental choice. In addition, the time needed to process parents' requests and the resulting uncertainty about school enrolments may cause delays to the planning process (Semple, 1980).

To conclude, several collective concerns are likely to influence an authority's approach to school admissions. Authorities do not want schools to be overcrowded. Equally, they do not want schools to be under-enrolled. They may want schools to contain a balanced academic and social mix. They will want admission procedures to be efficiently administered. And, at the same time, they may wish to enable parents to choose schools for their children. An authority will wish to take all these factors into consideration in determining its admissions procedure.

In contrast to the authority-wide approach, the *child-centred approach to school admissions* focuses on the circumstances of each individual child. The main concern is with the matching of individual children to particular schools. This can be achieved in one of two ways. Experts may assess the child's aptitude and ability and then match the child to the school that can offer the most appropriate course of education. Alternatively, parents can be given the responsibility for deciding which school their child should attend. The first of these variants on the child-centred approach was of central importance in the allocation of children to selective secondary schools but will not be considered further here. We focus instead on the second of the variants since this is central to the idea of parents' rights of school choice.

The concern to match individual children with particular schools presumes that schools are different in important ways and that one school may be more suitable for a given child than another. Schools may differ in a number of ways: first, schools may differ in the courses that are available, in the emphasis they place on particular subjects, in the ways in which subjects are taught, in the facilities they provide for particularly bright children or for slow learners, and in the extra-curricular activities they provide. Secondly, they may differ in the philosophies which the headteacher and the staff espouse, in their attitudes to religion, uniform and homework, in the disciplinary systems they employ, and in the extent to which parents are encouraged to participate in school activities. Thirdly, schools may differ in their outputs. Thus, for example, some schools achieve better examination results, or higher staying-on rates or greater success in finding jobs for school leavers than others. Fourthly, some schools are more effective than others in the sense that pupils perform better as a result of going there.[12]

In addition to these 'educational' differences, there may also be non-educational differences between schools. Thus, schools may differ in the social composition of their intakes – some may be single-sex or denominational schools, others may have primarily middle class or primarily working class catchment areas, and schools may vary in the proportion of pupils from ethnic minority backgrounds. Schools may also differ in their buildings and grounds – some may be in new, purpose-built accommodation while others may be on several sites, and some may have adjacent playing fields while others may have to share distant sports facilities. Finally, schools will differ in their locations – some will be more convenient or safer to get to while others will be less so.

The upshot of all this is that parents may have non-educational as well as educational reasons for preferring one school to another and for deciding that one school rather than another would be better for their child. Some parents may prefer a school with strong discipline and a vocational orientation although its examination record is relatively poor, on the grounds that their child is unlikely to go on to higher education but will benefit from the strong discipline and vocational courses which the school can offer. Other parents may prefer a more academic school with a better examination record, in spite of the fact that discipline is rather slack and the school offers few vocational courses, because they think that their child is likely to go onto higher education and would thrive academically in such an environment.[13]

The child-centred approach implies that parents' concerns should have priority over those of the authority. The presumption is that parents are best placed to decide what is best for their child and that the authority's concern to avoid under-enrolment or over-enrolment, or to achieve balanced academic or social intakes, should never prevent the admission of children to schools requested by their parents. Thus, the child-centred approach involves a rejection of the hierarchical relation between policy making and case-level decision making.

In the child-centred approach, authorities can look at policy in one of two ways. They can simply accept that school-admission decisions are prior to policy making. The authority would decide the best allocation of its resources given the distribution of pupils that results from parents' requests. An authority would respond to parents' requests by distributing its teaching and other resources in line with the school enrolments produced by those requests. Thus, an authority would be free to decide whether small schools should be given extra staff to maintain their curriculum and whether large schools should receive their full allocation of teachers to keep class sizes down.

Alternatively, schools could be allowed to respond to parents' requests in the same way that firms in competitive markets respond to the preferences of their customers. Schools would be run independently, making their own decisions and competing to attract parents. The prospects for each school would be tied to its ability to attract the 'business' of parents. The resources available to the school would be directly proportional to the number of pupils enrolled at the school, as if the pupils were paying fees. However, schools would be competing in terms of the quality and variety of their services rather than in terms of price. Schools that did well would prosper and expand while schools that did badly would contract. There would be pressure on these schools to improve but, if they failed to attract pupils, they would have to close just like businesses that fail to make a profit are eventually wound up. The authority's functions would be largely administrative and would comprise assisting schools in their operations, providing information to parents about schools and co-ordinating the distribution of resources to schools on the basis of their performance (Sexton, 1975; Midwinter, 1980).[14] The authority-wide and child-centred approaches to school admissions are both presented as ideal types. As such, they illuminate some of the key issues involved in school admissions and the potential for conflict between individual choice and collective policy goals, i.e. between the parents' focus on the admission of their child to the school of their choice and the authority's concern with the overall pattern of decision making. Each authority had to deal with these issues in formulating and implementing its school admission procedures. We have already seen that the 1944 and 1945 Acts gave parents few rights in relation to school admissions or, indeed, in relation to other aspects of education policy. Thus authorities were largely free to determine their own admission policies. Although no authority adopted either approach exclusively and some authorities favoured the less extravagant version of the child-centred approach, most authorities (not surprisingly) favoured the authority-centred approach and formulated their admission procedures accordingly. This position lasted until the enactment of the 1980 and 1981 Acts which gave statutory effect to the ideas outlined in the Parents Charter and established parental rights of school choice for parents.[15] The effect of the 1981 Act, which created stronger rights for parents than the 1980 Act, on case-level decision making and on the balance between the two approaches to decision making in three Scottish authorities is one of the main concerns of this book.

CLIENTS' RIGHTS IN SOCIAL WELFARE PROGRAMMES

We have already noted that rights impose duties on the agencies at which they are directed and shape case-level decision making. We have also noted that, although the implied right to free schooling was undoubtedly of great importance, there were few references to rights in either the 1944 or the 1945 Acts. This was in keeping with most of the other major pieces of social welfare legislation where there were likewise few references to clients' rights. These programmes, which were accountable through a Minister to Parliament, were enjoined to promote the collective welfare of all their clients. While they were trusted to do so, there were few problems but, with the decline of trust (also referred to above) critics began to argue for a strengthening of clients' rights as a means of furthering their interests.

Taking its cue from the civil rights movement, a welfare rights movement grew up in the United States in the 1960s. Advocates of welfare rights argued that the wide discretion exercised by officials in public agencies posed a serious threat to clients' interests and that the best way of furthering those interests was through the enactment and strengthening of legal rights.[16] Following the lead of Charles Reich (Reich, 1963, 1964, 1965 and 1966), they pressed for the introduction of proper procedural safeguards for the 'new property', i.e. to welfare benefits and services provided under various social welfare programmes, arguing that this was necessary to protect clients from abuses of discretion and, more generally, to further their interests.[17] Clients' rights became a major tool for social reformers in the United States who aimed to shift the balance of power in case-level decision making away from social welfare agencies and case-level officials towards clients and their representatives

(Scheingold, 1974; Handler, 1978). One result of this was that courts and legislatures established rights for clients in a number of social welfare programmes (Horowitz, 1977; Handler, 1979; Sosin, 1986).

During the 1970s, a welfare rights movement emerged in Britain. Concentrating on social security and, to a lesser extent on housing, public health and employment issues, it employed a variety of strategies ranging from organising take-up campaigns and representing clients at appeal tribunals and in court to pursuing a 'test-case strategy' and engaging in pressure group politics (Welfare Rights Working Party, 1975; Prosser, 1983; Whiteley and Winyard, 1988). Although the test-case strategy achieved few long-term gains, many clients benefited from these activities and, in some instances, their legal rights were actually strengthened.[18] However, it required the return of a Conservative Government in 1979 for the enactment of clients' rights to gather real momentum. This calls for some explanation.

The logic which underlay the strategy adopted by the welfare rights movement was as follows: officials exercised their discretion in ways that were detrimental to clients; appeals against those decisions would lead to more favourable outcomes; these outcomes would be facilitated by a strengthening of the appeals procedure and by successful appeals to the superior courts which would strike down the restrictive exercise of discretion. The logic which underlay the Government's strategy was almost exactly the opposite: officials exercised their discretion in ways that policy makers did not approve of; the enactment of legislation which specified clients' entitlements would ensure that policy makers' intentions were adhered to; and the adoption of a system of precedent and case law would ensure greater consistency and conformity with the legislation. While the welfare rights movement espoused a rights strategy in order to enhance clients' interests, the Government did so to curtail the discretion of officials and to ensure a greater measure of compliance with its policies (Prosser, 1981).

It is clear from the above that discretion may be seen as problematic in different ways by different groups (Bankowski and Nelken, 1981). Likewise, rights may be advocated for different reasons by different groups. Thus, a rights strategy may have attractions for a Government which seeks to limit some of the central concerns of the dominant collective welfare orientation in many social welfare programmes, including education.

One important feature of clients' rights is that they can be used to challenge an adverse decision. If clients believe that they have been wrongly denied their full entitlement, they can challenge the decision by appealing against it. The appeal body would have the power to substitute its own decision for the original one. Thus, appeal decisions can provide guidance for case-level decision makers while the prospect of an appeal would deter them from making incorrect decisions. Finally, rights of appeal would also enable clients to participate in the decisions that affect them (Fuller, 1978; Galligan, 1986).

Studies of clients' rights and case-level decision making in social welfare programmes point to several factors that may undermine this picture. First, clients frequently do not challenge decisions because they lack the legal or administrative competence to do so (Nonet, 1969; Cranston, 1986). Secondly, clients may not challenge decisions because they do not want to antagonise officials with whom they have a continuing relationship. Thirdly, appeal tribunals are frequently not independent of the agency whose decision is being appealed against. Moreover, appeals are often dominated by presenting officers representing the agency and influenced by the clerk, who is often employed by the agency. Fourthly, successful appeals by some clients often fail to bring about general improvements in case-level decision making. This is because social welfare agencies concede the cases they lose without revising their general approach to decision making (Jowell, 1973; Handler, 1979; Harlow and Rawlings, 1984). Finally, appeal procedures may be strengthened while substantive entitlements are reduced. Thus, clients may end up with stronger rights to fewer benefits or services (Prosser, 1977; Adler and Asquith, 1981).

A pessimistic assessment of these shortcomings might point to the failure of rights in social welfare programmes. Thus, while rights (in particular the right of appeal) may have benefited those individual clients who appealed, they have not transformed the treatment of clients in general. This is because officials continue to make case-level decisions more or less as they did in the absence of rights. Moreover, rights can impose substantial costs which may work to the detriment of clients. The existence of rights may eliminate discretion which could be used to help clients (Titmuss, 1971; Bull, 1980a). Officials may respond defensively to the possibility of an appeal, adopting more formal and bureaucratic modes of dealing with clients to insulate themselves from criticism (Simon, 1983; Harlow and Rawlings, 1984). Clients who gain most from the exercise of rights may be those who are least disadvantaged at the outset (Galanter, 1975). Moreover, those who gain may do so at the expense of others. Thus rights may limit the ability of social welfare programmes to achieve a reduction in inequalities.[19] Finally, the existence of rights may inhibit the efforts of reformers seeking more comprehensive improvements for clients. Thus, strengthening clients' procedural rights may confer the symbolic appearance of legality on the programmes in question and make it more difficult to achieve fundamental changes that could really enhance social welfare (Piven and Cloward, 1972; Prosser, 1977; Adler and Asquith, 1981; Simon, 1985).

The effects of parents' rights of school choice on the admission of children to schools will provide an opportunity for assessing the impact of clients' rights on a social welfare programme.

THE PLAN OF THE BOOK

Two key questions provide the foundation for our examination of parents' choice of school in Scotland. First, what roles should parents and education authorities play in decisions about which schools children attend? Addressing this question calls for an evaluation of parents' concerns for their children's education and authorities' concerns for educational provision more generally and the ways in which they influence admission decisions. Secondly, how do parents' rights of school choice affect school admissions decision making and how do the outcomes of decision making affect the operation of the authorities' schools? Unlike rights in some other social welfare programmes, parents' rights of school choice in Scotland have substantially changed the pattern of case-level decisions. Authorities can no longer manage schools' enrolments to avoid under-enrolment or to maintain links between schools and their communities. Examining the implementation of parents' rights of school choice in Scotland identifies the consequences of shifting the balance between authorities and parents in school admissions and more generally the balance between collective policy concerns and those of individual clients.

In Chapter 2, we discuss the statutory enactment of the Education Act 1980 (which established parents' rights of school choice in England and Wales) and the Education (Scotland) Act 1981 (which did likewise in Scotland). We describe the concerns that led to the legislation and the forces that shaped its content. At the end of this chapter, we set out the legal structure of parents' right of school choice established by the Education (Scotland) Act 1981. This provides the basis for our examination of the effects of parents' rights of school choice in Scotland.

In Chapter 3, we examine the implementation of parents' rights of school choice in three Scottsh authorities in the years 1982–1985. We describe the authorities' school admission practices prior to the 1981 Act and show how they incorporated parents' rights into their school admission procedures. We describe how the authorities have administered their school admissions and how parents' rights have changed the way in which authorities deal with parents' school requests. We focus on the key policy issues that have arisen, such as deciding what reasons could be used to refuse parents' school requests, dealing with school requests on behalf of children not yet of school age, and coping with the new patterns of enrolment that have resulted.

In Chapter 4, we present the findings of our survey of parents in the three authorities. We look at several key issues related to parental choice: the characteristics of parents who make school requests compared with those who do not, the kinds of considerations parents have in mind in selecting a school, the reasons parents have for rejecting and choosing schools, and parents' knowledge of their rights.

In Chapter 5, we examine the operation of parents' appeals when authorities refuse their school requests. We look at the patterns of refusals, appeals, and appeal decisions in the authorities and describe the conduct of appeal hearings based on our observations. We also examine sheriffs' decisions in Scotland as a whole, focusing on how the sheriffs' approaches to authorities' decisions relate to the purposes and effects of the 1981 Act.

In Chapter 6, we examine the patterns of movements between schools that have resulted from the parents' rights. We look at schools' educational characteristics and their districts' demographic characteristics, comparing schools that lose pupils with schools that gain. We also look at how the pattern of parents' school requests has affected the enrolments of particular schools, particularly how some schools are becoming seriously under-enrolled.

Finally, in Chapter 7 we look more broadly at the issues involved in parental choice of school and clients' rights in social welfare programmes. We examine the consequences of the 1981 Act's establishment of parents' rights of school choice in the light of views of what would happen held by advocates and opponents of the legislation. We also use our analysis of parents' rights of school choice under the 1981 Act to augment our understanding of how granting clients' rights can affect case-level decision making and the operation of social welfare programmes, and to anticipate the consequences of more recent legislative changes.

NOTES

1. In this book we use the term 'social welfare programmes' in a generic sense to refer to policies concerned with the distribution of benefits, e.g. social security and housing subsidies, or services, e.g. health care, social work and education. We likewise use the term 'clients' in a generic sense to refer to the recipients of these benefits and services. Neither of these terms is particularly felicitous, but we were unable to think of any more suitable ones. There are indications that the term 'users' may soon replace the term 'clients' as a general description of those who receive benefits and services.

2. In national insurance, and, more recently, in other areas of social security, the rights and entitlements of recipients were spelled out in detail; funding was largely independent of direct Exchequer control and a legal model of adjudication, based on clearly defined rights of appeal and the development of case law, was explicitly adopted.

3. In the field of industrial relations, Fox (1974) has likewise described how a decline in trust leads to a concern with rule

imposition in an attempt to secure compliance and, thus, accountability.

4. Arising out of his study of the US Disability Insurance programme, Mashaw (1983) has developed three models of decision making that are similar in many ways to the two orientations developed here. Mashaw's 'bureaucratic rationality' model roughly corresponds to our collective welfare orientation, while his 'professional treatment' and 'moral judgment' models are closely related to the expert judgment and individual autonomy versions of the individual client orientation. The three models of accountability developed by Kogan (1986) likewise have a number of similarities wth the two orientations developed above. Thus, Kogan's 'public or state control' model corresponds to our collective welfare orientation, while his 'professional control' and 'consumerist control' models correspond to the expert judgment and individual autonomy versions of the individual client orientation. However, the parallels should not be over-stated since Mashaw's professional treatment model, Kogan's professional control model and one version of his consumerist control model all embody important collective values and concerns. Our account of the two orientations to case-level decision making differs slightly from that in Tweedie (1989a).

5. The individual client orientation rarely confronts the fact that the aggregation of individual decisions may overburden the resources of the programme. In practice, decision makers usually cope with the problem of limited resources by adopting informal rationing techniques.

6. The 1944 Act remains in force, subject to a number of fairly substantial amendments, whereas the 1945 Act was consolidated, first in 1946 and subsequently in 1962 and 1980. For consistency we refer in this section to the relevant sections of the 1944 Act (for England and Wales) and the 1945 Act (for Scotland).

7. According to section 35, 'a person shall be deemed to be of compulsory school age if he has attained the age of five years and has not attained the age of fifteen years and a person shall be deemed to be over compulsory school age as soon as he has attained the age of fifteen'. This was amended in 1972 when the minimum school-leaving age was raised to sixteen.

8. Under section 8, 'sufficient' was defined to mean 'sufficient in number, character and equipment to afford for all pupils opportunities for education offering such variety of instruction and training as may be desirable in view of their different ages, abilities and aptitudes and of the different periods for which they may be expected to remain at school'.

9. As McPherson and Raab (1988) point out, the increase in the proportion of pupils admitted to (selective) senior secondary schools in Scotland unwittingly undermined confidence in selection.

As higher proportions of successive age groups were selected for senior secondary courses, so the number of dissatisfied 'borderline' cases was statistically bound to increase. Moreover, an expanding senior secondary school sector continued to drain (non-selective) junior secondary schools of resources, teachers and esteem.

The expansion of grammar schools in England and Wales had the same effect.

10. There is considerable debate about the effects of parental choice on educational attainment, in particular about the specific effects of parental choice on pupils who attend one school (the requested school) rather than another (the school which they would otherwise have attended) but also about its general effects on other pupils. No empirical evidence is yet available.

11. Simple rules can expedite decision making but only at the cost of limiting the number of factors that are taken into account. For example, setting admission limits and then, where a school would be over-subscribed, giving priority to children with siblings at the school or ranking all requests in terms of distance from home to school, would make possible the rapid processing of requests at the cost of ignoring other factors that might well be more relevant to deciding where children should go to school.

12. For a further discussion of school effectiveness, see Chapter 6.

13. The reasons parents give for choosing schools are discussed in Chapter 4.

14. This system would work rather like a voucher system, where the Government provides a sum of money to parents for each child, which parents can then add to if they wish and use to send their child to any local authority or independent school (Friedman, 1962; Beales, Blaug, Veale, West and Boyson, 1970; West, 1970; Maynard, 1975; Coons and Sugarman, 1978). The system described here applies only to local authority schools which compete in terms of what they can offer but not in terms of price.

15. See Chapter 2 and Appendices A and B.

16. The arguments of welfare rights advocates paralleled those of administrative lawyers who argued that the wide discretion exercised by officials in public agencies was a major source of injustice in public administration and that justice could best be enhanced by eliminating unnecessary discretionary powers and ensuring that necessary discretionary powers were properly confined, structured and checked (Davis, 1971).

17. In a footnote to *Goldberg* v *Kelly* 397 U.S.254 (1970), the United States Supreme Court said 'It may be realistic today to regard welfare entitlements as more like 'property' than a 'gratuity'. The footnote built on an attempt in the academic literature to assimilate state social welfare benefits with traditional notions of property. The argument for assimilating the two is that all property is 'state largesse' in that it derives from the state and cannot exist without the protection of the law. Thus Reich (1964) argued that the same protections ought to apply to social welfare benefits as to traditional categories of property.

18. Prosser (1983) concluded that the indirect effects of test cases, e.g. the diffusion of welfare rights skills and their use for campaigning purposes, were more important than their direct effects since a successful outcome was a matter of chance and could, in any case, be negated by the Government. Among the most successful campaigns were those that resulted in the abolition of the 'wage stop' and the reform of the 'cohabitation rule'.

19. Since, in the absence of rights, some clients will benefit more

than others while, when rights are present, other clients will derive most advantage, it follows that the introduction of rights will inevitably bring about some measure of redistribution among clients.

2

THE STATUTORY ENACTMENT OF PARENTAL CHOICE LEGISLATION

The roots of the legislation which established parents' rights of school choice in Scotland in 1981 can be traced to the emergence, in the early 1970s, of parental choice of school as a national issue in England and Wales. The Conservative and Labour parties unsuccessfully put forward various proposals for parental choice legislation during the 1970s before the Conservatives managed to introduce legislation in 1980 which established parents' rights of school choice in England and Wales (Tweedie, 1986a). The support that developed for parental choice during this period, particularly within the Conservative Party, stimulated the introduction of parental choice legislation in Scotland. Although the Education Act 1980 adopted a general approach to parental choice which the Scottish legislation followed, the separate development of the Education (Scotland) Act 1981 ensured that it had many novel features. Our account of the English and Welsh legislation shows, first, how political concerns led to the introduction of parental choice legislation and, second, that, because parental choice conflicted with other educational policy concerns, officials had to balance parental choice against these other concerns in the course of drafting the legislation.[1]

THE CONSERVATIVE PARTY AND THE POLITICAL APPEAL OF PARENTAL CHOICE IN ENGLAND

As we have seen in Chapter 1 above, the Education Act 1944 implicitly gave Local Education Authorities (LEAS) broad discretion to decide school admissions. There was one limit on the LEAS' discretion. Section 76 of the 1944 Act provided that LEAS 'shall have regard to the general principle that, as far as compatible with the provision of efficient instruction and training and the avoidance of unreasonable public expenditure, pupils are to be educated in accordance with the wishes of their parents'. Legal interpretations of section 76 required that LEAS 'should have regard' to parents' wishes about which school their child should attend. However, LEAS were allowed to decide that other factors justified refusing the parents' choice of school.[2] In short, the statutory balance was drawn strongly in favour of LEAS' discretion (Ministry of Education, 1950; Meredith, 1981)

Most LEAS made some efforts to comply with parents' choices of school. In these LEAS, parents' requests were turned down only when the school was full or when the school could not provide a suitable education for the child. Some LEAS, however, relied on zoning arrangements or banding by academic ability and refused parents' choices that were inconsistent with these policies.[3] In almost all LEAS, disputes occasionally arose between parents and the LEA over choice of school. Most LEAS provided some form of complaints procedure for parents who were dissatisfied with the school to which their child had been allocated (Lewis and Birkenshaw, 1979a and 1979b, Birkenshaw, 1985). Although some parents did complain to the Secretary of State, virtually all disputes between parents and LEAS were resolved at the local level (Stone and Taylor, 1977; Meredith, 1981).

Prior to the 1970s, school admission arrangements were regarded as a local issue. Although the Department of Education and Science (DES) received a number of complaints from parents about LEAS which had refused them their choice of school, officials persuaded ministers that choice of school was a local matter and, in virtually all these cases, the Secretary of State declined to order the LEA to admit the children to the school of their parents' choice.

It took the initiative of the Conservative Opposition in 1974 to convert parental choice into a national issue.[4] After the defeat of the Conservative Government in the February election, pressure grew among Conservatives for a re-evaluation of their education policies. Backbench MPS and party supporters argued that the Conservatives had gone along with Labour policy for too long. The appointment of Norman St John-Stevas as Education spokesman marked the re-orientation of Conservative education policy. St John-Stevas was charged with developing new policy initiatives that would lead to a new and distinctive Conservative education policy (TES, 28 June 1974). The Conservative policy initiative came at a time when many observers perceived growing dissatisfaction with the state education system. The scathing attacks on declining standards of education and discipline published in the 'Black Papers' (which sold in very large numbers), echoed the doubts of many parents and politicians (Cox and Dyson, 1971; Kogan, 1978). These doubts were often linked to concerns about secondary school reorganisation. Thus, the 'Black Papers' asserted that the replacement of selective schools with comprehensive schools was contributing to the decline in the quality of state education, particularly for those children who would previously have attended grammar schools.

St John-Stevas and his colleagues quickly realised the potential appeal of policies aimed at increasing parental involvement in schools. In this way the Conservatives could be seen to be responsive to the mounting concerns of parents. Establishing rights of school choice was given particular priority. Parents would be given more control of their children's education. This would enable them to avoid 'bad' comprehensive schools, and respond to some of the expressed concerns about secon-

dary school reorganisation. Moreover, the political attractiveness of
parental choice was complemented by its compatibility with traditional
Conservative values of individual freedom and parental responsibility.
St John-Stevas launched the 'Parents' Charter' in August 1974 and the
Conservatives included a Charter of Parents' Rights in their October 1974
Election Manifesto:

> A Charter of Parents' Rights: An important part of the distinct
> Conservative policy on Education is to recognise parental rights. A
> say in how their children are to be brought up is an essential
> ingredient in the parental role. We will therefore introduce
> additional rights for parents. First, by amending the 1944 Education
> Act, we will impose clear obligations on the State and local auth-
> orities to take account of the wishes of parents. Second, we will
> consider establishing a local appeal system for parents dissatisfied
> with the allotment of schools. [The charter goes on to promise
> parental representation on boards of governors, an obligation to
> form parent–teachers associations, and a requirement that schools
> publish prospectuses.] (Conservative Party; 1974)

The Conservatives twice put forward parliamentary proposals from
the Parents' Charter while in opposition. There was a Private Member's
Bill, the Education (Parents' Charter) Bill in 1974. The Bill would have
strengthened the duty of LEAS to follow parental wishes in education, set
up local appeal committees to hear parental complaints and required
schools to publish information for parents.

In 1976, the Conservatives introduced a set of new clauses relating to
parental choice as amendments to Labour's Education Bill in a strategy to
stall the Bill (H.C. Debs, Vol.912, cols.1345–86; Vol.914, cols.461–572;
and Vol.916, cols.1889–936). These amendments provided for a parents'
right of choice as long as there was room at the school. The amendments
also provided for independent appeal boards to hear parents' complaints
about allocations to school and for the publication of school information
that would help parents compare schools and therefore make better
choices (H.C. Debs, Vol.912, col.1345 and Vol.914, col.409).

In the course of putting forward these legislative proposals, the Conservatives developed a rationale for parental choice. Most importantly,
links were developed between parental choice and the quality of schools.
The key Conservative argument envisaged the play of 'market forces' on
schools – many parents choosing not to send their child to a school
would put pressure on that school to improve or close; large numbers of
parents requesting a school would signal that the school was doing well,
and that it should be expanded and copied by other, less popular
schools. As Sir George Sinclair, head of the Conservative Party's Committee on Parental Choice said:

> If the exercise of parental choice results in heavy pressure on one
> school, with an open withdrawal of confidence from some others,

surely that should be a storm warning to the local authority that it must do something about such schools, and quickly . . . To allow a school to be below standard for years is doing no service to the children or the neighbourhood . . . The spur to remedial action is the exercise of parental choice, which shows which schools are losing the confidence of the parents of the area. (H.C. Debs, Vol.912, col.1382. See also H.C. Debs, Vol.912, cols.1352–71)

Some Conservatives supported parental choice because it could result in the emergence of a new type of selective school system. Schools would offer different courses of study, some primarily academic and some primarily vocational, with selection determined, at least in the first instance, by parents' choices. Squaring the circle of 'selective' comprehensive schools, the Conservatives proposed that, where schools were over-subscribed, the headteacher would then select pupils on the basis of interviews and the child's record at primary school (H.C. Debs, Vol.912, cols.1348–50. See also St John-Stevas, 1977).

The rationale for parental choice and the details of its statutory form were worked out after the launch of the 'Parents Charter' in 1974. The Conservatives had political motives for originally adopting parental choice as a central part of their education policies. Public concern about state education and parents' demands for greater involvement underlay the attraction of parental choice. Parental choice could be advertised as a response to declining educational standards which did not require significant new spending. Parents would be given greater control of their children's education. And parental choice was an assertion of traditional Conservative values – individual freedom and parental responsibility.

This general point deserves emphasis. St John-Stevas, along with a few other Conservative MPs, backed parental choice primarily because he saw it as a promising basis for an electoral appeal and, secondly, because of its resonance with traditional Conservative values. The Conservatives' adoption of parental choice was not a direct response to complaints or demands from parents. Nor was it the product of the activities of pressure groups. Nor, at least initially, was it seen as a remedy for declining standards in education. Instead it was a skilful exploitation of many concerns that would draw support to parental choice and the Conservative Party. For these reasons, the Conservatives advocated parental choice legislation. This action put parental choice on the parliamentary agenda and provided the impetus that resulted in the 1980 Act.

LABOUR'S ATTEMPT TO STEAL THE CONSERVATIVES' CLOTHES WITHOUT CHANGING ITS OWN

Particularly after Margaret Thatcher became leader early in 1975, parental choice became a central plank in the Conservatives populist appeal to the electorate. This put pressure on the Labour Government and contributed to its decision to propose its own parental choice legislation.

The Government's first attempt to come to terms with parental choice was a draft circular issued for consultation in 1976. The draft circular was prompted by the Department of Education and Science's (DES's) concern over the large number of section 68 appeals [5] and the growing number of parents using school attendance procedures to challenge the LEA's refusal of their choice of school.[6] Prior to comprehensive reorganisation, the combined number of appeals to the Secretary of State had approached 100 per year. After reorganisation and into the 1970s, this number climbed to about 1000 per year – a ten-fold increase (Department of Education and Science, 1977b). This was in spite of the fact that the success rate was very low – for example in 1977, only two out of 1124 section 68 complaints and 24 out of 40 section 37 appeals were upheld (Passmore, 1983). School attendance procedures were particularly troubling because they gave parents who broke the law an advantage over parents who complained under section 68. (This is because section 68 orders could be issued only if the LEA acted unreasonably while school attendance decisions had to be decided in favour of the parents unless the LEA showed that admitting that one child would cause 'unreasonable public expense'.) The draft circular stated that section 37 and section 68 cases would be decided by identical criteria (Department of Education and Science, 1976). However, this strategy had to be abandoned when the DES's new legal advisor argued that the terms of the 1944 Act would not allow such an approach (Department of Education and Science, 1977b).

The new Secretary of State, Shirley Williams, concluded that legislation was necessary. A new circular was considered to be insufficient both politically and administratively. Williams and her Ministers thought that they should pre-empt the Conservatives and enact their own parental choice legislation and in this way claim the credit for themselves. Legislation could clarify the circumstances where parents were or were not entitled to their choice of school and so reduce the number of disputes as well as removing any incentive for parents to use the school attendance procedures. In addition, a new statute might prevent a future Conservative government from enacting a form of parental choice that would undermine the comprehensive school.

The Government and the LEAs had also by this time recognised the fundamental importance of falling school rolls. Primary and secondary school numbers were expected to drop by almost a third in the coming generation of pupils (Department of Education and Science, 1977a. See also Meredith, 1984; and Bondi, 1989). This meant that LEAs had an increased number of surplus places at schools. On the one hand, that meant there were more places at popular schools to satisfy parents' choices. Fewer parents' school choices would have to be refused because of the lack of accommodation. On the other hand, falling school rolls were seen as creating important management problems for LEAS. Surplus school places were expensive and small schools required extra teachers and resources so that the school could offer a full curriculum. Public spending reductions put further pressures on the LEAS to reduce expenditure in line with the falling school rolls. LEAS were uncertain of their existing authority to limit school enrolments and they wanted clear statutory authority to refuse parents' choices to avoid overcrowded schools and to protect the viability of smaller schools.

In October 1977, the Secretary of State issued a consultation paper, *Admission of Children to the School of their Parents' Choice* (Department of Education and Science, 1977b), that anticipated new legislation. LEAS would be able to set limits on the number of children who attended each school. Parents would have a statutory right to a place at the school of their choice unless the school's roll was at its limit or the LEA believed that granting the parent's choice would adversely affect the efficient provision of education or be in conflict with the comprehensive principle. LEAS would be required to provide local appeals and parents would have a further appeal to the Secretary of State.

These proposals came under heavy attack from within the Labour Party. Though some Labour Party officials opposed parental choice, most agreed that parents should be able to choose which school their child attended as long as this did not damage educational provision at any other school. They were particularly concerned that parental choice would distort the distribution of academic ability among the schools, thus undermining the comprehensive principle.

Strong reservations about parental choice were also voiced by several education pressure groups, led by the local authority associations – the Association of County Councils (ACC) and the Association of Metropolitan Authorities (AMA). They accepted the idea of limited parental choice and, since they saw legislation as inevitable, they did not want to be seen to adopt a stance of outright opposition. However, they wanted legislation that would give them clear authority to refuse parents' school choices when this was necessary to manage falling rolls efficiently. The DES endorsed the local authorities' point of view, and they agreed that new legislation was necessary, primarily to give LEAS the powers needed to manage school rolls and to eliminate the vexing resort to school attendance procedures. Once those ends were achieved, residual provision could be made for parental choice. The Secretary of State, the DES and the local authority associations all believed that parental choice legislation could be enacted in a form which would strengthen LEAS' ability to deal with falling rolls and limit educational expenditure without detriment to the principle of comprehensive schools or the provision of education more generally.

The Government included parental choice provisions in its 1978 Education Bill. The provisions followed the lines set out in the consultation paper: LEAS would be given powers to set planned admission limits (PALS) and parents would be given rights of school choice subject to those limits. The LEA would have to reconsider its decision if the parents submitted written objections. Parents could then obtain a review by the Secretary of State that was much like the section 68 review (Education Bill 1978, cl. 6–10).

Although the Bill was heralded by the Labour Government as establishing parental choice (H.C. Debs, Vol.959, col.1231), its primary effect would have been to give LEAS explicit powers to control school numbers. Pupils could be allocated among schools in whatever numbers the LEA thought most efficient. Parental choice could not threaten LEA planning because the LEA would have had statutory authority to refuse parents' requests to avoid exceeding a school's PAL. Parents would have had an appeal only in that they could have required the LEA to reconsider its decision since the appeal to the Secretary of State would have been little different from the existing section 68 procedures. The primacy that Labour accorded falling rolls rather than parental choice is captured in this statement by Gordon Oakes, Labour Minister of State for Education and Science.

> Given [falling rolls] the question is not whether admissions should be reduced but how that reduction should be administered. Are parents to be allowed to vote with their feet in a way that would ensure that less popular schools become unable to offer a full curriculum, thus contributing to the downward spiral of deprivation, or are LEAS to be encouraged to plan responsibly, even if this means appearing to be less responsive to the wishes of individuals or small groups in the short term. (Standing Committee E, cols.404–5)

The Conservatives immediately attacked the Bill, arguing that it would restrict parental choice rather than extend it. Their critique of the Labour Bill drew on the principle of parental responsibility and advocated the introduction of social markets into public services. This intensified their belief that the parental right of school choice should be strengthened and that an effective appeal system had to be provided for parents. Mark Carlisle, new Opposition spokesman on education, said:

> We fear that the proposed planned admission limits . . . will simply undo all the potential good in the other clauses and allow some local authorities to show a cynical disregard for parents' wishes . . . Our main criticism of the proposed planned admission limits . . . is that they will enable schools to turn away pupils even when there are empty places, in order to keep less popular schools open. (H.C. Debs, Vol.959, cols.1253–4. See also H.C. Debs, Vol.959, cols.1330–49)

The Labour Bill fell when Parliament was dissolved in April 1979. The Labour Government did not push the Bill because it expected that many

Labour MPs would refuse to support it on the grounds that parental choice would undermine many comprehensive schools. The Bill's significance comes from its linking of falling rolls with parental choice and the way it set the pattern for the Conservative proposals to follow.

THE ENACTMENT OF PARENTAL CHOICE LEGISLATION FOR ENGLAND AND WALES

The 1979 election returned the initiative to the Conservatives, who were committed to legislation that would shift the balance toward parents and away from the LEAS. The 1979 Conservative Manifesto stated:

> Extending parents' rights and responsibilities, including their right of choice, will also help raise standards by giving them greater influence over education. Our parents' charter will place a clear duty on government and local authorities to take account of parents' wishes when allocating children to schools, with a local appeals system for those dissatisfied. Schools will be required to publish prospectuses giving details of their examination and other results.
> (Conservative Party, 1979)

The incoming education ministers shared a commitment to parental choice legislation, but two had strong reservations. The new Secretary of State, Mark Carlisle, believed that parental choice had to be balanced against other educational concerns and that LEAS were in the best position to do that. Carlisle did not believe that establishing a social market in the state education system would bring about a major improvement in educational standards. The Minister of State for Schools, Lady Young, who had a local authority background[7], shared Carlisle's perspective. Rhodes Boyson, one of the Parliamentary Under-Secretaries at the DES and a long-time proponent of parental choice and educational vouchers,[8] was deliberately given responsibility for higher education and not for schools. Boyson believed that parental choice could establish a market in education and in that way raise educational standards. However, he recognised that a strong market form of parental choice was not acceptable to his ministerial colleagues or to mainstream Conservatives.

In drafting their own legislation, the Conservatives started with the Labour Bill. The Conservatives had disagreed with the Labour Bill on two main points: the strong control that PALS gave LEAS over parental choice and the lack of an effective appeals system. These two issues were priorities for the Government's attention as they were seen as crucial to the aims of strengthening parental choice and distinguishing the new legislation from the Labour Bill.

Ministers were uncertain whether PALS could be changed because they recognised that LEAS needed some powers to manage falling rolls. However, after the debate over the PALS contained in the Labour Bill, DES officials came to believe that PALS, and the necessary procedures for appealing PALS to the Secretary of State, would involve too much controversy and too many demands for intervention by the Secretary of State. They also believed that statutory PALS as limits on parents' choices were over-balanced in favour of the LEAS. The DES officials proposed abandoning statutory PALS and relying instead on a general exception to the LEAS' duty to comply with parents' choice of school. This exception would be based on the effect of compliance on the efficient use of resources by the LEA. LEAS would be able to set informal admission limits based on their judgments about what constituted 'efficient' education. If parents appealed a refusal that was based on the limits, the LEA would have to justify the refusal by reference to the efficient use of resources. Ministers agreed immediately as the proposal met all their concerns: it would give some parents more choice; it would not interfere much with LEAS' operation of their schools; and it was demonstrably different from Labour's approach.

At the same time, DES officials were developing provisions to meet ministerial concerns that parents should have an effective appeal at the local level. Neither ministers nor officials were attracted to the Labour Bill's reliance on reconsideration by the LEA and an appeal to the Secretary of State. The officials first proposed that each LEA should set up an independent appeal committee. Although it would be a committee of the LEA, the majority of its' members would be 'independent', that is they would not be elected members of the LEA or LEA staff. The appeal committee would recommend to the LEA whether or not it should place the child in the school requested by the parents.

The Secretary of State agreed to this proposal. However, the local authority associations protested that independent appeal committees would undermine the LEAS' responsibility for providing education. They proposed instead that the appeal committees should have an LEA majority, which would give LEAS more control, and in exchange suggested that these appeal committees be able to make binding decisions in individual appeals. The Secretary of State agreed to the changes, though he insisted that the chairperson of the appeal committee could not be a member of the LEA's education committee. He refused to compromise on this, despite pressure from the local authority associations, because he thought it was essential that the appeal committee was seen to be independent of the LEA (Bull, 1980b).

This arrangement between the Secretary of State, the DES, and the local authority associations settled the major provisions of the proposed legislation for parental choice in local authority schools. They were all satisfied with the compromise and agreed that it would enable LEAS to manage falling rolls, particularly since the LEA had a majority on the appeal committee. The Secretary of State could also derive satisfaction from the fact that he had strengthened the right of parents to choose schools and thus accomplished one of the Government's manifesto promises.

Some Conservatives argued that these arrangements went too far in compromising the rights of parents. Some of the Secretary of State's advisors wanted fully independent appeal committees that had powers to make binding decisions. They also wanted to draft the exceptions to the LEAS' duty more restrictively. They feared that LEAS could too easily refuse parents' choices under the Secretary of State's proposals. The Secretary of State rejected their arguments on three grounds. First, he was convinced that LEAS must be able to limit parental choice to some extent. He was particularly concerned that 'absolute parental choice' would result in 'rump schools' and that the children left at those schools would suffer. Secondly, the Secretary of State agreed with the LEAS' complaint that reducing spending and expanding parental choice were incompatible goals. He felt that reducing education spending had to take precedence. Thirdly, the Secretary of State believed that ultimately the LEAS had to be trusted to implement parental choice. There was no way that LEAS could be forced to accept it.

The Government included these provisions in the Education (No.2) Bill 1979 which formed part of its first legislative programme. There were no major amendments, although the Government itself moved an amendment to section 7 to put the appeal committees under the supervision of the Council on Tribunals and the Commissioner for Local Administration (the Local Authority 'Ombudsman') (Standing Committee D, cols.564–645).

The 1980 Act placed duties on all English and Welsh LEAS to allow parents to express a preference about which LEA school they wished their children to attend (Education Act 1980, s.6(1)). It required LEAS to admit children to the school chosen by their parents unless one of the following statutory exceptions existed:

(a) if compliance with the preference would prejudice the provision of efficient education or the efficient use of resources;

(b) if the preferred school is an aided or special agreement school and compliance with the preference would be incompatible with any arrangements between the governors and the local education authority in respect of the admission of pupils to the school; or

(c) if the arrangements for admission to the preferred school are based wholly or partly on selection by reference to ability or aptitude and compliance with the preference would be incompatible with selection under the arrangements. (Education Act 1980, s.6(3))

The 1980 Act also required LEAS to establish local appeal committees to hear the appeals of parents who were denied their choice of school. The appeal committees were to consist of three, five or seven members. A bare majority of members could be drawn from members of the LEA, but the remaining members had to be parents or persons knowledgeable about education in the LEA. The 1980 Act set out in draft form the procedures the appeal committee was to follow and placed some restrictions on the composition of appeal committees. Most importantly, the chairperson of the appeal committee could not be a member of the LEA's Education Committee. The appeal committee procedures were set out to provide an informal hearing at which parents could appeal and make whatever representations they wished (Education Act 1980, s.7 and Sched. 2. See also Bull, 1980b). Finally, the 1980 Act required LEAs to publish information for parents about their admission arrangements and about each of their schools. The information about admission arrangements included the number of pupils the LEA intended to admit to the school, the procedures for parents to request a school, and notice of the parent's rights of appeal should the LEA refuse their request. LEAs were also required to provide basic information about schools to aid parents in selecting a school (Education Act 1980, s.8).

COMPROMISES IN THE ENGLISH LEGISLATION

The Conservatives came into Government in 1979 committed to enacting a statutory right of parental choice. The Government introduced legislation that established rights of parental choice, but did little to disturb LEA control of school admissions. The Conservatives could therefore claim that they had fulfilled their manifesto promise and given parents new rights. At the same time, the Government had acceded to the central concerns of the LEAS.

Government ministers recognised that the new rights of school choice would not shift the balance between parents and LEAS very much but accepted that no more could be done. There were three primary reasons for this. First, the Labour Bill proposed in 1978 linked the issues of parental choice and the LEAs' management of falling rolls. The use of the Labour Bill as a starting point and the continued influence of the DES and the local authority associations (in particular, the Conservative-controlled ACC) established falling rolls as the top priority. Recognition of the importance of falling rolls restricted how far the Conservatives could shift the balance toward parents. Secondly, the Ministers responsible for the parental choice legislation were not committed to a strong form of parental choice. The Secretary of State believed that parents should have more choice of school, but not so much that LEAs had to run schools inefficiently or that the children in unpopular schools suffered. Lady Young agreed. Boyson advocated a strong form of choice but he was unable to convince his ministerial colleagues. Thirdly, the proposals for parental choice came at a time when the Government was committed to radical reductions in public spending. Falling school rolls may have made parental choice possible, but they also led to a strong drive to reduce spending (Hewton, 1986). In the end, spending reductions were given priority over extending parental choice. The Secretary of State realised that the two were incompatible and chose to restrict parental choice so that LEAS could reduce spending with a minimum of cuts to teaching activities.

Two broad conclusions can be drawn from this account of the making of the English parental choice legislation. First, the political appeal of parental choice provided the impetus towards legislation once the Conservatives had put the issue onto the parliamentary agenda. Both Conservative and Labour politicians recognised the symbolic value of supporting a stronger role for parents in school admissions. This was sufficient to ensure that some form of legislation would be enacted. Secondly, parents' rights of school choice were enacted in a qualified form because Ministers, civil servants and LEAS were concerned about the effects of parental choice on unpopular schools and educational spending. They concluded that the importance of reducing educational expenditure and strengthening the ability of LEAS to manage falling school rolls would have to limit the operation of parental choice. Against this background, we can now turn to an examination of the making of the Scottish parental choice legislation.

THE SCOTTISH DIMENSION

The Conservatives' commitment to parental choice legislation not only produced the Education Act 1980 but also resulted in the Education (Scotland) Act 1981, which established parents' rights of school choice in Scotland.[9] The impetus for the 1981 Act came primarily from English concerns about parental choice of school in the mid-1970s, and parental choice of school was not a contentious issue in Scotland in the same way as it was in England. However, the Conservatives' commitment in their 1979 Election Manifesto to strengthening parents' rights of school choice applied to Scottish as well as to English schools, and some Scottish Conservatives, particularly the Minister for Education, Alex Fletcher, jumped at the prospect of introducing parental choice legislation in Scotland. In spite of the fact that pressure for the Scottish legislation came primarily from England, the tradition of Scottish autonomy in respect of education resulted in legislation that was different from the English legislation in a number of important ways.[10] Fletcher's strong support for parents' rights, coupled with the relatively weaker influence of Scottish local authorities, produced parents' rights that were more specific and more restrictive than those established by the 1980 Act.

INDIFFERENCE TO PARENTAL CHOICE IN SCOTLAND

The dearth of politicians with strong interests in education among the depleted ranks of Scottish Conservative MPS after the party's defeat in the 1974 general election meant that Scottish interests were not represented among those Conservatives who set out to create a new and distinctive approach to education in the mid-1970s. In any case, there was less public concern in Scotland with educational standards or with the introduction of comprehensive schooling and less support for an attack on collectivism in practice or for the espousal of an individualistic ethic.[11] As a result, the Parents' Charter did not immediately take root in Scotland and, although there were some disputes in authorities which rigidly adhered to the catchment-area principle, they were spasmodic and localised.[12]

Many of these disputes involved appeals to the sheriff under the attendance order procedure (Himsworth, 1980). Although they undoubtedly reflected a certain amount of local concern and generated a good deal of local interest, they signally failed to provoke any national pressure for legislative change. However, they eventually contributed to the mobilisation of support within the Scottish Conservative Party for parental choice.[13] In the Leith Academy case (*Grieve* v *Lothian Regional Council*, 1978 SLT (Sh.Ct) 24), which was a 'test case' against Lothian Region, the successful parents received considerable support from Conservative councillors in Lothian Region. On their initiative, Scottish Conservative councillors came out in favour of a new Education Act which would give parents the right to have their children admitted to the school nearest to them or to any school where accommodation was available, such a right to be enforced, if necessary, through an 'admission order' from a sheriff (TESS, 11 March 1977). It was only at this point that Scottish Conservatives began to sense what their English counterparts had grasped three years previously, namely that parental choice was an issue they could and should exploit.

From this point on, the Conservatives wasted little time. In a discussion paper submitted to the Conservative Party Education Policy Committee in January 1978, John MacKay (who was himself a teacher at Oban High School as well as parliamentary candidate for Argyll) argued that parents of children in P7 (their last year at primary school) should all be asked to list three choices of secondary school in order of preference; that authorities should consider parental choices in terms of six factors (the agreed school roll, with enrolment being allowed up to the maximum permitted number; the neighbourhood element; the attendance of brothers and sisters at the school; personal compassionate circumstances; the cost of travel; and any other points raised by parents) and that disputed cases should be considered in three stages (first by an informal panel set up by the authority; secondly through an Appeals Sub-committee of the Education Committee or an Appeals Board; and thirdly by a sheriff whose decision would be final). In support of these proposals, MacKay referred to falling school rolls which would create spare capacity in schools and to an 'inevitable' process of specialisation among comprehensive schools. His aim was to avoid further cases like the Leith Academy case but he favoured a gradual approach, granting parental choice first to the parents of children entering P1 (the first year of primary school) and S1 (the first year of secondary school) and only extending these provisions to other parents after consultation with education authorities, School Councils and teachers' organisations.

MacKay's discussion paper was followed in May 1978 by a statement of Conservative policies for Scotland entitled *Onward to Victory* (Scottish Conservative Party, 1978). This contained the pledge that:

Conservatives will stand firmly by the right of parents to have their children educated in the school of their choice. The decline in the school population will provide an opportunity to offer parents a reasonable selection of schools within the state system.

There was, however, no real evidence of any detailed thinking about what this pledge would mean in practice. In September 1978, Fletcher (who was Opposition spokesman on Scottish Affairs) and MacKay (who, by this time had become Chairman of the Education Policy Committee of the Scottish Conservative Party) published a Conservative Party paper on education, entitled *Scottish Education – Regaining a Lost Reputation* (Fletcher and MacKay, 1978), in which they reiterated their support for greater parental choice in terms that had now become familiar:

We wish to give all parents greater freedom of choice in the school their children attend by relaxing the rigid system of catchment areas and boundaries, including local authority boundaries.

They noted that the decline in school rolls would create spare classroom space. In order to offer as wide a choice as possible, they encouraged schools to 'develop particular strengths in groups of subjects' and suggested that schools 'could then issue a prospectus outlining not only those strengths but also their philosophy and practice'. Although the paper did not go into detail, it was sufficient to align the Conservative Party in Scotland with any commitments the national party might wish to make in its manifesto for the forthcoming general election.

From the above account, it will be clear that there was much less interest in parental choice during the 1970s in Scotland than there was south of the border. There are several reasons for this. It would appear that there was greater acceptance of the neighbourhood school and the catchment-area principle. At the same time, most education authorities operated reasonably flexible admissions policies and were prepared to make exceptions in individual cases. Moreover, where this was not the case and parents had to resort to the attendance order procedure to secure the admission of their child to the school of their choice, education authorities were normally prepared to adjust their policies in the light of an adverse court judgment. Thus, for example, following a successful action by three Dunbarton parents (*Kidd* v *New Kilpatrick School Council*, 1978 SLT (Sh.Ct) 56), Strathclyde Region revised its notes of guidance for School Councils, emphasising that zoning arrangements were not sacrosanct and pointing out that there was no point in considering requests for exceptional admission or transfer if no exceptions could be made (TESS, 24 June 1977). The main counter-example was Lothian which, after regionalisation in 1975, adopted a strong neighbourhood school principle and was very reluctant to make any exceptions to it.[14]

Because parental choice was so much less of an issue in Scotland in the mid-1970s and because, in any case, the Scottish Education Department (SED) did not get drawn into local disputes in the same way as the DES (since there were no provisions in the Scottish legislation analogous to those of sections 37 and 68 of the 1944 Education Act) Labour ministers in the Scottish Office could and largely did ignore the issue. After local government reorganisation in 1975, the new Regional education authorities were required to submit their transfer schemes to the Secretary of State for approval. In the case of one education authority, the SED was unhappy with the original proposal, which prescribed two grounds on which parents could request an alternative school, on the basis that the authority was required under section 30 of the 1962 Act (formerly section 20 of the 1945 Act) 'to take into account the wishes of the parent' but raised no objections to the Region's restrictive policy as formulated below:

> Pupils will normally be transferred from primary school to the secondary school designated in the authority's Scheme for the Provision of School Education. Parents or guardians may alternatively request placement in another school ... Requests by parents or guardians for placement in a school other than that designated will be considered but are unlikely to be granted except in special circumstances such as where brothers and sisters will be in attendance at the school requested when the pupil transfers or where the Director of Education recommends ... on the grounds that the transfer under normal arrangements would be contrary to the educational or other interests of the child.

Three years later, there was still very little pressure on the Labour Party in Scotland to propose its own form of parental choice legislation and the Scottish Office took the view that provisions analogous to those contained in the 1978 Education Bill (see above) were not needed in Scotland. According to a Scottish Office Press Notice dated 24 November 1978

> In England and Wales, the law on school admission is confusing and to some extent contradictory, and the extent to which parents can express a preference varies widely from area to area. No similar need for legislation exists in Scotland.

The Scottish Conservatives' commitment to parental choice in 1977 and 1978 posed too little of a threat and, in addition, came too late to produce any pre-emptive response from the Labour Party in Scotland.

All this was to change with the return of a Conservative government and the appointment of Fletcher as Parliamentary Under-Secretary of State (junior Minister) for Education and Industry in the Scottish Office in May 1979. The Conservative Manifesto for Scotland (Scottish Conservative Party 1979) elaborated on the statement in the national manifesto (see above) in two ways, first by promising that

> Rigid catchment areas will be relaxed as the number of children falls, though parents should continue to have the right to have their child educated in the local school . . .

and, secondly, by indicating that

> . . .there should be easy transfer between schools that have differing strengths in a particular range of subjects.

Thus two of the arguments which were first expressed in Fletcher and MacKay's 1978 discussion paper found their way into the Scottish Manifesto. Moreover, the appointment of Fletcher as Minister for Education made it virtually certain that these manifesto commitments would be acted on. As an Edinburgh MP, he had been on close terms with Conservative councillors in Lothian Region and had taken a keen interest in the cases of parents who had removed their children from school and appealed to the sheriff against the Region's refusal to allow them to send their children to the schools of their choice. Lothian's intransigence contributed in no small measure to his dislike of catchment areas and to his unwillingness to trust local authorities to adopt a more flexible approach to parental choice.

THE ENACTMENT OF PARENTAL CHOICE LEGISLATION FOR SCOTLAND

The first indication of Fletcher's intentions came when he met members of the Convention of Scottish Local Authorities (COSLA) Education Committee in August 1979.[15] He argued that falling school rolls presented an opportunity for relaxing school catchment areas and widening parental choice of school, and expressed the view that an extension of the rights and responsibilities of parents would be good for overall educational standards. Fletcher stressed parents' need for more information, including details of examination results, to enable them to make informed choices and invited comments on a two-tier appeal system, administered locally by the education authority, in which parental applications would be considered first by School Councils and subsequently by an appeals committee with an independent element. COSLA's response was unenthusiastic. Dr Malcolm Green (Chairman of COSLA's Education Committee) pointed out that authorities were already required to 'have regard to' parental wishes and argued against the imposition of a uniform system. He could see no problem about making more information available but pointed to some of the difficulties which increased parental choice might create for authorities, emphasising that limits would have to be placed on the number of places available at each school.

The Minister suggested that further discussions should take place at official level between the SED and COSLA in order to clarify the issues involved, investigate likely difficulties and possible means of resolving them, and set out (possibly in the form of a draft circular) the steps that might be taken by authorities to implement his proposals. Thus, at this stage, it would appear that he was not necessarily thinking in terms of legislation. Green accepted the invitation, on the understanding that the COSLA representatives would merely feed in their expertise without committing COSLA in advance to whatever proposals the government came up with.

When the first meeting took place in October, it was made clear that the SED's aim was to produce a Consultative Paper on which COSLA and other interested parties would be asked to comment. Whether legislation would follow would depend on the outcome of the consultations and the willingness of authorities to enter into voluntary arrangements. Discussion focused on the scope authorities had to allow greater parental choice by relaxing their existing policies on admissions and catchment areas, the possibility of a two-tier system of appeals, the feasibility of pilot schemes in which parents could choose one of a number of schools within an enlarged catchment area, and the information parents would require in order to exercise choice. SED officials acknowledged that problems would arise but reiterated the Minister's hope that authorities would no longer refuse parents if space was available at the school of their choice. They also accepted that any new arrangements should still preserve the general principle that priority should be given to parents who wished their children to be educated at the local school and take into account the physical capacity of schools, bearing in mind the desirability of ending the use of annexes and temporary accommodation, and the need to determine the optimum annual intake, with some capacity retained for incomers to the area. However, there was clearly very little enthusiasm for the idea of 'free choice', even on a pilot basis.

While his officials were engaged in discussions with COSLA, Fletcher developed his own ideas on parental choice in an address to the Annual Conference of the Scottish Parent-Teacher Council (SPTC). He reaffirmed the government's commitment to a 'Parents' Charter' and his intention to produce a consultative paper on the subject. However, he explained that government spending policies would make it impossible to extend to all parents the freedom to choose schools for their children, since local authorities could not be asked to staff half-empty schools or incur additional expenditure to extend parental choice. However, he also stated that his 'longer term aim' was to introduce a system whereby all parents would be asked to choose a school, even if this involved opting for their local school, and he envisaged a much greater degree of specialisation (and thus of differentiation) between secondary schools. Although the SPTC favoured a more flexible system of school admissions and transfers, it is clear that it was not prepared to go that far. In a joint memorandum on the Parents' Charter which they had already submitted to the Minister, the Scottish Consumer Council (SCC) and the SPTC had argued against 'free choice' and in favour of a 'limited choice' and had urged the government to give greater consideration to ways of extending and developing choice within schools.

Prior to the publication of the Consultative Paper, the Minister had outlined his ideas to COSLA and the SPTC and a series of discussions had taken place between SED officials and Directors of Education (in their role as advisors to COSLA). The Minister had some continuing contact with the Conservative Group on Lothian Regional Council but there appears to have been very little direct contact on the issue of parental choice between the SED and the DES, either at ministerial or at official level. Policy was developed independently by a small group of officials within the SED who met regularly with the Minister. Fletcher was almost certainly more 'bullish' than his officials and had to compromise on a number of issues. However, his officials experienced little difficulty in supporting the general principle of parental choice or in translating this into a workable policy.

The Consultative Paper, *Admission to School : a Charter for Parents* (Scottish Education Department, 1980) was published in March 1980[16]. At a press conference to launch the paper, Fletcher questioned whether low rates of exceptional admissions and transfers in Scotland reflected widespread satisfaction with the existing arrangements, as the education authorities, in particular, insisted. He claimed, instead, that it indicated a high level of apathy, which was engendered by existing practices. He also invoked the beneficial consequences of market forces, asserting that 'a touch of consumerism is no bad thing for a nationalised industry' (TESS, 7 March 1980).

The introduction to the paper made it clear that account had been taken of the need to reduce existing levels of educational expenditure (para. 2), and claimed that the proposals would enable disadvantaged children to escape from the deprived areas in which they were currently trapped (para. 3). The paper itself did not propose the abolition of zoning schemes or catchment areas but argued that, pending legislation to this effect, 'all authorities should accept an obligation to meet parents' wishes if this can be done within the existing accommodation and staffing resources of the school in question' (para. 6). It accepted COSLA's argument that authorities needed to determine planned capacity and annual intake limits for each school, and agreed that the former could be less than the school's physical capacity where an authority wished to end the use of annexes, temporary buildings or other unsatisfactory accommodation (para. 9). It sought views on whether or not places should be reserved for incomers to the catchment area (para. 10). In order to deal with over-subscribed schools, authorities would be required to devise guidelines for determining which cases should be given priority (para. 22). Priority would still be given to children from the catchment area. However, where some children from outside the catchment area were refused admission, authorities were to set up appeal procedures involving, in the first instance, headteachers, School Councils and, subsequently, committees of the authority with the same constitution and powers as those proposed in the (English) Education (No.2) Bill (see above, paras. 23–9). The Consultative Paper also listed the information (including examination results) which authorities would have to provide for parents (paras. 15–18) and concluded by giving local authorities, teachers associations and bodies representing parents twelve weeks in which to submit their comments.

The Consultative Paper reflected a number of developments in the government's position. First, legislation was promised, if not immediately, then at least at some time in the future. This reflected the Minister's concern to ensure that all parents could exercise choice at all stages, his worry that some education authorities would not agree to this voluntarily, and the fact that his existing powers were limited to amending an authority's policy on transfer to secondary school. In addition to these general considerations, the Consultative Paper was no doubt also influenced by the continuing dispute between the Secretary of State and Lothian Region over Lothian's transfer scheme. Secondly, although the Consultative Paper encouraged authorities to consider adopting wider catchment zones, it no longer contained any specific references to the piloting of 'free choice' schemes. Likewise, although it encouraged schools to develop their own ethos, it was noticeably cautious about curricular diversity. These two changes can be taken to reflect the moderating influence of the SED. Thirdly, in borrowing only one provision (concerning the constitution and powers of appeal committees) from the English legislation, strong evidence is provided for the separate elaboration of parental choice legislation in Scotland.[17]

The Consultative Paper was given a fairly cool reception. Altogether, some fifteen organisations responded, of whom four were teachers' unions and three were headteachers' associations (Macbeth, Strachan and Macaulay, 1986). Four proposals received general support: retaining catchment areas (once again, there was little enthusiasm for the adoption of wider catchment zones); giving authorities the power to set admission limits; reserving places for incomers to the catchment area; and requiring the provision of information. On the other hand, there was widespread criticism of the government's approach on the grounds that it would raise expectations which would not be satisfied. There was also a general concern about the effects of the proposals on the reputations of individual schools, especially in deprived areas, and on staff morale. In addition, fears were expressed that the 'Parents' Charter' would bring back a 'two-tier' system of secondary schools. Many reservations were also expressed about the publication of examination results. COSLA took the view that the existing practices satisfied the 'broad interests' of parents and pupils. It opposed the statutory imposition on local authorities of standard practices and procedures, such as those relating to appeal procedures, and criticised the Consultative Paper for tipping the balance too far in favour of individual parents. On the other hand, the scc argued that in some respects the Consultative Paper did not go far enough. Thus, it criticised the government for ignoring the issue of under-age admissions to primary schools, and argued that parents should be given a statutory right of appeal to the sheriff.[18] This would eliminate the undesirable practice of keeping children out of school in order to invoke the attendance order procedure (Scottish Consumer Council, 1980).

In July 1980, in a written parliamentary answer, Fletcher announced that he proposed to introduce legislation much along the lines of his Consultative Paper, the only major change being the provision of an appeal to the sheriff by a parent who was aggrieved by a decision of an appeal committee. Thus, when the Education (Scotland) (No.2) Bill was laid before Parliament in December 1980, it contained few surprises.[19] Education authorities would still be able to allocate children to schools, but parents would be given a right to make a placing request for another school and the authority would be required to grant such requests unless one of seven grounds for refusal applied. The most important of these seven exceptions applied to circumstances where the school was over-subscribed and the admission of the child would 'exceed the planned admission limit for that school or that stage of education' (cl. 28A(3)(a)(i)), or 'require engaging an extra teacher in the school or give rise to significant expenditure on extending or otherwise altering the accommodation at or facilities provided in connection with the school . . .or be likely to be seriously detrimental to order and discipline in the school or the educational well-being of the pupils there' (cl. 28A(3)(a)(ii) and (v)). However, the authority could still grant a placing request even if one of the grounds for refusal existed. Education authorities would be required to publish their admission arrangements and the order of priorities which would apply if a school were over-subscribed (cl. 28B(1)). Where a placing request is refused, parents would be able to refer the case to an appeal committee set up by the authority (cl. 28D(1))[20] and subsequently to a sheriff. The powers of the appeal committee and the sheriff were to be identical to those of the authority and, where an appeal was upheld, the decision would be binding on the authority (cl. 28E(4) and 28F(5)). The only provision in the Bill which was not foreshadowed in Fletcher's parliamentary answer or in the draft of the legislative proposals was a novel requirement that where an appeal is upheld and analogous placing requests have been refused, the authority must review their decisions in such cases and, where they do not reverse their decision, the parents who have been refused must be given a further right of appeal (cl. 28E(5) and 28F(6)).

In arguing against the Bill, the Opposition (comprising Labour members and Gordon Wilson for the SNP) did not launch a frontal attack on the ideology underlying the proposed legislation or give much direct support to the stance adopted by Lothian Region. They stressed that they were not opposed to the principle of parental choice, although they thought that it had to be balanced against other considerations. They argued that legislation was unnecessary, since most authorities already operated flexible admissions procedures and upheld the majority of appeals. Tacitly accepting that Lothian Region's strict catchment-area policy was an exception, they likened the Bill to 'a sledgehammer that was being used to crack a nut'.

The Opposition believed that the proposed procedures would be cumbersome and expensive to operate, and held that they could not be justified while the government continued to reduce expenditure on education. They argued that the Bill was irresponsible in that it would raise parents' expectations beyond the point where they could be real-ised, so that many parents would be disappointed. They opposed the introduction of an appeal to the sheriff and, rather surprisingly, would have preferred appeals to go to the Secretary of State. And, finally, they feared that the proposed legislation would undermine the comprehen-sive principle and lead to the re-emergence of a two-tier pattern of junior and senior secondary schools (H.C.Debs, Vol.998, cols.1002–76 and First Scottish Standing Committee, cols.40–468).

Of the fifteen organisations which responded to the Consultative Paper, only a handful made clause-by-clause criticisms of the Bill or prepared detailed amendments.[21] Moreover, only the scc and, to a much lesser extent cosla, made any attempt at lobbying. The Govern-ment successfully moved one amendment, at the instigation of the scc, to the effect that a placing request could only be refused if a local authority had to take an additional teacher into employment.[22] By contrast the Opposition moved a large number of amendments, many of which had been proposed by cosla, but none of them was successful. In every division, voting proceeded along party lines.

The lack of support for Lothian reflected the geographical distribution of Opposition mps, most of whom came from the West of Scotland.[23] However, it was significant that none of the Region's six Labour mps participated in the debates or spoke up in favour of the Region's stance. The leading Opposition speakers, representing constituencies in Strath-clyde, Central and Tayside Regions, may well have concluded that, in spite of their objections to the Bill, they could live with it since it would not, in practice, pose any significant threat to the majority of education authorities.

Thus the Opposition came to terms with the Bill. However, the truce did not last very long. The whole impact of the Bill, and the balance it sought to strike between the rights of individual parents and the collec-tive responsibilities of education authorities, was fundamentally altered by the Government's announcement at the Report Stage that it proposed to delete the provision (in cl. 28A(3)(a)(i)) which would have enabled an authority to fix admission limits for its schools and for each stage within them (H.C. Debs, Vol.6, cols.213–16).

It is not absolutely clear what caused the Government to change its mind at this late stage. In moving the amendment, Fletcher referred only to press reports that education authorities regarded the provision as 'an important safeguard against the worst excesses of the Parents' Charter' and that COSLA had argued that 'without the safeguard, there would be an exodus from unpopular to popular schools' (H.C. Debs, Vol.6, col.215). However, an amendment along these lines had been proposed by the SCC (Scottish Consumer Council, 1981) and the SPTC, who pointed out that authorities could have used the provision to reinforce rigid catchment area policies and to deny or seriously restrict choice. The Government may well have been influenced by this.

Opposition MPs were predictably furious. COSLA was equally incensed, not only by the amendment but also by the stage at which it was introduced. Their co-operation with the Government had throughout been on the understanding that any legislation would contain such a provision. However, despite intensive lobbying, it was clear that the Government would not back down. The Bill went to the Lords in June 1981 (H.L. Debs, Vol.421, cols.1181–1209). A number of further amendments were moved in Committee but only one was successful (H.L. Debs, Vol.424, col.249). This had the effect of debarring members of the education authority or its education committee from chairing an appeal committee. This amendment was, once again, the result of SCC lobbying. The Bill received its Royal Assent in October 1981, some 14 months after the statutory enactment of parental choice in England.

COMPARISONS BETWEEN THE SCOTTISH AND THE ENGLISH LEGISLATION

The general structure of the parental choice provisions of the Education (Scotland) Act 1981 is in many ways similar to that of the Education Act 1980. (The relevant parts of the two pieces of legislation are set out in full in Appendices A and B.) In Scotland, as in England, parents were given the right to request that their children be admitted to a particular school or schools; education authorities were required to comply with parental requests unless a statutory exception to this general duty applied; dissatisfied parents were given the right to appeal to a statutory appeal committee and, if the latter found in favour of the parent, its decision was to be binding on the authority; and education authorities were required to provide parents with information about their allocation procedure and the criteria for admitting children to over-subscribed schools, about the school to which their child had been allocated and about any other school if the parents asked for it.[24] However, there were also some important differences between the two pieces of legislation.

First, while the English legislation gave every parent the right to express a preference for a particular school and to give reasons for their preference (Education Act 1980, s.56(1)), the Scottish legislation gave parents the right to make a placing request but made no reference to the giving of reasons (Education (Scotland) Act 1981, s.28A(1)). Scottish education authorities are required to formulate 'guidelines to be followed ... in the event of there being more placing requests made ... than there are places available' (Education (Scotland) Act 1981, s.28B(1)(c)) but there is no statutory requirement that the guidelines should refer to the reasons offered by the parents or to the circumstances of the children concerned. The significance of the distinction is that the reference to reasons in the English legislation serves to qualify choices while the absence of any reference to reasons in the Scottish legislation suggests that the fact of choice is really all that matters.

Secondly, the statutory exceptions to the authorities' duty to comply with parents' requests were broad and general in England but much more specific in Scotland. In England, the primary exception, which applied when compliance with parents' requests would 'prejudice the provision of efficient education or the efficient use of resources' (Education Act 1980, s.6(3)) enabled an authority to justify a refusal by referring to conditions at schools other than the one requested by the parents or to conditions in their schools generally. By contrast, in Scotland, where the primary exceptions applied when compliance would entail either the employment by the authority of an additional teacher, or significant extensions or alterations to the school or 'be likely to be seriously detrimental to order and discipline at the school or the educational well-being of the pupils there' (Education (Scotland) Act 1981, s.28A(3)(a)), the authority could only refer to conditions at the school requested by the parents.[25] Not only were the grounds for refusal more narrowly defined in Scotland, the standards for refusal are actually higher. Thus, the Scottish legislation referred to 'serious detriment' while the English legislation referred only to 'prejudice'.

Thirdly, whereas parents in Scotland could appeal against an adverse decision of an appeal committee to the sheriff (Education (Scotland) Act 1981, s.28F), parents in England had no further right of appeal. The right of appeal to the sheriff in Scotland is important for at least three reasons: parents have a second chance if the appeal committee confirms the authority's decision; sheriffs are independent of the authority and are unlikely to be predisposed to the authority's concerns, unlike the appeal committees which include a majority of authority members; and appeals to the sheriff involve independent judges interpreting and applying the authority's duty directly to the parents' request. Appeals to the sheriff are not strictly reviews of the authority's decisions, but are *de novo* decisions of whether the authority has grounds for refusing the parents school request under the 1981 Act. The authority must convince the sheriff that it has grounds to refuse the parents' request. Sheriffs would not be bound by the authority's interpretation of the grounds of refusal. An unanticipated consequence of the existence of a right of appeal to the sheriff has been to enable the parents of children under school-age to challenge decisions to refuse their entry on age grounds. Following the decision of a sheriff in a 'test case' that requests from under-age children were to be treated as placing requests, many parents have appealed against such refusals. In these cases, the relevant exception to the authority's duty to comply is 'if the education normally provided at the specified school is not suited to the age, ability or aptitude of the child' (Education (Scotland) Act 1981, s.28A(3)(b)).

Fourthly, the statutory duties of appeal committees (and sheriffs) are more clearly defined in the Scottish legislation. In Scotland, they are obliged to uphold the appeal unless they are satisfied that one or more of the statutory grounds for refusal applies (Education (Scotland) Act 1981, ss.28E(1)(a) and 28F(5)(a)) and, where one or more grounds does apply, they can confirm the authority's refusal only if they are satisfied 'that, in all the circumstances, it is appropriate to do so' (Education (Scotland) Act 1981, ss.28E(1)(b) and 28F(5)(b). In England, on the other hand, the statutory duty is much less clearly defined.[26]

Fifthly, where an appeal is upheld in Scotland, the authority is required to review the cases of all parents in similar circumstances who have not appealed and, if its decisions are unchanged, it has to grant the parents a further right of appeal. There is no comparable provision in the English legislation.

CONCLUSIONS

It is somewhat ironic that, although the primary impetus for parental choice legislation came from England, the Scottish legislation appears to have resulted in stronger rights for parents. The explanation for this irony lies partly in the greater salience of parental choice in England and the fact that the previous (Labour) Government had already produced an English, but not a Scottish Bill; partly in the different perspectives of the ministers responsible for the two pieces of legislation; and partly in the relative influence of English and Scottish local authorities. Since the DES had already produced a Bill for the previous (Labour) Government and the new (Conservative) Administration was under pressure to legislate quickly, DES civil servants argued that the most expeditious way of proceeding was to amend Labour's 1978 Bill and DES ministers agreed. However, because the previous Government had decided against introducing parental choice legislation for Scotland, this option was not available to Scottish Office ministers. Moreover, Scottish Office ministers were not under the same pressure to legislate quickly. Thus, unlike his

English counterparts, the Scottish Education Minister could start the legislative process from scratch.

The Secretary of State for Education and Science, Mark Carlisle, was rather lukewarm in his support for parental choice. Although he recognised the Government's manifesto commitment and was committed to the principle of parental choice, he was concerned that it should not give rise to additional spending or result in an inefficient use of resources. Moreover, at the end of the day, he was prepared to trust English LEAs to implement the legislation in good faith. On the other hand, the Scottish Education Minister, Alex Fletcher, was very strongly committed to parental choice. Having been closely involved in the disputes over parental choice of school in Edinburgh, it is clear that he did not trust the education authorities and was thus determined that legislation should specify all the exceptions to the authority's general duty to comply with parental requests. He was able to do so, in part because COSLA (which was Labour controlled) had less influence over the Scottish Office than the English local authority associations, in particular the Conservative controlled Association of County Councils (ACC), had over the DES. Thus, as we have seen, COSLA was unable to prevent the Government from removing, at a very late stage in the parliamentary process, a key provision in the Bill which would have allowed education authorities to fix the maximum number of pupils to be educated at a school or at a stage of education in a school and to refuse a placing request where the maximum number has already been reached.

COSLA's lack of influence with the Government, and the Government's own populist tendencies, allowed organisations representing parents (SPTC) and consumers (SCC) to exercise considerable influence over the Government and it is significant that these two organisations lobbied successfully for all the amendments that were adopted. Those who had come to regard themselves as 'insiders' in the policy process strongly resented the influence of these two 'outside' organisations.[27] Although the Government had gone through the motions of consulting the 'insiders', the 'outsiders' clearly had a greater impact on the final outcome.

McPherson and Raab (1988) conclude their epic study of post-war educational policy making in Scotland by suggesting that the increasing political assertiveness of Government had led to a decline in the traditional forms of 'partnership' between the SED, education authorities and teachers. Our account of the making of the Scottish parental choice legislation supports that conclusion. Thus the issue is no longer whether 'pluralism' or 'corporatism' best describes the process of decision making within the policy community, a term they use to denote the 'set of persons and groups which stretches across the divide between government and outside interests and which is directly involved in the making and implementation of policy'. It is rather whether, at least in relation to policy making, the traditional educational policy community is being by-passed altogether. Although one of the aims of the parental choice legislation may have been to reduce the influence of education authorities and teachers by increasing the local influence of parents, the demise of the educational policy community could have far-reaching implications for Scottish education.[28]

NOTES

1. Our account of the genesis and passage of the English legislation is based on interviews conducted with most of the key participants (listed below) and an examination of files kept by the Association of County Councils (ACC) and the Association of Metropolitan Authorities (AMA). Since some of the interviews were given, and the ACC and AMA files were made available on the understanding that we would not reveal the identities of those involved, this account contains no attributable material. We interviewed the following:

   Margaret Beckett (Minister of State for Education and Science, 1976-1979 as Margaret Jackson)

   Alan Beith (Liberal Spokesman on Education)

   Andrew Bennett (Member of the Standing Committees for the 1978 Labour Bill and the 1979 Conservative Bill)

   Rhodes Boyson (Member of the Conservative Backbench Education Committee 1974–1979 and Parliamentary Under-Secretary for Education and Science 1979–1981)

   Tyrrell Burgess (education journalist and member of the Labour Party's National Executive Committee, Education and Science Sub-committee 1970–1979)

   Mark Carlisle (Opposition Spokesman on Education 1978–1979 and Secretary of State for Education and Science 1979–1981)

   Bert Clough (Education Secretary, Labour Party)

   Gordon Cunningham (Education Officer, Association of County Councils)

   Geoffrey Duncan (Schools Secretary, General Synod of the Church of England)

   Keith Hampson (member of the Conservative Backbench Education Committee 1974–1979)

   Lady David (Opposition Whip and Spokesman for Education in the Lords)

   Eric Midwinter (National Consumer Council)

   Roger Morgan (Department of Education and Science)

   Robert Morris (Deputy Education Officer, Association of Metropolitan Authorities)

   Gordon Oakes (Minister of State for Education and Science 1977–1979)

   Christopher Price (Member of Standing Committees for the 1978 Labour Bill and the 1979 Conservative Bill)

John Ranelagh (Conservative Research Department 1975–1978)

John Rowe (National Union of Teachers)

Clive Saville (Department of Education and Science)

Stuart Sexton (Advisor to Norman St John-Stevas, Mark Carlisle, and Sir Keith Joseph)

Peter Sloman (Education Officer, Association of Metropolitan Authorities)

Shirley Williams (Secretary of State for Education and Science 1976–1979)

Lady Young (Minister of State for Education and Science 1979–1981).

2. Lord Denning's judgment in *Watt v Kesteven County Council* [1955] 1 Q B 408 is universally regarded as the correct interpretation of section 76 (see Chapter 1).

3. For an account of the diversity of allocation procedures in England and Wales, see Stillman and Maychell (1986), Chapter 3.

4. In 1969, the Labour Government raised the possibility of establishing an independent appeals system for parents as part of a new Education Bill. The Government wanted parents to have some means of complaining about their child's school allocation that did not involve the Secretary of State. This proposal received only moderate support, even from parents' groups. The Government's preparations for consultations about the Bill were cut off by the General Election called in 1970. (*The Times*, 25 March 1969; Middleton and Weitzman, 1977).

5. Under section 68 of the 1944 Act, parents could complain to the Secretary of State for Education and Science about decisions of the LEA. The Secretary of State had authority to overturn the LEA's decision if it was considered to be unreasonable (see Chapter 1).

6. Some parents withheld their children from school in disputes over school admissions. Under section 37 of the 1944 Act, LEAS would then seek an order requiring parents to send their children to a named school. Parents could request a change in the named school (to the school of their choice) and, if no agreement was reached between the parent and the LEA, the Secretary of State had to decide which school was named (see Chapter 1).

7. From 1967–1972, Lady Young was Leader of the Conservative Group on Oxford City Council.

8. Educational voucher schemes would provide all parents of school children with a publicly-funded voucher that they could use to pay fees at private as well as state schools. The establishment of vouchers would create a state-financed market in education. See Friedman, 1962; Beales, Blaug, Veale, West and Boyson, 1970; West, 1970; Maynard, 1975; and Coons and Sugarman, 1978.

9. Our account of the background and enactment of the Scottish legislation is based on interviews conducted with many of the key participants (listed below) and an examination of files kept by the Convention of Scottish Local Authorities (COSLA) and the Scottish Consumer Council (SCC). For the reasons outlined in Note 1 above and in order not to reveal the identities of the

individuals concerned, this account also contains no attributable material. We interviewed the following:

Graham Atherton (Scottish Consumer Council)

Denis Canavan (Member of the Standing Committee for the
English and Scottish Bills)

Pat Cox (Scottish Education Department)

Alex Fletcher (Parliamentary Under-Secretary of State for
Education and Industry in the Scottish Office)

William Livingstone (Secretary to Education Committee,
Convention of Scottish Local Authorities (COSLA))

Martin O'Neil (Opposition Spokesman on Scottish Education
and Member of the Standing Committee for the Scottish Bill)

David Robertson (Director of Education for Tayside Region
and Adviser to COSLA)

David Semple (Director of Education for Lothian Region and
Adviser to COSLA).

10. Kellas (1984) describes Scottish education as 'one of the best-
defined arenas of Scottish life and one that most maintains the
boundaries of the Scottish political system'. Nevertheless, particularly on 'grand' issues, the policy agenda is often, as in this
case, a UK policy agenda. On this issue, see Keating and Midwinter (1983), Parry (1987) and McPherson and Raab (1988).

11. This greater degree of confidence in the educational system can
be explained in terms of the potent and lasting influence of the
'Scottish myth', i.e. the widespread (but not necessarily well-
founded) belief in the superiority of Scottish education and, in
particular, of the general curriculum, the common school and
the 'lad o' pairts' (McPherson and Raab, 1988). However, the
general preference among Scots for collective forms of social
and political organisation is clearly also an important factor.

12. This difference between England and Scotland can be highlighted by comparing the contents of the *Times Educational Supplement* (TES) with those of its Scottish counterpart, the *Times
Educational Supplement Scotland* (TESS) over the period 1974–1979.
While there were more than 200 references to parental choice in
the TES, there were a mere twelve in the TESS.

13. After one early case (*Davison v Dunfermline District Education
Sub-committee*, (1974)) the successful parent was subsequently
elected to Fife Regional Council as a Conservative councillor.
However, that was in 1974 and his election does not appear to
have had any wider repercussions.

14. For an administrative defence of the neighbourhood school
principle, see Semple (1980).

15. This was the first of several meetings between the Minister, SED
officials, elected members of COSLA's Education Committee and
Directors of Education (in their role as advisers to COSLA) at
which the Minister outlined the government's thinking in general terms and sought a response from the Convention.

16. Previous Consultative Papers dealt with curriculum development, education for the 16–18s and the assisted places scheme.

17. The separate elaboration in Scotland of issues drawn from the
UK policy agenda is, arguably, the dominant mode of educational policy making for issues that have high political salience. According to McPherson and Raab (1988), educational
expansion, the movement towards national certification and the

move to comprehensive secondary education can all be described in this way. For a comparison between secondary school
reorganisation and parental choice, see also Adler, Petch and
Tweedie (1987).

18. In the Consultative Paper (Scottish Education Department,
1980), the Government had stated that there were no proposals
for changing the existing attendance order procedure.

19. Other provisions in the Bill dealt with special educational
needs, the assisted places scheme, changes in the powers of the
Secretary of State and the duties of education authorities, the
examination board, teachers' pay and conditions of service, and
educational endowments.

20. Comprising 3, 5 or 7 members. Members of the authority or its
education committee could not outnumber non-members by
more than one. Appeal committees were placed under the
general supervision of the Scottish Committee of the Council on
Tribunals.

21. COSLA, the EIS, the SCC and the SPTC all prepared detailed
amendments to the Bill.

22. The SCC pointed out (Scottish Consumer Council, 1981) that the
wording of the Bill would have enabled an authority to reject
placing requests if it chose not to transfer staff from under-
subscribed to over-subscribed schools. The amendment was
intended to prevent authorities from refusing placing requests
in these circumstances and to encourage transfers of staff.

23. The Standing Committee which considered the Bill comprised,
in addition to the Labour Chairman (Harry Gourlay), nine
Government supporters and eight members of the Opposition
(seven Labour and one SNP). They represented constituencies
in the following Regions: Central (3), Fife (2), Tayside (2) and
Strathclyde (Glasgow and Kilmarnock) (2). No Lothian MPs
served on the Committee .

24. A general, non-technical discussion of the parental choice provisions in the 1981 Act can be found in Atherton (1987), a
comprehensive guide to education law in Scotland written from
a consumer perspective.

25. The three exceptions have to be combined because none is
sufficient standing alone. Numbers of pupils at the school
would never make it necessary for an authority to employ an
additional teacher or extend the school's buildings unless concern for quality of education (the avoidance of serious detriment) is incorporated into the idea of necessity. Likewise,
numbers of children at the school would never cause serious
detriment to education at the school if the authority could
simply add new teachers and extensions to the facilities. Curi-
ously, the SED did not recognise this situation. They interpreted
the 'seriously detrimental' exception to apply only to cases in
which the behaviour or special educational needs of the particular pupil involved was likely to cause disruption at the school.
See SED Circular 1074 (Scottish Education Department, 1981).

26. In the only case of judicial review to reach the courts so far (R v
South Glamorgan Appeal Committee ex parte Evans (1984)) Justice
Forbes read the 1980 Act to require that (English) appeal committees adopt a two-stage consideration. They were first to
decide if the admission of that one child would have prejudiced

efficient education at the school. He insisted that the decision
'be limited to the one child under consideration'. On the issue of
prejudice he wrote, 'the onus seems to me to be clearly on the
education authority'. So the appeal committee must be convinced that the admission of the single child would cause prejudice. If not, it must uphold the appeal of the parent. If the appeal
committee found that prejudice would result from admitting
the child, they were to move on to the second stage, determining whether the prejudice caused was 'sufficient to outweigh
the parental factors'. From this it is not clear how much weight
should be assigned to the 'parental factors', but it is clear that a
finding of prejudice, even prejudice that can be attributed to the
admission of the one child being considered, is not sufficient.
The local authority associations and the Council on Tribunals
issued a revised Code of Practice (Association of County Councils, 1985) which followed the South Glamorgan decision in
recommending a two-stage decision procedure although it did
not adopt the focus on the single child, saying that 'where two
or more appeals are being decided together in respect of the
same school, this process may involve considering the consequences of allowing all or only some appeals.'
For a further discussion of the South Glamorgan case, see Chapter 7 and Tweedie (1986b).

27. After the government had successfully moved the deletion of
clause 28(3)(a)(i) John Pollock, General Secretary of the EIS (Educational Institute of Scotland), was quoted as saying 'The
government is using outside organisations in order to slip
through vital amendments which would fundamentally affect
Scottish education in years to come without consultation and
with the minimum of fuss' (*The Scotsman*, 16 May 1981).

28. The long-running and bitter dispute over teachers' pay and
conditions was due, at least in part, to teachers' frustration at
their virtual exclusion from the policy community.

3

THE IMPLEMENTATION AND ADMINISTRATION OF THE 1981 ACT

The Education (Scotland) Act 1981 replaced much of the discretion that education authorities had exercised over school admissions with a regime of parents' rights. Authorities could refuse parents' school requests only if a statutory ground of refusal applied. And parents could appeal against authorities' refusals to appeal committees set up by the authorities and then to the sheriff. Finally, authorities had to provide parents with information about their schools and their admission arrangements. [1] However, many features of the authorities' existing procedures could be left in place. Most importantly, authorities could continue to base school admissions on catchment areas or feeder schools, initially allocating all children to schools on the basis of their residence or prior school, and then transferring children if parents made a placing request for a different school and no statutory ground of refusal existed. All Scottish authorities used catchment-area or feeder-school schemes before the 1980 Act and no authority changed the basis of its admissions scheme after the Act. Changes in their admission procedures came in three main areas: grounds for refusing parents' requests, appeals, and information for parents.

In this chapter, we consider the way three authorities – Burns, Watt and Maxton – incorporated the requirements of the 1981 Act. In each case, we examine the basis of the pre-1981 Act admissions scheme and then discuss how the authorities altered their procedures in the course of implementing the 1981 Act. We also look at how the new procedures and the placing requests they gave rise to have affected school admissions and the operation of the authorities' schools generally.

In this examination, we see how the three authorities adopted primarily collective welfare orientations in school admissions, both before and after implementation of the 1981 Act. They demonstrated little concern for which schools particular children attended, instead focusing on how the pattern of school admissions related to their central policy concerns. And, for most decisions, they relied on simple rules and procedures, choosing administrative efficiency over individualised consideration of admissions. However, we also see how each authority's approach to school admissions and how it implemented the 1981 Act depended very much on the circumstances of the authority. For instance, in two of the case study authorities – Watt and Maxton – the 1981 Act resulted in few policy changes or disputes. Although there were a substantial number of placing requests in both Regions, particularly in Maxton where the incidence of placing requests was among the highest in Scotland, policy-makers have been prepared to live with the consequences of parental choice. In Burns, however, large numbers of placing requests and long-standing political controversy over parental choice put issues of implementation at the centre of educational policy-making. Our discussion of implementation begins with an extended examination of Burns Region as it provides for the most complete examination of the implementation of the 1981 Act. The experience of Burns with the 1981 Act is, of course, not typical of all other Scottish authorities. Indeed, it is Burns' special difficulties with parental choice that make it an especially useful case study. After our discussion of Burns, we examine Watt and Maxton Regions to highlight the particular issues that have arisen in these authorities and to develop a more balanced understanding of the implementation of the 1981 Act.

PARENTAL CHOICE AND THE 1981 ACT IN BURNS REGION

Burns Region is one of several in Scotland that include both a large urban area and substantial rural areas.[2] In Burns, most of the urban area is contained in one geographical division which is the focus of this case study (Burns City). Our discussion focuses on Burns City's primary schools and its twenty non-denominational secondary schools. The city also contains a number of prominent independent secondary schools which are attended by almost twenty per cent of secondary school pupils and a disproportionately high number of the most able children.

PARENTAL CHOICE BEFORE THE 1981 ACT

Beginning in 1975, when the recently created Burns Region took over responsibilities for education, the Labour administration operated a restrictive catchment area policy in school admissions. All children were initially allocated to the school for the area in which they lived. Although parents could request an alternative non-district school, the Director of Education granted such requests only if the child had an older sibling at the school, had a medical certificate from the Regional Health Board, or had attended a selective primary school.[3] No exceptions were granted if the school was full. Burns adopted this policy in order to build links between schools and their communities, to prevent some schools benefiting at the expense of others and to try to ensure that all schools contained pupils with the full range of interests and abilities.

For the secondary schools in Burns City, the number of non-district requests declined steadily from 1976 to 1980. Presumably, parents learned of the Region's strict catchment-area policy and, unless they could cite one of the three recognised reasons, made fewer requests. This explanation is supported by the increase in the proportion of requests granted by the Director during this period. At the same time, the drop in the number of children entering secondary school reduced the number of schools that were full so that, by 1980, no school reached its admission capacity. More places became available for non-district requests, but Burns' policy prevented many children from moving into non-district schools (see Table 3.1).

Parents could appeal requests refused by the Director to the Transfer Committee, composed of five elected and three appointed members of the Education Committee. (Early on, Burns had established a practice of allowing appeals to committees of elected members concerning any application of policy by officials.) The Transfer Committee evaluated parents' requests in order to ascertain whether special circumstances existed. The appeals were decided on parents' written submissions as summarised in a report by the Education Department. Education officials were present at meetings to explain the Director's decision and to answer any questions. Parents were not allowed to attend.

The Transfer Committee considered each appeal separately. Many of the appeals cited common reasons, such as the proximity of the school to the child's home, ease of travel, the fact that the child's friends would be going to the requested school, or a simple and unelaborated preference for the school. In virtually every case, these reasons standing alone were not sufficient to sustain an appeal. The Committee routinely upheld appeals in a few special categories such as medical reasons involving some external support (such as a doctor's letter), single parent families, siblings attending the requested school (where the Education Depart-

Table 3.1. Transfers to secondary school in Burns City, 1976–1981

	1976	1977	1978	1979	1980	1981
Transfer places	5 452	5 373	6 085	5 159	4 953	4 592
Pupils	5 280	4 957	5 918	4 768	4 503	4 108
(% of places)	96.8	92.3	97.2	92.4	90.9	89.5
Non-district school requests	644	425	443	309	281	362
(% of pupils)	12.2	8.6	7.5	6.5	6.2	8.8
Requests granted administratively	222	215	255	178	138	360
(% of requests)	34.5	50.6	57.6	57.6	49.1	99.4
Refusals to schools with places	181	148	60	133	143	0
(% of refusals)	42.9	70.4	31.7	100	100	0

Note: In 1981, Burns' secondary transfer admissions were operated under a Transfer Scheme modified by the Secretary of State for Scotland to include the statutory grounds of refusal contained in the 1981 Act.

ment had refused the request because the school was full), pupils attending formerly selective primary schools (refused because the associated school was full), and (less frequently) pupils who wanted a specific education course which was available only at the requested school.[4] The Transfer Committee sometimes upheld appeals involving no special parental reason because it wanted to bolster the enrolment of the schools being chosen. One such school was considered too small and two others were located in depressed working class areas that the Labour administration wanted to strengthen. In addition, the Committee upheld a number of requests for reasons specific to the child's or the family's circumstances. These appeals included a child who had been repeatedly bullied by pupils at his district school, one whose father worked as a policeman in the area of the district school, and one who was responsible for picking up his handicapped brother near the requested school.

The Transfer Committee upheld an increasing proportion of appeals in succeeding years. They upheld only 13 per cent of appeals in 1976 but over 61 per cent of appeals in 1980 (see Table 3.2).

The increased rate of successful appeals reflects both the changing substantive composition of appeals and the Transfer Committee members' increasing receptiveness to appeals. Fewer appeals involved schools that had reached their capacity. Also, some Committee members believed that many parents had discovered what reasons had worked in the past and then gave these reasons in support of their case (presumably short of making themselves into a single parent family or adopting children at the desired school). These Committee members were particularly sceptical of parents who cited medical reasons or a preference for a specific educational course. Each year, a higher proportion of appeals

Table 3.2. Secondary transfer appeals in Burns City, 1976–1981

	1976	1977	1978	1979	1980	1981
Pupils	5 280	4 957	5 918	4 768	4 503	4 108
Requests refused administratively	422	210	189	133	143	2
Appeals to Transfer Committee	184	160	112	63	73	1
(% of refusals)	43.6	76.2	59.3	47.4	51.0	50.0
Appeals upheld	24	64	64	35	45	0
(% of appeals)	13.0	40.0	57.1	55.6	61.6	0

Note: In 1981, Burns' secondary transfer admissions were operated under a Transfer Scheme modified by the Secretary of State for Scotland to include the statutory grounds of refusal contained in the 1981 Act.

fitted into the established categories of successful reasons. At the same time, new Committee members were often more sympathetic to parents and less disposed to refuse requests on the principle of maintaining neighbourhood schools on the grounds that a few pupils here or there did not make much of a difference. (The Labour Administration decided against enforcing party discipline on these votes, as they did in all policy areas where individuals could appeal officials' decisions to a committee of elected members.)

The experience with parents' school requests in primary school admissions was similar to that in secondary transfer. By 1977, primary school intakes had passed their peak. There was no general shortage of places, although a few schools were oversubscribed each year. The proportion of non-district requests at primary entry declined from 11.4 per cent in 1977 to 7.4 per cent in 1981. The Director granted requests almost exclusively in cases where an older sibling attended the requested school. Only 11 of 974 requests allowed administratively from 1977 to 1981 did not involve an older sibling at the school (see Table 3.3).

The Transfer Committee also heard parents' appeals relating to primary entry beginning in 1977. Parents appealed a large majority of decisions to refuse requests, over 80 per cent in 1978 and 1979. The Transfer Committee decided these appeals following the same procedure used in secondary transfer appeals. It looked at each appeal in

Table 3.3. Entrants to primary school and appeals in Burns City, 1977–1981

	1977	1978	1979	1980	1981
Entering pupils	5 219	4 875	4 344	3 916	3 872
Non-district school requests	593	393	327	289	285
(% of pupils)	11.4	8.1	7.5	7.4	7.4
Requests granted administratively	325	241	160	127	121
(% of requests)	54.8	61.3	48.9	43.9	42.5
Requests refused administratively	268	152	167	162	164
(% of requests)	45.2	38.7	51.1	56.1	57.5
Requests refused to schools with places	246	152	159	161	163
(% of refusals)	91.8	100	95.2	99.4	99.4
Appeals to the Transfer Committee	136	125	134	109	111
(% of refusals)	50.7	82.2	80.2	67.7	67.7
Appeals upheld	73	57	68	46	49
(% of appeals)	53.7	45.6	50.8	42.2	44.1

turn, deciding whether the parents had given sufficiently strong reasons for their preference. The circumstances that moved the Transfer Committee were similar to those in secondary transfers, particularly single parent families and difficulties in access to school. The Transfer Committee upheld nearly half of the appeals it heard.

1981: A YEAR OF TRANSITION

Shortly after issuing the consultative paper, *Admission to School – A Charter for Parents* (Scottish Education Department, 1980), the Secretary of State specifically requested Burns to comply with the principles it contained. After Burns rejected his request, the Secretary of State directed it to prepare and submit a revised Transfer Scheme. (The Education (Scotland) Act 1962 gave the Secretary of State powers to require education authorities to submit new Transfer Schemes and to modify those Transfer Schemes as he saw fit before approving them.)[5] At this time, Burns was already embroiled in an acrimonious dispute with the Secretary of State over finances and spending (Heald, Jones and Lamont, 1981; Crompton, 1982) so it thought it could not afford to resist him on this issue. Burns submitted a revised Transfer Scheme that eased restrictions on parental choice, but the Secretary of State rejected the changes as insufficient. He modified the Transfer Scheme so that it provided that parents' requests would 'normally be granted if there is accommodation in the secondary school desired by the parents'. This became Burns' operative policy for secondary transfer in 1981. Application of the new scheme resulted in the acceptance of all but two parents' requests for non-district secondary schools in that year (see Table 3.1). Those two requests were turned down because the school was at the maximum intake level fixed under the Transfer Scheme. One parent appealed but the appeal was dismissed by the Transfer Committee. Burns maintained its strict catchment area policy for the other stages of education, including primary entry, as they were not subject to the Secretary of State's order.

BURNS' IMPLEMENTATION OF THE 1981 ACT

The shift from local authority discretion to parents' rights in the 1981 Act radically transformed the operation of school admissions in Burns. Burns now carried the burden of having to justify refusals of parents' requests, rather than parents having to justify exceptions to its policy. The statutory grounds of refusal limited the reasons the Region could use to justify refusals. Most importantly, the grounds of refusal precluded refusing parents' requests to promote neighbourhood schools, to protect comprehensive intakes, or to protect enrolments at undersubscribed schools.

Burns objected to the 1981 Act's parental choice provisions, fearing that the Act would result in many parents sending their children to

schools with especially good reputations while many schools in disadvantaged areas would have too few pupils. However, Alex Fletcher's
rebuff of the COSLA's pleas to reinstate the admission levels clause (see
Chapter 2), coupled with the Secretary of State's modifications of Burns'
1981 transfer policy and the continued acrimony between the Region and
the Secretary of State over finances and spending, set the context for the
Region's implementation of the 1981 Act. Despite concerns about the
effects, Burns' Labour Administration quickly resigned itself to the strict
terms of the Act. Adoption of new policies to comply with the Act was
anti-climactic, especially considering the controversial history of parental choice in Burns. The Labour Administration viewed implementation
as a technical rather than a political matter: how to comply with the Act
while maintaining, in so far as possible, the principal features of the
existing admission policies. It simply accepted the advice of the Director
of Education and the Regional Solicitor as to what changes were required
under the Act. It did not make any formal proposals for resistance. The
majority of the Labour group viewed as futile suggestions about working
out a plausible interpretation that would maintain some control over
school admissions. Education officials, the Regional Solicitor, and some
Labour members concluded that parents' rights of appeal, particularly
the appeal to the sheriff, provided an effective means of challenging
restrictive interpretations of parents' rights of school choice. Since parental choice had been such a contentious issue in Burns City, they
expected a high proportion of parents to appeal if their requests were
refused. The publicity concerning the 1981 Act had also reinforced
parents' conviction that they could choose which schools their children
attended.

Burns grafted the requirements of the Act onto the existing procedures
for school admissions. Children would continue to be allocated to their
catchment-area school. Parents would be notified of their child's allocation and their right to request a different school. (Notice was required
by the 1981 Act.) Parents' requests would be dealt with by the Education
Department. The Department would grant all requests unless there
appeared to be a statutory ground of refusal.

Requests where a possible ground of refusal existed would be forwarded to the Placing Request Committee (the successor to the Transfer
Committee). Where parents' requests for a school outnumbered the
places available at the school after catchment-area pupils had been
admitted, the Department would forward all requests for that school to
the Placing Request Committee. The Committee would decide which
requests would be refused and which granted. Regional policy also set
out criteria for deciding which pupils should be admitted to over-subscribed schools (as required by the Act). Priority was given to catchment-
area pupils. Officials chose not to put the remaining criteria in order. The
Placing Request Committee was charged with having regard to a list of

nine factors including medical reasons, siblings already in attendance at the school, an educational course available only at the school, and the proximity of home to school.[6]

Burns' arrangements for appeal committees generally followed the terms of the 1981 Act and the associated regulations. It decided to appoint five-member appeal committees drawn from three panels: three members from the Regional Council or the Education Committee, one member from a panel of parents suggested by the local Federation of Parent–Teacher Associations, and one member, who would chair the appeal committee, from a panel of people experienced in education. Burns decided that the three Council or Education Committee members would include one councillor from the Education Committee, one councillor not on the Education Committee and one non-councillor on the Education Committee to ensure a suitable balance. Finally, it decided that the chair of the appeal committees would be permanent to lend continuity and develop expertise in the appeal procedures.

Burns also had to plan how to determine the admission levels where they could justify refusing parents' requests under the Act. It decided not to set firm limits on all schools' enrolments, because falling rolls meant that most schools would always have unfilled places. It decided to carry over the nominal limits for secondary schools adopted at the Secretary of State's command in 1981 and evaluate whether the limits should be maintained if and when requests threatened to push admissions beyond the limit. It also adopted nominal limits at primary schools based on the number of available classrooms and a maximum of thirty-three pupils per class in most schools. Under this approach, few schools were likely to be over-subscribed because falling rolls created surplus capacity in almost all schools. However, the experience at two open-plan primary schools with class sizes of thirty-three convinced officials that the Region would have a good chance to establish 'serious detriment' if classes had more than thirty pupils. Burns adopted limits of thirty pupils per class in those schools. It decided that any other problems could be evaluated when they arose.

Finally, the 1981 Act required authorities to publish information to parents concerning the arrangements for school admissions and the character of particular schools. The statutory provisions and the subsequent regulations specify in considerable detail the information that must be provided to parents. For instance, brochures for particular schools were required to include information about their location, the headteacher, arrangements for parents' visits, provisions for religious instruction, extra-curricular activities, the curriculum, the school's policies on homework, uniform, and discipline, and examination policies and results.

Burns, like other authorities, resisted these information requirements because of the expense and effort involved in producing them. They were particularly concerned about school brochures. However, once the requirements were in place, Burns implemented them straightfor-wardly. Burns produced three information sheets for parents: *Placing in Schools* – which outlined parents' rights of choice (including the grounds of refusal and the right of appeal) and the Region's policies on infor-mation, special educational provision, and school transport; *Guidelines on Placing in Schools*, which set out the procedures and policies for deciding admissions to over-subscribed schools; and *Starting School*, which explained the statutory provisions and the Region's policies con-cerning entry to primary school. Burns remitted to each school the responsibility for producing school brochures that met the requirements of the statutory regulations.

Burns viewed providing information to parents as an administrative task, simply organising the publication of the types of information required by the 1981 Act and subsequent regulations. The Education Committee passed on the responsibilities to the Director without debate. The only controversial issue involved the publication of secondary schools' examination results. Burns opposed the inclusion of exam-ination results as required in the 1981 Act, but the regulations and an SED circular imposed clear obligations and even set out the format for pre-senting the results, so the Director only had to see that the information was collected. The clarity of the statutory requirements resulted in full compliance. Some schools produced brochures that went beyond the information required by the regulations, but for the most part, Burns Region provided only what was required.

In sum, Burns' response to the 1981 Act was to formulate procedures and policies consistent with the Act and to put off questions of how to deal with conflicts between parents' requests and their other concerns. The Act was specific and clear about authorities' duties. The Secretary of State had shown his willingness to respond harshly to resistance. And the appeal committees and the sheriffs were unlikely to uphold refusals not solidly grounded in the terms of the 1981 Act. The Labour Adminis-tration and the Education Department saw little choice but to accept the primacy of parents' school requests.

Local government elections were held shortly after Burns had adopted its new school admission policy and decided parents' schools requests for August 1982. No party won a majority. The Conservatives formed the administration with the support of the Alliance. However, the Alliance qualified its support for the Conservative Administration, agreeing only to let the Conservatives form an administration, but going its own way on matters that came before the Council. Because of this arrangement, the Conservatives could not count on support for their policies and, in a few vital votes, they were unable to implement their policies. Both the Conservatives and the Alliance supported parental choice. Thus, even without the 1981 Act, it is likely that Burns would have substantially loosened restrictions on parental choice. The Labour Administration's capitulation in 1982 indicated that the 1981 Act was sufficient in itself to force opponents of parental choice to grant parents' requests in virtually all circumstances. Moreover, the course of events after 1982 suggests that the Labour group, if they had maintained control of the Regional Council, would have acted in substantially the same way as the Conservative Administration did. The transformation of Burns' policy on parental choice should be attributed to the 1981 Act, not to the changing political control of the Regional Council.

FALLING ROLLS, REORGANISATION AND INTAKE LIMITS

By 1980, Burns had begun to recognise the problems that would be posed by falling school rolls. A working party set up by the Director of Education reported in October 1982 on the implications of falling rolls for secondary education and the possible responses that Burns might make. The report forecast that rolls in Burns City's secondary schools would drop from 27 040 in 1981 to 18 100 in 1991, a decline of 33 per cent. The consequences of this drop would be amplified because some schools were already dangerously small. The report identified 750 pupils as the point where secondary schools begin to suffer significant curriculum restrictions and require extra funding, and 500 as the point where under-enrolment reaches a crisis point, given current curriculum and funding constraints. It projected that three city schools would be at or below 500 pupils by 1991 and that an additional nine schools would be at or below 750 pupils. These schools would require substantial curriculum restrictions as well as increased funding.

The report also considered how Burns might respond to falling secondary school rolls. By 1991, 10–12 000 surplus secondary school places would exist (out of a total of 30 000 places). The number of surplus places could be reduced if nine secondary schools vacated annexes and temporary accommodation and consolidated on single sites. However, several of the schools with annexes or temporary units had, in the past, attracted many requests from parents and it was difficult to see how enrolments at those schools could be limited under the 1981 Act. The effects of parental choice were seen as likely to postpone the closure of annexes and temporary units at these schools and frustrate efforts to protect the rolls at other schools.

Events during the consideration of reorganisation demonstrated to officials that they would have to include formal means of limiting parents' school requests. Prior to 1984, Burns had used only nominal admission limits for its secondary schools. All of its secondary schools had surplus places and the Department did not foresee the need to refuse any parents' requests. In 1984, however, the number of parents making requests increased dramatically. Three schools received the most requests, over one hundred in each case. Requests to one school,

Dalgleish High School, increased from 74 in 1983 to 171 in 1984, pushing its expected intake from 217 to 291. Dalgleish High School was over-subscribed by sixty-one pupils according to the Department's staffing and building use plans. However, the Department was doubtful about its ability to refuse parents' requests without having established admission limits prior to asking parents to request schools. They decided that they had to accommodate the sixty-one extra pupils in Dalgleish High, converting some of the school's dining rooms into classrooms.

Shortly after this decision by the Department, the Education Committee considered three reports dealing with possible responses to falling rolls in three areas of Burns City. The reports focused on schools that were nearing dangerously low levels of enrolment. They listed several options, including closing two under-enrolled schools and vacating annexes and temporary units in a number of schools. The reports paid particular attention to the likely effects of parents' requests on the various options. They noted, for example, that enlarging the catchment areas of under-enrolled schools might not increase their enrolment much because parents could simply request a place at another school.

Controversy immediately arose over the reorganisation proposals, particularly over two options which involved school closures. Both the schools were situated on council housing estates and served disadvantaged communities. There had been considerable efforts by Burns and by local residents to strengthen community ties in these neighbourhoods. Community activists and the Labour group on the Council saw the possiblity of closure as an attack on these communities.

The Conservative administration eventually proposed that one school be closed because its enrolment had declined to such a level that severe curriculum restrictions would have to be made. However, Labour and the Alliance voted to keep the school open because of the strong community opposition to its closure and the difficulty of making alternative arrangements for the children. Because of the split on the Council, the Education Committee could not get a majority to close any school against local opposition or to adopt other strong measures to deal with falling rolls and under-enrolled schools.

Burns did adopt intake limits at three popular schools as part of its plan to vacate annexes and temporary accommodation at several schools. The Dalgleish High School episode (discussed above) convinced it that, in order to prevent severe overcrowding, it would have to refuse parents' requests at some schools and that formal limits on admissions were necessary to justify refusals. Up until this time, it had accepted parents' requests as simple constraints on education policy – policies were decided and adjustments made after the pattern of parents' requests became clear. The Labour group proposed the imposition of intake limits well below the capacity of the schools' main buildings because that would help several schools with low enrolments. However, the Conservative and Alliance members rejected these low limits because of the limited grounds of refusal in the 1981 Act and the likelihood of successful appeals. No intake limits were proposed for schools other than the three most popular ones because there was little chance of those schools' main buildings being over-subscribed.

Falling secondary rolls posed significant problems for Burns' schools, particularly the ones whose rolls had fallen or showed signs of falling below a viable minimum level. The curriculum would inevitably have to be restricted at these schools and teaching costs per pupil would rise significantly. These problems were in many cases exacerbated by the pattern of parents' school requests. Several of the under-enrolled schools in Burns City lost significant numbers of pupils due to parents' requests, though one school with a small catchment-area population was kept viable by requests from other areas (for details, see Chapter 6). Strong support for schools under threat of closure and the political situation in the Regional Council prevented Burns from closing schools to reduce the number of surplus places and to protect the rolls of the remaining schools. The only response to falling rolls that could be agreed was the vacation of several school annexes and the setting of intake limits at three schools to make this possible.

ADMINISTERING SCHOOL ADMISSIONS

During these considerations of policy, Burns had to administer the annual cycle of primary school admissions and secondary school transfers as well as deciding requests for school places at other stages. These case-level decisions constitute Burns' real policy in a fundamental way. That does not mean that case-level decisions were inconsistent with Burns' official policies. With a few minor exceptions, school admissions decisions were consistent with the formally adopted policies. However, the official policies did not dictate answers to all questions that arose in the admissions process. For example, because the criteria for determining non-district admissions to over-subscribed schools were not ranked, the Placing Request Committee had to decide which criteria would receive priority in deciding admissions to particular schools. Furthermore, it does not imply that outcomes constitute the whole of decision-making. The style or character of decision making which influences the way parents feel about the outcome of their request and how they react to decisions is also important.

Each year's admissions process began the previous November. The Department sent letters to the parents of all children who would transfer to secondary school the following year. The letter indicated the school to which the child was allocated, i.e. the school for the catchment area that included the child's residence. The letter also informed parents of their rights to make a placing request. (Prior to 1985, the letter included a form on which parents could request an alternative school. Hoping to reduce the number of placing requests, the Department decided to remove the form, instead including in the letter an explanation of how parents could obtain one.)[7] Parents were also sent the brochure for their district school and informed of the dates for parents' nights at their district school and other nearby schools.

For primary admissions, officials took out advertisements in the local newspaper and put up notices in public places advising parents of primary-age children of the procedures for enrolling their child in school. Parents were to register with the headteacher of the school they wanted their child to attend. Where the parents wanted a school other than their district school, they also had to send in a form to the Education Department.

The next stage in the primary school admissions process was a mechanical one. Two officials handled all requests for Burns City, keeping a running count of expected enrolment for each school. They received periodic reports from primary headteachers about the district pupils who had asked to enrol at each primary school. The address that parents gave was accepted as proof of the child's residence in the district. The officials also received all the placing-request forms from parents who wanted a place at a non-district school and used the two lists to determine the prospective admissions for each school.

No action was taken with regard to the list of prospective admissions until after the administrative deadline for making placing requests. The primary-school lists were turned over to the Divisional Education Officer (DEO). The DEO used these lists in deciding how many first year classes would be offered in each school. For most primary schools, the maximum class size was thirty-three, the 'normal' maximum specified in the teachers' contract. As discussed above, two 'open-plan' primary schools were given limits of thirty per class because experience had shown that class sizes of thirty-three resulted in overcrowding and disruption. The DEO used every available classroom in a school, if needed, unless doing so would require significant roll reductions in future years. The DEO used composite classes, where one class included pupils from two year groups, to accommodate district pupils but would not create new composite classes solely to grant more placing requests. The DEO was able to accommodate almost all district children and almost all placing requests by shifting a few teachers from some under-subscribed schools into other, over-subscribed schools.

The operation of admissions at secondary transfer was roughly similar to that at primary entry. The Department kept a running count of prospective admissions to all schools. After the administrative deadline for placing requests had passed, the records were all passed to the DEO. There was a great deal of flexibility in secondary school admissions because of the large number of surplus places due to falling rolls. The DEO determined whether the prospective admissions to schools exceeded their available accommodation. For most schools, the places available far outnumbered prospective admissions. Prior to the setting of admission limits for 1985, only once did the prospective admissions outnumber the places available at a secondary school. This was the case of Dalgleish High School, described above, where additional places were created to accommodate all requests. In 1985, three schools were over-subscribed so that some requests had to be refused.

The Director sent out acceptance notices to the parents who had requested schools that were not over-subscribed. The Department also accepted all district pupils into over-subscribed schools. It forwarded all non-district requests for these over-subscribed schools to the Placing Request Committee. The Department was responsible for administering the education service and most decisions about the number of places available at each school fell within this responsibility. However, the Department was reluctant to make decisions which were potential sources of dispute, particularly when the decisions were not considered relevant to the educational aims of the Department. The Department was only concerned with numbers, not with which children attended which school.

The Placing Request Committee was responsible for determining which non-district pupils were to be admitted to over-subscribed schools. On the basis of written reports summarising parents' reasons for choosing schools and occasional supplementary information provided by Education Department officials at the meeting, the Committee considered all the placing requests for over-subscribed schools. It viewed its task as filling the available places at a school from the list of placing requests and then putting the remaining placing requests on a waiting list in order of priority. It did not consider whether more places might be added to a school to accommodate more requests. Nor did it consider each placing request on its own merits (unlike the pre-Act Transfer Committee).

Several points about the Placing Request Committee' considerations of placing requests should be noted. It accepted its role as determining which children should fill the spaces deemed to be available by the Department (after district children had been admitted). It consistently gave priority to requests for children with siblings already at the school. Other criteria were used less consistently. After children with siblings had been admitted, the Committee's consideration of placing requests consisted of a search for factors that discriminated between requests so that the correct number of requests could be granted. In some sessions, the Committee granted requests that involved attending a feeder school, having a cousin at the school, or wanting an educational course at the school. In other sessions, completely different criteria determined who was admitted.

The Department and the Placing Request Committee worked with a modest amount of information, essentially information provided by the parents and what general information the members could recall, such as whether or not particular streets were busy. When Committee members asked for more details, officials explained that they only had the information given by the parent on the form and that they were in no position to investigate parents' claims. They explained that the selection of which children should be admitted was not worth the effort.

Giving priority to district children and, secondarily, to children with siblings at the school were viewed as important by the Department and by the Placing Request Committee. Both were considered to have an educational basis. Though individual members sometimes proposed other criteria, such as medical reasons, there was never any consensus about them. Sometimes they were taken into account and at other times not. What mattered above all was the number of places at the school.

Parents also asked for school places at stages other than primary entry and secondary transfer. Most commonly these cases involved parents moving into an area and requesting that their child attend the district school. The requests were routinely granted as long as there was room at the school at the stage requested. The DEO applied the same standards to determine enrolment limits as they did in entry and transfer cases. Primary schools were limited to thirty-three (or thirty in special cases) per class. Composite classes were held to thirty. Secondary school places were limited by the number of classes existing at the school, with no more than thirty pupils in each class and no more than twenty pupils in each classroom for practical subjects.

As in cases of primary entry and secondary transfer requests, only the Placing Request Committee had the authority to refuse a placing request. If the DEO decided that a request should be refused, either because there was no accommodation or because of the pupil's disciplinary problems, he forwarded the request to the Placing Request Committee. The Committee always followed the recommendation of the DEO in these matters, usually without discussion. The only requests that were given much scrutiny involved pupils who had disciplinary problems at their current school where officials were concerned that the request may have been an attempt to extract the pupil from a difficult situation rather than having to deal with it. The Committee's discussion did not focus on whether to grant the request but on evaluating the manner in which Education Department officials had dealt with the problem. Officials were often rebuked by councillors for the ways in which they had dealt with a problem pupil. However, such requests were not granted against the recommendation of the official.

Parents whose requests were refused at any stage were allowed to make a request for another school and would be offered a place if room was available. Until their request was granted, their child remained on the roll of the district school and so could not lose this place because they had made a placing request. The parents were also told of their right to appeal.

PARENTS' RIGHTS AND UNDER-AGE ADMISSIONS

The parents' rights of school choice contained in the 1981 Act also raised questions about Burns' policy for under-age admissions. The 1981 Act required authorities to allow a parent to make a placing request for a 'child' and further required that each placing request be granted unless a statutory ground of refusal existed. The word 'child' was not explicitly defined in this context and many parents have made placing requests on behalf of children under the statutory school age. Even though there is no contemporary evidence that the government sought to extend the rights of parents of under-age children, Scottish authorities have had to decide whether to treat under-age requests as statutory placing requests and, if they are treated as statutory placing requests, what statutory grounds of refusal can be used to refuse those requests.

Until the 1981 Act took effect, the Education (Scotland) Act 1962 covered under-age admissions. The 1962 Act required parents of children who had reached five years of age by the statutory commencement date in August to send these children to school and also required authorities to provide schools for them. Under the 1962 Act, an authority could also allow parents to send their children to school if they had reached four years of age by a date set by the authority. Burns adopted 28 February as the cut-off date: children who turned four before 28 February would be automatically admitted to primary school. Parents could request admission for children who turned four after that date. Burns' policy was to refuse admission unless 'the child would suffer lasting educational detriment and then only after every other alterna' e had been carefully examined'. Under-age applications were submitted to the Transfer Committee. Between 1977 and 1981, the Transfer Committee upheld only one of the thirty-one under-age admission requests in Burns City.

In its implementation of the 1981 Act, Burns did not consider that the Act affected under-age admissions. It continued its policy of denying admission to under-age children unless the Placing Request Committee decided that it would cause lasting educational detriment to the child. Burns also refused to allow parents to appeal refusals by the Placing Request Committee to the statutory appeal committee, holding that under-age requests were not statutory placing requests.

All but one of the other Scottish authorities had also refused to include under-age applications as placing requests. This practice was challenged by many parents. Two sheriffs in other authorities held that under-age requests did constitute statutory placing requests, but Burns continued to resist as these sheriffs' decisions were not binding on it. However, Burns capitulated after the SED issued a circular (Scottish Education

Department, 1984) endorsing the reasoning in the sheriffs' decisions as the original legislative intention, and threatening to treat authorities as in default of their duties if they failed to consider under-age applications as placing requests under the 1981 Act (Petch, 1987).

Burns changed its consideration of under-age applications in 1984. Officials decided to maintain their practice of admitting under-age children only in exceptional circumstances. Placing requests involving under-age children (assuming the school had places) could be refused only if 'the education normally provided at the school is not suited to the age, ability, or aptitude of the child'. Officials decided to interpret this ground of refusal *disjunctively*, so that placing requests on behalf of under-age children could be refused on the basis of age alone. Officials feared that considering 'age, ability, or aptitude' *conjunctively* would require them to admit many more under-age children as well as to undertake assessments of each child for whom a request was made (see Chapter 5). Burns continued to refuse admissions to under-age children unless preventing the child from entering school would cause 'lasting educational detriment'. Less than forty under-age applications were made each year and the Placing Request Committee granted only four in two years. Fifteen parents appealed, but in all cases the appeal committee upheld the refusal. One parent also appealed to the sheriff, who upheld the refusal.[8] The inclusion of under-age applications as placing requests did not significantly affect Burns' treatment of under-age applications or its provision of education generally, even though officials considered it a major threat. By adopting the narrow, disjunctive approach, this threat was avoided.

THE CONSEQUENCES OF PARENTS' RIGHTS IN BURNS REGION

Parents' rights of school choice transformed the pattern of school admissions in Burns. Before the Act, parents were discouraged from making non-district placing requests and requests were granted only in special circumstances. After the Act, more parents made placing requests and, until 1985, few placing requests were refused. The Act converted Burns' restrictive parental choice policy into one in which parents' requests were given virtually absolute priority.

After 1982, the number of parents making requests increased substantially at the same time as the number of requests refused dropped almost to zero. At secondary transfer, the proportion of parents making requests went up from 6.1 per cent in 1980 (the last year of Burns' restrictive policy) to 13.7 per cent in 1982 (the first year of the Act) and to 22.1 per cent in 1984. Alongside the almost threefold increase in the proportion of parents making requests, the proportion of requests granted increased from 49.1 per cent in 1980 to 100 per cent in 1982, 1983, and 1984. Not until 1985, after the Region had adopted intake limits at three schools, were any requests refused (see Table 3.4).

Table 3.4. Secondary transfers and appeals in Burns City, 1982–1985

	1982	1983	1984	1985
Transfer pupils	4 176	3 878	3 602	3 144
Placing requests	573	642	796	666
(% of pupils)	13.7	16.6	22.1	21.2
Requests granted administratively	573	642	796	595
(% of requests)	100	100	100	89.3
Requests refused administratively	0	0	0	71
(% of requests)	0	0	0	10.7
Appeals	–	–	–	12
(% of refusals)				16.9
Appeals upheld	–	–	–	3
(% of appeals)				25.0

Note: In order to maintain comparability with Tables 3.1 and 3.2, in this table Burns City includes only those schools within the boundaries of the city division when Burns Region was created in 1975.

At primary entry, the effects of parents' rights have been nearly as dramatic. In 1981 (the last year of the Region's restrictive policy), 7.4 per cent of parents made requests. Of these requests 42.5 per cent were granted administratively and a total of 59.6 per cent were granted after appeal to the Transfer Committee. In 1982, 12.6 per cent of parents made requests, 97.3 per cent of which were granted administratively. By 1985, 22.3 per cent of parents made requests, 96.2 per cent of which were granted administratively (see Table 3.5).

The dramatic changes caused by the 1981 Act are sharply illustrated by comparing the pattern of parents' requests before 1982 with the pattern afterwards. At both primary entry and secondary transfer, the proportion of parents making placing requests has increased. The only exception to the steady upward trend involves secondary transfer requests in 1985 which declined slightly after intake limits were placed on the three most popular schools and placing request application forms were removed from the material sent to parents. In addition, the proportion of requests granted increased sharply. The most striking evidence of the effect of the Act relates to the number of children who were admitted to non-district schools. At primary entry, 21.5 per cent of city children started in non-district schools in 1985 compared to 4.4 per cent in 1980 (see Figure 3.1). At secondary transfer, 19.0 per cent transferred to non-district schools in 1985 compared with 4.1 per cent in 1980 (see Figure 3.2).

Parents' rights of school choice certainly altered the manner in which Burns took account of parents' concern over which school their child

Table 3.5. Primary entrants and appeals in Burns City, 1982–1985

	1982	1983	1984	1985
Entering pupils	3 518	3 817	4 180	3 440
Placing requests	444	563	669	767
(% of pupils)	12.6	14.7	16.0	22.3
Requests granted administratively	432	553	659	738
(% of requests)	97.3	98.2	98.5	96.2
Requests refused administratively	12	10	10	29
Appeals	6	5	3	11
(% of refusals)	50.0	50.0	30.0	37.9
Appeals upheld	0	5	0	0
(% of appeals)	0	100	0	0

Note: In order to maintain comparability with Tables 3.1 and 3.2, in this table
Burns City includes only those schools within the boundaries of the city
division when Burns Region was created in 1975.

attended. Burns could no longer balance parents' interests in choice
against their own commitment to neighbourhood schools, to the maintenance of comprehensive intakes, to protecting under-enrolled schools
from becoming too small or to administrative convenience. Only a physi-

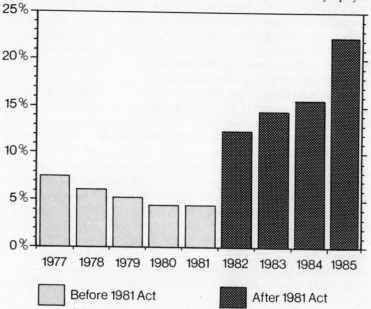

Figure 3.1. Percentage of primary entry (P1) pupils admitted to non-district
schools in Burns City, 1977–1985.

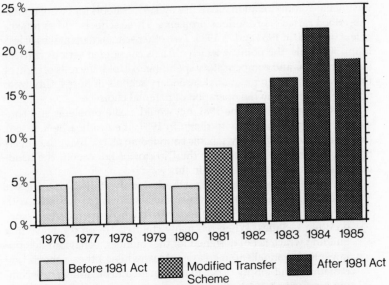

Figure 3.2.   Percentage of secondary transfer (s1) pupils admitted to non-
district schools in Burns City, 1976–1985.

cal lack of space and the desire to vacate unsuitable or deteriorating
temporary accommodation and distant annexes could be used to justify
refusing parents' requests. Statistics describing the pattern of admissions and requests detail the triumph of parental choice in Burns. Only
130 of 5 034 parents' school requests have been refused in the four-year
period following implementation of the Act in 1982. Even those parents
whose requests were refused were placed on a waiting list (and frequently received a place) at their requested school, while parents who
were refused entry for one school could still get places at other non-
district schools.

The effects of parents' rights extend beyond the decision to grant more
parents their choice of school. Evaluating the effects of parents' rights of
school choice calls for an examination of the impact of placing requests
on school intakes. A detailed analysis of the effects of the 1981 Act on
admissions to secondary schools in Burns City can be found in Chapter
6. Many schools' rolls were not significantly affected, and twelve of the
twenty non-denominational secondary schools in Burns City had first
year intakes which remained within what officials considered to be an
acceptable range, that is their intakes were neither too large (according to
the physical capacity of the school) nor so small as to result in curriculum
and staffing difficulties. Three schools were substantially over-subscribed due to parental choice. However, Burns placed intake limits on
these schools in 1985 to eliminate overcrowding and allow them to take

unsuitable accommodation out of use by 1991. Schools that were under-subscribed raised more serious problems. Three schools had s1 intakes of less than 100 in 1984 and/or 1985. Two other schools had intakes of less than 150 pupils, the point at which officials considered serious curriculum reductions and compensatory spending. All told, the rolls of eight of the twenty non-denominational secondary schools in Burns' City were adversely affected by the operation of parental choice.[9]

Burns recognised that the 1981 Act would create problems and considered best how to deal with them. In 1984, the headteachers of four (under-enrolled) secondary schools sounded an alarm about the effects of parental choice. In a letter to the Director of Education, the headteachers summarised the effects in this way:

> Favoured schools are bursting at the seams, overflowing into huts or forced into maintaining annexes. Such schools are supplied with extra classroom space but no account is taken of the added pressure on other facilities. When too many children are on the move in a building which is not designed for that number, behaviour deteriorates and vandalism increases. Meanwhile, other schools are remaining half-empty. Also, management and planning are becoming increasingly difficult ... The morale of the staff in the schools adversely affected is given a dreadful knock, a blow which comes year after year. Despite their best endeavours, the staff of such schools see local parents rejecting their work, young colleagues being compulsorily transferred ... Once begun, the downward or upward spiral can become very rapid and irreversible, i.e. the more who opt out, the more will continue to opt out ... It simply cannot be halted. [We] believe that the principle of comprehensive schooling is being undermined in some areas of the city; and the concept of the community school is going out the window.

The headteachers went on to propose ways of limiting the number of parents who made a placing request, although they conceded that there was little Burns could do under the 1981 Act. They proposed that all huts and annexes should be phased out, that primary headteachers should be required to support their local school and punished where they did not, and that in writing to parents the Director should emphasise loyalty to the district school and make it more difficult for parents to make requests by not including a request form among the transfer materials sent to parents. (This last suggestion was implemented for the 1985 admissions.)

The letter from the headteachers prompted a review of the effects of parental choice and rekindled the Labour group's efforts to resist. The schools being most harmed were in disadvantaged working class areas, so the Labour group used the headteachers' letter to criticise the Conservative administration and central government for damaging working class schools.

In 1985, the Education Department produced a report on the effects of parental choice. The report focused on six secondary schools, three of which were over-subscribed because of parents' requests and three of which were seriously under-subscribed. The report noted that intake limits had been placed on the three overcrowded schools so that, if those limits were not successfully challenged by an appeal committee or the sheriff, the overcrowding at those schools would begin to ease. The report then turned to the problems that existed at the under-enrolled schools:

> Perhaps more serious are the problems created for schools which lose substantial numbers of pupils owing to the operation of parental choice. In such cases the effects of falling pupil rolls are exacerbated, and planning ahead becomes more difficult for the authority and the schools. Experience to date indicates these schools are situated, in the main, in areas of public housing on the periphery of the city, and their role within the communities they serve is limited by the loss of pupils through parental choice. Accommodation becomes underutilised and the range of curricular provision more difficult to sustain. The stability of staffing is affected, and as staffing levels fall, so do the size of departments, the responsibility allowances for promoted posts, and the complement of promoted staff, especially in senior management and in guidance. As reduced rolls progress through these schools, the numbers staying on voluntarily beyond school leaving age in s5 and s6 (the fifth and sixth years) will decline and may represent a smaller proportion of the cohort on entry at s1 compared to other schools. Thus it could become increasingly difficult and expensive to maintain the range of course provision and to attain viable group sizes.

The report then explained that Burns' options for eliminating the adverse effects of parental choice were limited. The report, as the Director emphasised in presenting it, saw little hope for limiting parental choice beyond the new intake limits based on vacating annexes and temporary units. Nothing could be done directly to protect under-enrolled schools. Even the Labour group conceded that the restrictive terms of the 1981 Act frustrated effective resistance. Furthermore, Burns had limited resources for mitigating the effects of parents' requests on under-enrolled schools. Some extra money was being spent to shore up teaching at these schools, but this money was tight because of stringent central government controls over local authority spending and the large number of competing claims on limited resources. School maintenance and special projects at all schools had already been cut drastically.

Debate in Burns often focused on the concentrated effect of parental choice on schools in disadvantaged working class areas, compounding the already substantial difficulties faced by pupils in these areas. Schools in disadvantaged areas were losing pupils, resources, and teachers to schools in more advantaged areas. (As we show in Chapter 6, the three schools which lost most pupils were located in three of the most disadvantaged areas of the city, where unemployment and other manifestations of social deprivation were highest, and income and educational attainment were lowest.) Supporters of parental choice saw this pattern as evidence of pupils in disadvantaged areas taking advantage of the 'ladder of opportunity' made available by school choice. However, even supporters conceded that those pupils continuing to attend these schools were likely to receive a sub-standard education. Their answer to this problem was to close these schools, so that all children would have to go to better schools. However, they could not get a majority for closing any school. Labour opponents of parental choice argued that these schools should receive extra support so that they could contribute to the rebuilding of the communities they served. They claimed that parents' rights of school choice and spending limits prevented this.

Parents' rights of school choice in Scotland resulted in parents' school requests being given almost absolute priority in Burns despite the possibility of substantial damage being caused to many of the Region's schools. The specific and concrete limits contained in the statutory grounds of refusal coupled with the prospect of sheriffs' appeals led Burns to grant virtually all parents' requests, even though in the event most refusals were upheld on appeal. In Burns, the 1981 Act strongly shifted the balance in school admissions toward parents' choice of school and away from the Region's efforts to maintain balanced rolls and neighbourhood schools. (For a further discussion of appeals involving over-subscribed schools and under-age pupils, see Chapter 5.)

PARENTAL CHOICE AND THE 1981 ACT IN WATT AND MAXTON REGIONS

The examination of parents' rights of school choice in Burns reveals a number of difficult issues that can arise: information for parents, procedures for making placing requests, admission limits for schools, curriculum planning, priorities for admission to over-subscribed schools, vacation of unsuitable annexes and temporary units, school closures, under-enrolled schools, appeal committee membership and procedures, and under-age admissions. However, these issues did not arise immediately in all authorities. Authorities have generally responded to the 1981 Act by adjusting their existing procedures for parental choice to meet the form required by the Act: increasing information for parents, changing their standards for deciding placing requests, and appointing panels from which appeal committees could be drawn. They did not decide many of the difficult policy issues that could arise. Instead, they waited until they were confronted with a concrete problem, such as a school for which there were more placing requests than places for new pupils. Most authorities have tried to accommodate all placing requests, so many potential issues have not emerged and have not been resolved. In this way, Burns was atypical of most Scottish authorities. Although Burns approached implementing the 1981 Act in a piecemeal fashion like other authorities, high rates of requests in the city and strong, though minority, opposition to parental choice resulted in many issues having to be resolved. Other authorities had to decide only a few of these issues and did so in ways different from Burns. We present case studies of Watt and Maxton Regions, focusing on particular issues that they have confronted to provide a deeper understanding of how the 1981 Act has been implemented and administered by Scottish authorities.[10]

PARENTAL CHOICE BEFORE THE 1981 ACT IN WATT REGION

Watt, which is one of the smaller regions in Scotland, contains a number of urban areas within a predominantly rural hinterland. The urban population is centred on two large industrial towns (or burghs) and a new town. Within the region there are sixteen non-denominational secondary schools, including two junior high schools which cater for s1–s4 only, and two Roman Catholic secondaries. At primary level there are a total of 147 schools, 15 of which are Roman Catholic. The dispersed nature of the population means that many of the rural schools are small in size, with only a handful of pupils enrolled each year. Since local authority reorganisation in 1975, Watt has had a Labour administration with a large overall majority.

In considering the entry and transfer arrangements that operated in Watt prior to the 1981 Act, two distinct phases have to be recognised. In the years immediately following reorganisation and the creation of the region, the policy in operation, both at primary and at secondary level, was of rigid zoning by catchment area. This policy was generally held to be strictly enforced. School rolls were on the whole near to capacity and there was a desire to minimise movement across catchment area boundaries. The only general exception was made for those attending a feeder primary who could opt for the appropriate secondary school despite a home address outwith the catchment area. Other exceptions did, however, occur and Education Committee meetings for the period record a number of successful appeals, particularly at primary level. In other instances, however, the policy was more rigidly enforced, with the requirement, for example, that children be compelled to attend the correct secondary school after a change of address.

Requests relating to secondary transfer came before a Transfer Board composed of councillors, teachers and the Director of Education. For entry in 1978, for example, seventeen requests were received for exceptional transfers to secondary: ten were approved, six were refused and one was referred for further information. At the same time there were twenty requests for transfer from Roman Catholic primary schools to non-denominational secondary schools; four were approved, fourteen refused and two referred. The following year (1979), the Transfer Board dealt with twenty-five requests for exceptional transfers: fifteen were approved, five refused and five deferred. The numbers involved therefore were small and almost insignificant as a proportion of total numbers. Choice did, however, periodically emerge as a contentious issue, for example when parents complained to the Commissioner for Local Administration (the local authority 'ombudsman') about the way in which the physical capacity of a school had been assessed, or when a vocal critic of any measures to reduce parental choice withheld his children from school and successfully appealed to the sheriff under the attendance order procedure (see Chapter 2).

About the beginning of 1978, the attitude of Watt towards parental choice, particularly at primary level, began to shift. On the initiative of the Education Department, and with the knowledge of the committee chair, the majority of requests at primary level began to be accepted. After a year's 'trial', a report was presented outlining the potential for greater flexibility created by falling rolls and, anticipating that national legislation was imminent, the Region decided to proceed with the implementation of a scheme of parental choice for primary schools from August 1980. For P1 entrants at that date and for those moving home, the opportunity to select a preferred school was offered, provided that there was sufficient capacity at the selected school once zoned pupils had been accommodated, and provided parents were willing to pay the transport costs. Allocation of available places was made by the appropriate School Council in accordance with guidelines provided by the Education Department and there was a right of appeal to the Schools Sub-committee. For transfer to secondary school, previous practice was maintained, except that a child already at an 'outwith' primary school would transfer to the secondary school 'fed' by that primary school. The attitude of the authority was that legislation appeared inevitable and that they should be seen to be responsive, gradually loosening controls in preparation for its enactment. In the event, the opportunity to exercise a choice was taken by 2.9 per cent of the parents of P1 pupils who enrolled in August 1980 and 3.8 per cent of those who enrolled in August 1981. No requests had to be turned down because of lack of places.

Perhaps influenced by the steps they had already taken, Watt's response to the SED Consultative Paper of March 1980 was more favourable than many others:

> In broad terms the proposals in the Paper, which are similar in many respects to the scheme of parental choice of primary school which my council has decided to adopt with effect from August this year, are acceptable to the Council.

Detailed practical suggestions were submitted which accorded with their own scheme. At secondary level Watt's response was somewhat more cautious, expressing concern about the damage that parental choice

could inflict upon a balanced comprehensive system. 'A hierarchy of popularity based on tradition, fashion and prejudice is not unlikely'.
It was argued that proposals should be deferred until the primary scheme could be assessed.

At the later stages of consultation, Watt submitted that both the proposed regulations and the procedures for appeal committees were unduly complex. The format for publishing examination results was considered to be misleading and placing requests were considered to be inappropriate for special education. In common with other authorities, Watt considered it unrealistic to expect to implement parental choice without additional expenditure.

IMPLEMENTATION OF THE 1981 ACT

The issue of parental choice was not considered to be of major salience in Watt and the arrangements for implementing the 1981 Act were remitted to the Director. The policies adopted by the Director continued to allocate children to primary and secondary schools on the basis of residence. Indeed district pupils are guaranteed a place at the district school, and no district enrolment would be refused on the grounds of lack of accommodation. Extra places are even reserved (see below) for new housing developments within a school's catchment area. At secondary level, the zoning scheme which is adopted for each school may reflect an attempt to create a balanced social mix for each catchment area (see Petch, 1988). School capacities are calculated by the headteacher on the basis of the number of available classrooms and the maximum class sizes, taking into account, at primary level, composite classes and special needs. Placing requests in Watt are submitted to the headteacher of the desired school.

The numbers of requests that have been received in the four years 1982–1985 and the proportion of pupils which these represent are detailed in Table 3.6. After an initial rise, the number of placing requests has levelled off, both at primary entry and secondary transfer, with the percentage making requests somewhat higher at primary than at secondary. This level of placing request activity is much more characteristic of Scotland as a whole than the higher levels recorded in Burns and Maxton Regions.

If a school is over-subscribed, the decision as to who should be admitted rests with the School Council responsible for that school. No criteria or principles for admission are laid down by the authority. In practice, requests have had to be refused at only one school, a primary school in Watt Burgh, where, because of lack of space, eight placing requests had to be turned down for August 1984 and four for August 1985. No requests have had to be refused at secondary level. The strategy adopted by the School Council meeting in 1984 demonstrates the difficulty of dealing with the problem of potential over-enrolment. The capacity of the school was calculated on the basis of five composite

Table 3.6. Primary entrants and secondary transfers in Watt Region, 1982–1985

	1982	1983	1984	1985
Primary entrants				
Placing requests	194	334	400	410
(% of pupils)	4.9	7.7	8.7	8.8
Requests granted administratively	194	334	396	406
(% of requests)	100	100	99.0	99.0
Requests refused administratively	0	0	4	4
Appeals	–	–	4	0
Appeals upheld	–	–	0	–
Secondary transfers				
Placing requests	213	272	272	275
(% of pupils)	4.0	5.1	5.3	6.0
Requests granted administratively	213	272	272	275
(% of requests)	100	100	100	100

Note: Statistics for primary entrants and secondary transfers refer only to August admissions. Placing requests for P1 and S1 during the course of the year are not included.

classes of twenty-nine pupils, two homogeneous classes of thirty-three pupils and six homogeneous classes reduced to twenty-nine pupils because of the integration of a deaf child. An allowance of twenty places was made for children who were expected to move into houses within the catchment area which were due for completion during the forth-coming session. Only then were the remaining places available for allocation and eight requests had to be refused, four for P1 and four for subsequent stages. In the event the School Council could not find any basis on which to select amongst the requests and decided to select names from a hat.

Five of the eight parents whose requests were refused subsequently appealed. In accordance with the statutory requirements a panel had been established from which appeal committees would be drawn. Five members of the panel were to hear any one appeal, three coming from the group representing members of the authority and the education committee (ten in total) and two from the group of parents (six repre-sentatives) and persons with experience in education (four in number). A member of the last category acted as chair of the appeals committee, with the Director of Administration acting as clerk to the committee. On the only occasion on which the appeal committee has had to sit, the five appeals were all rejected by a majority of three to two.

Under-age admission has not been an important issue in Watt. Indeed there appears to have been some reluctance to acknowledge the existence of SED Circular 1108 (Scottish Education Department, 1984). Prior to the legislation the policy of the authority was to adhere strictly to the cut-off date for admissions. In practice, however, individual headteachers may have exercised discretion, particularly where nursery and primary classes were in the same building. A two-date entry and a high level of nursery provision (85 per cent) probably also reduced the demand for such under-age entry. Policy after the Act was to continue to discourage parents from seeking such admission. A letter sent to potential applicants states:

> We have developed a cautious approach to early entry to primary school as a result of studying children who have previously done so, and it is our firm belief that acceleration into formal education does not operate to the benefit of most children.

A two-page set of notes accompanies this letter, setting out clearly the answers to a number of questions which parents pose. Interestingly, no reference is made to the requirement that a request for a primary school place for an under-age child must be treated as a placing request with an associated right of appeal. Any child whose parents do seek early admission is referred for assessment to an educational psychologist and only very rarely would the child be admitted.

THE CONSEQUENCES OF PARENTS' RIGHTS IN WATT REGION

The attitude of Watt towards parents' rights of school choice has been rather low key. Thus it has been regarded as an issue of minor importance which, while it is not actually encouraged, has at least to be tolerated. Annual reports to the Schools Sub-committee of the Education Committee on the operation of the scheme reflect this general tenor, highlighting particular local circumstances but concluding that overall the impact has not been problematic.

> It is not anticipated that pressure from placing requests will cause any problems over the next few years as primary rolls remain static and the secondary population falls.

Overall parental choice has had few significant effects on education in Watt. Relatively few pupils have changed school and, apart from the one primary school, no school has been overcrowded, although some popular schools have been unable to vacate temporary huts or annexes. An attempt to reduce the number of temporary accommodation units at one popular secondary school by 're-zoning' several primary school catchment areas was blocked by parental opposition (Petch, 1988). However, parental choice has figured relatively little in the controversy surrounding this proposal.

At secondary level, there was little movement in the rural hinterland. In the urban areas, the Region itself noted that longer-established secondary schools gained at the expense of less well-established ones. By 1985, three well-established schools experienced net gains of 40–50 pupils. However, because of falling school rolls, there was space in these schools and the extra pupils could all be accommodated. In one case, the gains were at the expense of two schools which lost 20–25 pupils each, in the second, it was at the expense of a single school which lost in excess of 50 pupils while, in the third, the losers were the two junior high schools. Of the three all-through comprehensives which lost pupils, two had intakes of less than 150 pupils and on the criterion used in Burns, could be described as under-enrolled. The two junior high schools lost one quarter and one third of their first-year intakes (which were reduced to 79 and 46 respectively) and were no longer regarded as viable. However plans for the replacement of these two schools by an all-through comprehensive were well advanced.

Except for secondary schools serving predominantly rural areas, Watt regards a roll of 750–800 as the minimum required to maintain a viable secondary school. Most of the urban non-denominational secondary schools in the region have rolls well in excess of this minimum but two schools are fast approaching this threshold. These schools had problems which pre-dated the 1981 Act but, in both cases, these problems have been substantially amplified by parental choice. However, Watt has so far taken no steps to deal with the problem.

PARENTAL CHOICE BEFORE THE 1981 ACT IN MAXTON REGION

Maxton is a medium sized Region with a population twice the size of Watt and half as large as Burns. Much of the Region is rural but it also contains a number of small towns, a large town and a city. Administratively, the Education Department was divided into three geographical divisions, one centred on a number of small towns, one on the large town and one, in effect, comprising the city (Maxton City). Just as our analysis of school choice in Burns Region focused on Burns City, so our discussion of school choice in Maxton Region will focus on Maxton City. Within the city, there are ten non-denominational and three Roman Catholic secondary schools, and a total of 38 non-denominational and 14 Roman Catholic primary schools. From regionalisation in 1975 until the local elections in May 1986, Maxton Region had a Conservative administration with a sizeable overall majority.

Maxton Region operated a liberal policy on school admission prior to the 1981 Act. Each primary and each secondary school had its own catchment area and children were allocated to the school serving the area in which they lived. However, parents were free to approach any school, and the headteacher would normally admit the child as long as there was sufficient room in the school. Each child was placed in one of three priority categories (Category 1 comprised children who lived in the catchment area; Category 2 consisted of children with siblings at the school; while Category 3 consisted of children from outwith the catchment area) but this three-fold categorisation was rarely, if ever, used. If the headteacher was in any doubt or thought that the child should not be admitted, the matter then passed to the Divisional Education Officer (DEO). If the DEO refused to admit the child, the parents could then appeal to the Education Committee which would appoint an *ad hoc* sub-committee with powers to make a final decision on the matter.

As far as children of school age were concerned, the system seems to have operated in a fairly flexible manner. Unfortunately, records are no longer available. Thus we cannot say for certain how many parents sought to have their children admitted to a school outwith their catchment area. It is clear that more requests related to primary school than to secondary school but numbers were probably fairly small. As far as entry to primary school or transfer to secondary school were concerned, no requests were ever turned down and there were no appeals to the special sub-committee. Much the same applied to 'in term' transfer requests, i.e. to requests during the school year, although, particularly if the child was at secondary school, the parents were sometimes counselled against taking precipitate action and advised to wait until the end of the school year. For the Region, and equally for parents, the two areas in which problems did arise were in respect of children with behavioural problems who were seeking to transfer from one school to another, and under-age children who were seeking early admission. Both types of cases involved the Director of Education and there were a number of appeals to the *ad hoc* sub-committee from the parents of under-age children.

Maxton's response to the parental choice legislation was rather more muted than that of some other authorities. However, the Region was opposed to the legislation on the grounds that its 'fairly loose and informal procedures appear to have worked quite satisfactorily and the rather elaborate procedures being proposed would appear [to Maxton] to be adding an unnecessary burden'. In common with many other authorities, Maxton was also strongly opposed to the publication of examination results.

MAXTON'S IMPLEMENTATION OF THE 1981 ACT

Soon after the 1981 Act received the Royal Assent, the arrangements for dealing with placing requests under the new legislation were considered by the Education Committee. It was agreed that all placing requests should be dealt with in the first instance by the appropriate Divisional Education Officer who would be under instructions to give them favourable consideration where possible. However, where the DEO felt that it was necessary to refuse a placing request, he or she could only do so with the approval of the School Council for the school concerned.[11] The Region also had to set up appeal committees although it was assumed that there would be very few appeals. Committees of three would be set up on a Divisional basis, as required, with the membership drawn from two lists comprising: Regional Council members or appointed members of the Education Committee; and parents of school-age children or persons with experience or knowledge of education nominated by a School Council.

Since 1982, Maxton has allowed parents' choice of school to determine school admissions. An upper ceiling for the roll of each school in terms of the number of available classrooms and the maximum class size (33 in primary schools with 29 for composite classes, and 30 in secondary schools with 20 for practical classes) is calculated, and projected intakes estimated by extrapolating from previous years' statistics. As long as there was room in the school, everyone would be admitted. However, if there was no room (or if the DEO wished to invoke one of the behavioural grounds for refusing the placing request)[12], the approval of the School Council would have to be obtained.

THE CONSEQUENCES OF PARENTS' RIGHTS OF SCHOOL CHOICE IN MAXTON CITY

Over the four years from 1982–1985, the number of placing requests for primary entry and secondary transfer increased quite markedly (see Chapter 6 below). Thus, among the non-denominational schools, in Maxton City, the proportion of primary entrants who were subject to a placing request increased from 17.5 per cent in 1982 to 24.6 per cent in 1985 while the proportion of secondary transfers went up from 14.0 per cent to 23.7 per cent over the same period. Without exception, all these placing requests were granted. Thus, although children were still placed in one or other of three priority categories, this was a rather meaningless exercise. The annual totals are set out in Table 3.7.

The combination of falling school rolls and parental choice of school produced a number of very sharp declines in intakes (to primary and to secondary schools) and a much smaller number of large increases. However, Maxton's commitment to parental choice of school meant that the Region was unwilling to address the problems which arose from these movements. At primary level, the Region sought to deal with the problem of falling school rolls in Maxton City by closing a number of primary schools (Adler and Bondi, 1988). Parental choice of school was clearly not an important consideration since the majority of pupils at one of the schools (123 out of 193 in 1983–1984) came from outwith its catchment area and none of the schools selected for closure was among those that had experienced really large net outflows of pupils. The various Action Groups that opposed the closures were very imaginative in their use of legal remedies, and organised the submission of 750 placing requests for

Table 3.7. Primary entrants and secondary transfers in Maxton City, 1982–1985

	1982	1983	1984	1985
Primary entrants				
Placing requests	280	377	371	402
(% of pupils)	17.5	24.7	23.5	24.6
Requests granted administratively	280	377	371	402
(% of requests)	100	100	100	100
Secondary transfers				
Placing requests	291	336	413	402
(% of pupils)	14.0	16.6	21.8	23.7
Requests granted administratively	291	336	413	402
(% of requests)	100	100	100	100

Note: Statistics for primary entrants and secondary transfers refer only to August admissions. Placing requests for P1 and S1 during the course of the year are not included.

the schools in question.[13] The Action Groups hoped that their placing requests would all be refused and that parents would be able to appeal against the refusals to an appeal committee and subsequently to the sheriff. Thus, they were very disappointed by the Region's decision to grant the requests, subject to the proviso that the school remained open.

The eventual decision in 1985 to close four primary schools in Maxton City resulted in the imposition of an intake limit of 60 pupils for one primary school whose catchment area was enlarged to include that of one of the schools that was closed. Two years previously the DEO had discussed the possibility of restricting the number of first-year pupils at one very over-subscribed secondary school whose first-year admissions for 1983 were considerably in excess of its estimated intake and likely to outstrip the available third-year accommodation which would be needed two years later. However, the School Council was indecisive and, with no political will to confront the problem, the DEO had let the matter drop.

Parental choice of school was also an important consideration in the decision to rebuild a second over-subscribed secondary school. Unlike the previous school (which had a first-year intake of 374 in 1984) this school (with a first-year intake of 175) was not particularly large. However, it was housed in very inadequate accommodation. The original plan had been to build a school large enough to accommodate its catchment-area population of about 500 pupils. However, the school had been gaining about 50 pupils per year from an adjacent school which was, as a result of this, substantially under-enrolled. The Director outlined a series of options which, in addition to the original proposal, included proposals for a new school for 700 pupils (which could draw up to 200 pupils from the adjacent catchment areas) and a merger with the adjacent school. The first of these options was supported by the Conservatives and adopted by the Region while the second was supported by Labour. Although electoral considerations were important[14] so were attitudes to parental choice of school. As a result of the Region's *laissez-faire* approach to school admissions, two secondary schools (both mentioned above) out of ten were seriously over-subscribed while three (with intakes of 81, 92 and 109 in 1985) were substantially under-enrolled (see Chapter 6).

Maxton was not so *laissez-faire* in its approach to under-age admissions. Like most other Regions, Maxton did not at first treat requests for under-age admission to school as statutory placing requests. All children who reached four years of age by 28 February were automatically admitted to primary school the following August. Children who reached four after the cut-off date were considered on a case-by-case basis. Parents of under-age children who requested early admission were interviewed by the Convener of the Education Committee and the Director of Education. Both were opposed to early admission, on the grounds that children do not, on the whole, benefit from going to school early, although they did make a few exceptions, mainly for social reasons.

Maxton reluctantly changed its policy after the Sheriff Principal's decision in the Boyne case (*Boyne and Boyne v Grampian Regional Council* (1983)) and SED Circular 1108 (Scottish Education Department, 1984) supporting his ruling. It maintained its policy of admitting all children who turned four before 28 February, and of admitting younger children only when their parents presented a strong case for an exception. In 1984, a special sub-committee of the Education Committee was set up, comprising the Convener, the Vice Convener and one member from the appropriate Division, to consider all under-age requests. In the first two years, the sub-committee admitted two under-age children out of the forty-four requests that were made in the Region (see Table 3.8). The requests that were allowed both involved children living in relatively isolated rural areas where nursery provision was not available and were conditional on an assessment by an educational psychologist that the child was ready for primary school education.

Because under-age requests were treated as statutory placing requests, parents could appeal against the sub-committee's refusal. Several parents have done so and the appeal committees have generally been sympathetic. In the first two years, fourteen parents appealed and the appeal committees upheld the parents in eleven cases. The appeal committees focused on each individual case, evaluating whether the child would profit from attending school. This approach was very different from the Region's policy of discouraging under-age admissions, but

Table 3.8. Under-age placing requests and appeals in Maxton Region, 1984–1985

	1984	1985	Total
Placing requests	19	25	44
Requests considered by Sub-committee	18	24	42
Requests granted by Sub-committee	1	1	2
Requests refused by Sub-committee	17	23	40
Appeals	8	6	14
Appeals upheld	6	5	11
Appeals refused	2	1	3
Total granted	7	6	13
Total refused	11	18	29

the appeal committees also stated that they did not intend to criticise Maxton's policy or to establish precedents for future appeals and Maxton has not changed its policy in response to the appeal committee decisions.

CONCLUSIONS

In some ways, the 1981 Act has not greatly affected the administration of school admissions in the three authorities. All three authorities continued to use the procedures for admissions that they had used prior to the legislation taking effect. Indeed, for most parents, each year's admission process was very similar to those that had existed prior to the 1981 Act. Parents were notified of their child's allocation to their district school and given an opportunity to request a non-district school. Most parents accepted the allocation to their district school and, for those parents who requested a different school, most requests were granted. Only in Burns was there a substantial change in the outcomes of placing requests and, even there, most requests had been granted prior to the 1981 Act.

The two major changes caused by the 1981 Act involved the standards used by authorities to decide parents' placing requests and the availability of appeals to the appeal committee and the sheriff should the authority refuse the request. Authorities could refuse requests in only limited circumstances (primarily when the requested school was overcrowded). This produced a substantial decrease in the number of requests refused by Burns and stimulated a large increase in the number of placing requests in that authority and in Maxton and lesser, but still significant, increases in Watt. The 1981 Act clearly strengthened parents' abilities to obtain places at non-district schools.

Parents also gained access to a new set of appeal mechanisms. They could challenge refusals by the authority. However, the appeal committees did not play a significant direct role in school admission decisions because the authorities granted most parents' requests and because the appeal committees were generally supportive of the authorities' very limited efforts to impose admission limits at primary and secondary schools (see Chapter 5). However, the existence of appeal committees reinforced the statutory restrictions on authorities' powers to refuse parents' placing requests and discouraged authorities from construing the statutory grounds of refusal broadly or trying to ignore parents' rights in making school admission decisions. Appeals to the sheriff played an even more limited role. Only two appeals were lodged in the three authorities and in both cases the sheriffs supported the authority. However, like the appeal committees, the prospect of review by the sheriff led authorities to make restrictive interpretations of the statutory grounds of refusal. Appeals and the restrictive statutory grounds of refusal combined to result in strengthening parents' ability to obtain a place for their child in their school of their choice.

NOTES

1. For a more detailed discussion of the requirements of the 1981 Act, see Chapter 2.
2. This account of school admissions and parental choice in Burns Region is based on our field research. As a condition of access, we agreed to protect the anonymity of the authority, its schools, its elected members and its officials. We therefore make no references to specific sources. In the course of our field research in Burns Region, we interviewed the Director of Education, the three Senior Education Officers responsible for overseeing school admissions throughout the Region, the Divisional Education Officer responsible for Burns City, the education officers who administered school admissions throughout the Region, the Regional Solicitor, the Depute Regional Secretary responsible for clerking the Education Committee, the Placing Request Committee and the Education Appeal Committee, the (Conservative) Chairperson of the Education Committee, the leader of the Labour group on the Regional Council, the Labour spokesperson on education, and the permanent chairperson of the Appeal Committee. We also observed the meetings of the Education Committee, the Placing Requests Committee, and the Education Appeal Committee. Finally, officials generously provided us with complete access to Education Committee minutes and reports and internal Departmental memoranda going back to the origins of the Region.
3. Under arrangements that existed before Burns was created, some children went to selective primary schools and then went

on to the associated selective secondary school. The Region had eliminated the selective status of these schools, but, at the request of the Secretary of State for Scotland, allowed the children already enrolled in them to continue on to the associated secondary school even though it was not their district school.

4. Out of 49 appeals with verified medical reasons from 1976 to 1980, 47 were upheld. Of 41 single parent family appeals after 1977, 40 were upheld. 38 of 39 sibling appeals and 8 of 8 former selective pupil appeals were upheld.

5. Education (Scotland) Act 1962, ss.7, 30, 70.

6. The nine factors were as follows: certificated medical reasons; ease of access for the disabled; brothers/sisters or other relatives either in attendance or having previously attended the school requested; educational course not available at the district school; nature or place of the parents' employment; behavioural problems; road safety, ease of travel and proximity of home to school; attendance at feeder primary school (s1 requests only); and parental affinity with the aims, philosophy and religious beliefs of the school.

7. This change was proposed by four Burns headteachers who were concerned about the effects of parental choice and argued that the automatic distribution of the form encouraged parents to submit placing requests. Their concerns are discussed in detail below.

8. For a further discussion of appeals involving under-age requests, see Chapter 5.

9. The effects of parental choice of school on the provision of education result from changes in school rolls and are a consequence of having too many children in some schools and too few in others. Estimates of these effects can be based on school numbers. However, no direct measures of the effects of overcrowding and under-enrolment due to parental choice yet exist. This is largely because the cumulative impact of parental choice will take several years to make itself felt. The major effects of overcrowding come when admissions are high several years in a row. The major effects of under-enrolment are felt in the third and fourth years and, to an even greater extent, in the fifth and sixth years when the curriculum becomes more specialised and the subject groups become smaller. The extent of damage to the provision of education caused by parental choice was not immediately apparent.

10. The accounts of school admissions and parental choice in Watt and Maxton Regions are based on our field research. In contrast to Burns Region, no undertaking to protect the anonymity of these authorities, their schools, their elected members or their officials was either requested or granted. However, in order to fulfil our commitments to Burns, we decided that we could not disclose the identities of these two authorities and our account makes no references to specific sources. Our account of parental choice and the 1981 Act in Watt is based on Education Committee minutes, reports and internal Departmental memoranda; and interviews with the Senior Depute Director of Education, the Senior Assistant Director of Education with responsibility for primary education, and the headteacher of the

only over-subscribed school in the Region. Our account of Maxton is likewise based on Education Committee minutes, reports and internal Departmental memoranda; and on interviews with the Director of Education; the Divisional Education Officer responsible for Maxton City and the education officer who administered school admissions in the city; the Assistant Chief Executive who acted as Clerk to the Education Appeal Committee; the (Conservative) Convener of the Education Committee and the Labour spokesperson on education.

11. On the advice of the Chief Executive, the position was subsequently changed. The powers of School Councils were enhanced, although whether they were to decide on the imposition of intake limits or determine whether individual children should be refused admission, remained quite unclear.

12. cf. Education (Scotland) Act 1981, ss 28A3(a)(iii), (iv) and (v). See Chapter 2 and Appendix B.

13. This was based on the assumption that the placing request provisions in the 1981 Act would take precedence over the school closure provisions. Either Maxton would grant all the requests, in which case the schools would have to stay open, or they would refuse, in which case the decisions could all be appealed to an appeal committee and then, if necessary, to the sheriff. Maxton took counsel's opinion. Counsel took the view that, as long as no final decision had been taken to close the schools in question, the placing requests could all be accepted with a rider that the Region could not guarantee at this stage that all the schools would necessarily be open in the next session. Although the Action Groups subsequently took the view that the attachment of a rider in effect constituted a refusal, and that the decisions could therefore be appealed, other developments prevented them from putting this to the test.

14. The over-subscribed school was located in an area represented by the Conservatives which they needed to hold in order to retain their control over the Region. The merger option, which Labour privately favoured, had little support in the area. However, this was unimportant for Labour since their chances of displacing the Conservatives in this area were miniscule.

4

PARENTS' RESPONSES TO THE 1981 ACT

The exploration in Chapter 2 of the factors which lay behind the 1981 Act highlights the extent to which assumptions were made about, for example, the considerations which motivate parents in their choice of school and the decision-making strategies which they adopt. Political ideology inevitably colours such assumptions, and arguments were very often advanced on the basis of conjecture and speculation rather than empirical evidence.

In this chapter we report some of the detailed results obtained from surveys conducted with parents of children about to start primary school (Petch, 1986a) and of children transferring from primary to secondary school (Petch, 1986b). We shall concentrate in particular on the social characteristics of those who exercised choice under the 1981 Act, on parents' knowledge of and attitudes towards the parental choice legislation, on the sources of information on which parents drew, on the decision-making strategies which they employed, and on the explanations which parents offered for the choices which they made. We shall hope thereby to provide a more accurate account of parental choice behaviour than that which lies behind a manifesto commitment.

A preliminary exploration of notions of choice was included in a number of the studies for the Cambridge Accountability Project (Elliott, Bridges, Ebbutt, Gibson and Nias, 1981a, 1981b) and both Stillman and Maychell (1986) in England and Macbeth, Strachan and Macaulay (1986) in Scotland have reported on empirical research which was carried out at the same time as our own project. In addition, Johnson (1987) has recently explored in depth the perspectives of twenty-five families who have made use of both private and state sectors. Elliott and his colleagues (see above) drew an interesting distinction between determinants of school choice which can be termed 'product criteria', for example examination results, which refer to outcomes, and factors which reflect what they termed 'process criteria', for example the happiness of the child, which are indicative of the capacity for human relationships. Associated with this distinction, they identified parents sympathetic to a technological perspective and others who accord more with a humanistic perspective, concerned less with measures of outcome but more with the happiness of the child. This same distinction was picked up by Stillman and Maychell. Their sample of 2 245 parents offered 7 689 reasons in an open explanation of their choice of school, which they classified into 97 groups. Overall 68 per cent of reasons were categorised as process reasons, 18 per cent as product reasons and 14 per cent as references to geographical variables. Whereas 90 per cent of parents included process reasons when choosing a school, product reasons were cited by only 54 per cent. Macbeth, Strachan and Macaulay concluded that the reasons parents offered for choosing schools were fairly equally divided between those which reflected assessments of schools and those which were non-school reasons, the majority of the latter referring to convenience. Amongst school-based reasons, the most specific tended to be offered by 'requesters' whilst 'non-requesters' professed more generalised explanations.

SELECTING A SAMPLE

The data presented in this chapter are derived from surveys in selected areas of the three Scottish education authorities where the implementation of the 1981 Act was studied in detail. Home interviews were conducted in the Spring of 1984 with 410 parents who had a child starting primary school in August of that year and with 619 parents who had a child transferring to secondary school at that date. Given the scarcity of data both on the characteristics of those who were exercising choice and of the explanations which motivated this behaviour, it was felt necessary to conduct a fairly large-scale survey. The intention was to structure the survey such that approximately 50 per cent of the parents surveyed would have exercised their right of choice, while the other 50 per cent, either by deliberate choice or by default, were intending to send their children to the district school.

The decision to concentrate on choice at entry to primary school and transfer to secondary school reflects the much higher incidence of placing requests at these two stages (see Chapter 6). This is not to deny the importance of requests made at other stages (included by Macbeth, Strachan and Macaulay, 1986), although many of these appear to to be associated with a change of home address, with the child remaining at the same school. In addition to sampling only at P1 entry and S1, it was also decided to exclude Roman Catholic schools. The catchment areas for such schools tend to be larger and the opportunities for movement between different schools are correspondingly reduced.

In selecting the sample of parents to be interviewed, the strategy was simplified in comparison to Stillman and Maychell (1986) by the fact that in the three regions (as indeed throughout Scotland) all pupils are allocated to a district school according to their home address. For any school, therefore, the population can be divided into three groups, namely children from the catchment area who are allocated to the school and accept it, those who are allocated and opt out by making a placing request for another school, and those from outwith the catchment area whose district school is elsewhere but who select the school by making a placing request for it. The level of placing request activity associated with different schools was felt to be a potentially important variable, and one which should be taken into account in the sampling process. It was decided therefore not to sample across the entire population of the three study regions, but to concentrate on a number of target schools in specific case study areas, stratifying the sample to ensure that schools with different patterns of movement were included: high losers, high gainers, schools where gains were balanced by losses and schools with little movement in or out. A second level of stratification was introduced to allow for potential differences between different geographical areas, including at both primary and secondary level examples of a city, a town (burgh), and a new town environment.

The detailed sampling procedures varied by area, but for each target school the aim was to survey a sufficient number of 'stayers', those not making a placing request, and an enhanced number of 'requesters', those making placing requests, both in and out of the chosen schools. The primary sample is illustrated in Table 4.1, with each of the case study areas drawn from a different region. In the city sample (Maxton) a cluster of eight adjacent schools was selected. These formed a north-south transect just west of the city centre, served a mix of socio–economic groups and were chosen so as to minimise movement outwith the cluster. In the burgh sample (Watt), in addition to the four primary schools where a sufficiently large group of 'stayers' was included, parents were also chosen from the entire population of entrants across all the primary schools. This was in an attempt to explore notions of choice at the community level, allowing for an understanding of choice behaviour within an entire system. In Burns New Town and Watt Burgh all those making placing requests were approached; in Maxton City, where the number making placing requests into a specific school exceeded ten, the number approached was restricted to that level.

The secondary sample is detailed in Table 4.2. The city sample again comprised schools serving a wide range of socio-economic groups, a cluster of six schools in the south and west of Burns City being selected to include a variety of placing request activity and to minimise movement outwith the cluster.

The strategy for obtaining and approaching the desired sample had to vary between the three regions. In one region (Burns) a requirement was imposed that we had to make an initial approach to parents to obtain their consent before they could be included in the potential sample from which the final selection was made, a directive which affected the primary new town sample and the secondary new town and city samples. Moreover, this consent was required on an 'opt-in' rather than 'opt-out' basis, a constraint which places the initiative with the parent. The original stipulation at secondary level was to obtain parental consent by

Table 4.1 Composition of P1 entry sample, August 1984

School	DS population	PR in	DS interviewed	PR interviewed
Burns New Town				
A	35	6	15	4
B	44	1	14	0
C	36	13	15	11
D	61	1	15	1
Outwith	–	6	–	5
TOTAL	176	27	59	21
Maxton City				
E	14	22**	12	9
F	22	0	10	0
G	5	17**	5	4
H	28	8	14	5
J	15	10	17***	6
K	13	24**	9	7
L	34	6	11	4
M	25	4	10	4
Outwith	–	17	–	18***
TOTAL*	156	108	88	57
Watt Burgh				
N	36	3	17	3
P	30	1	12	1
Q	8	12	9***	9
R	34	15	16	13
Others (22)	684	62	53	44
Outwith	–	3	–	3
TOTAL	792	96	107	73

DS= Attended District School
PR= Made Placing Request (for the school)

* 5 district pupils who made placing requests for schools outwith the cluster were excluded
** Only 10 PR parents approached
*** Changes due to late decisions

sending letters home with the children through the feeder primary schools, but this was subsequently modified by obtaining permission to draw names from centralised lists. We were therefore able to obtain the names of all those who had made placing requests into or out of each of the secondary schools in our cluster. Letters were sent out by post and parents who were willing to be included in the sampling frame had to

Table 4.2 Composition of S1 transfer sample, August 1984

School	DS population	PR in	DS interviewed	PR interviewed
Burns City				
A	185	26	23	13
B	201	23	23	10
C	130	47	27	20
D	115	147	25	42
E	193	37	21	17
F	250	2	19	1
Outwith	–	40	–	30 + 18*
TOTAL	1 074	322	138	151
Burns New Town				
G	235	1	23	–
H	211	17	22	11
J	163	11	21	6
Outwith	–	18	–	14 + 1*
TOTAL	609	47	66	32
Maxton Burgh				
K	215	48	20	24
L	273	30	23	21
M	219	14	21	8
Outwith	–	–	–	0 + 3*
TOTAL	707	92	64	56
Watt Burgh				
N	226	2	20	2
P	270	21	21	20
Q	357	19	22	17
Outwith	–	8	–	7
TOTAL	853	50	63	46

DS= Attended District School
PR= Made Placing Request (for the school)
* to private school

return a reply-paid postcard. A postal approach yields a lower response rate but against this had to be offset the more complete coverage.

A decision had to be taken on the number of parents who should be approached for consent. It was hoped that an assumption of a 40 per cent response rate would be sufficiently pessimistic and, as our aim was to obtain interviews with 25 'stayers' at each of the six target secondary schools, initial letters were therefore sent to 63 sets of parents for each school. In addition all parents who had made placing requests either into or out of these schools were approached. From the parents who responded positively, the appropriate number were selected for interview. The response to the first mailing was less than expected[1] and arrangements had to be made for a follow up; despite this the minimum of 25 'stayers' was not attained for three of the six schools. Table 4.3 provides further details of the response to this request for consent in the three sample areas in this region.

In the other two regions, Maxton and Watt, the access arrangements were more favourable and any problems were of an administrative nature only. In Watt, for example, no centralised lists were held and names and addresses of parents had to be obtained by visiting each of the

Table 4.3 Obtaining consent in Burns Region

		Willing	Unwilling	No reply	Number approached
PRIMARY ENTRY					
Burns New Town	PR No.	22	1	4	27
	%	81.5	3.7	14.8	100
	DS No.	99	8	69	176
	%	56.3	4.5	39.2	100
	TOTAL No.	121	9	73	203
	%	59.6	4.4	36.0	100
SECONDARY TRANSFER					
Burns New Town	PR No.	34	3	10	47
	%	72.3	6.4	21.3	100
	DS No.	82	25	79	186
	%	44.1	13.4	42.5	100
	TOTAL No.	116	28	89	233
	%	49.8	12.0	38.2	100
Burns City	PR No.	191	21	110	322
	%	59.3	6.5	34.2	100
	DS No.	181	34	164	379
	%	47.7	9.0	43.3	100
	TOTAL No.	372	55	274	701
	%	53.1	7.8	39.1	100

PR= Made Placing Request
DS= Attended District School

26 primary schools and three secondary schools individually. In these regions, once the total populations were assembled, a sample of parents was drawn and letters informing them of the survey, together with a supporting letter from the region, were sent out, the population being over-sampled in order to allow for substitution for refusals and other non-contacts. The fact that, for example, 130 of the 150 Maxton City parents who were initially approached agreed to take part illustrates the scale of the reduction in response rate which resulted from the restrictions imposed in Burns.

The survey interviews were conducted by interviewers from a survey research organisation who had been briefed by the research team. The intention was to interview one parent only in each household[2] and to obtain interviews with equal numbers of mothers and fathers.[3] In the first sample area, we specified which parent was to be approached in each household; subsequently at the request of the interviewers, and on the assumption that any bias would be minimal, interviewers had to achieve a quota, save for single parents, of equal numbers of mothers and fathers. In the primary survey, 222 of the 410 parents interviewed (54.1 per cent) were mothers; in the secondary survey, the proportion was 372 out of 619 (60.1 per cent).

There was considerable discussion of the best date at which to interview parents. It was finally decided that interviews should take place in the period, usually about one month, between the closing date for the receipt of placing requests and the date on which decisions were to be announced. These dates varied between regions and the exact timing of the surveys varied accordingly. It was felt that, at this stage, the decision-making process would still be very fresh in the parents' minds. Moreover their responses would be unaffected by their reactions once the outcome of their placing request was known. It was also argued that there were fewer ethical objections to interviewing at this stage in the process, after the major decision-making period but at a date when, if parents were alerted to a course of action of which they had been unaware, a late application was still possible. This timing did, however, preclude gaining any response from parents on their satisfaction or otherwise with their decision once it had been carried through, and did not allow for those who changed their minds before the school year commenced. Such changes between sampling and interviewing may account for some slight discrepancies in our data.

DESIGNING THE QUESTIONNAIRE

The questionnaire on which the interview with parents was based represented an attempt both to obtain basic data from a sufficiently large number of parents to enable general conclusions to be drawn with some confidence, and also to explore in some depth certain of the key issues relating to choice. To this end, the schedule contained a mix of fixed-choice and open-ended questions, and used a dual format of both structured and unstructured questions on certain of the key items. Parents were questioned on the extent to which they thought choice should operate, on the reasons, if any, for which authorities could and should refuse requests, on their sources of information during the decision-making process, and on their knowledge of placing request and appeal procedures. It will be obvious, therefore, that particularly for those who considered exercising choice, the questionnaire was a somewhat lengthy document and interviews were frequently upwards of an hour in length.

In designing the questionnaire considerable thought was given to the extent to which parents who had not made a placing request should be made to consider the decision-making process. It was decided that three groups should be distinguished: those who made a placing request (*requesters*), those who considered alternative schools but remained with the district school (*considerers*)[4] and those who did not consider any alternative (*non-considerers*). Of the 619 parents interviewed at secondary level, 328 (53 per cent) were non-requesters remaining with the district school (264 non-considerers and 64 considerers) and 291 (47 per cent) were requesters. At primary level a somewhat lower proportion of interviews were with requesters, 150 of the 410 or 36.6 per cent. Of the 260 non-requesters (63.4 per cent), 228 were non-considerers, 32 considerers (See Table 4.4).

Different paths through the questionnaire were provided for each of these groups and, in addition, the number of different schools which a parent considered was taken into account. Only the considerers and requesters were asked about their reasons for making the choice they did and only requesters were asked to cite the reasons for rejecting the district school. Although it was recognised that the non-considerers may have positively made a choice in favour of the district school, it was felt that the danger of imposing a choice structure on those for whom there had been no such consideration outweighed the advantages of attempt-

Table 4.4 Distribution into response categories

	Primary Entry Number	%	Secondary Transfer Number	%
Requesters	150	36.6	291	47.0
Non-requesters	260	63.4	328	53.0
Of whom				
Considerers	32	7.8	64	10.4
Non-considerers	228	55.6	264	42.6
TOTAL	410	100	619	100

ing to pursue such hidden elements of choice. The schedules for primary and secondary levels followed the same broad outline but obviously differed in, for example, potential reasons for choice and sources of information. Information about pre-school experiences was collected in the primary survey whereas the secondary survey concentrated on experiences at primary school.

In presenting results from the two surveys, we have adopted the convention of weighting to the total population of each study area. The weighting has been done at the level of the individual target school (except in Watt Burgh) and therefore ensures maximum validity for each interview. Weights were calculated for both requesters and non-requesters for each school, the latter multiplying to the catchment area intake for the district school and the former grossing up to the total number of placing requests for the school. The assumption of representativeness which is built into the weighting procedure should be borne in mind throughout the discussion, with the mechanics of the weighting procedure explaining small variations in certain totals.

THE CHARACTERISTICS OF REQUESTING AND NON-REQUESTING PARENTS

Behind much of the political rhetoric relating to choice lies a set of assumptions about the characteristics of those parents most likely to take advantage of the provisions in the legislation. Such individuals are generally perceived to come from the higher socio-economic groups, to have themselves undergone further education, to be likely to own their own home, and to have leanings towards the right of the political spectrum. In short, the expectation for many is that the legislation will appeal to middle-class parents, well-accomplished in using administrative procedures for their own benefit. However, at both primary and secondary level, the evidence suggests that such assumptions are inaccurate. The legislation has been utilised by a much broader section of the population than is commonly believed (and was perhaps originally envisaged), with the 'middle-class' stereotype appearing to exist only in a few specific contexts. Elsewhere there is sufficient variation to suggest that perhaps only at the level of the individual school can a full understanding be gained of the identity of those parents who choose to send their children to the district school and those who choose to send them elsewhere.

In searching for the identity of requesters, a large number of different variables were examined, both at area level and at school level. These ranged from socio-economic variables such as income, housing tenure and educational attainment, through indices of parental participation and of administrative competence, to responses designed to elicit the value attached by individual parents to educational provision and to the attainment of educational qualifications. All these indices, it should be noted, related to characteristics of the parents themselves rather than to any attributes of the schools. (School level analysis is presented in Chapter 6.) For each of these variables the characteristics of the requesters, both into and out of each target school, were compared with the characteristics of those remaining with the district school. Although we shall make some attempt to generalise for the two stages of entry, it is important to bear in mind that, whatever differences there may be between requesters and non-requesters at the school level, these are largely masked by the process of aggregation.

Parents' Characteristics: Primary Entry

Table 4.5 illustrates the breakdown by social class of requesters and non-requesters in each of the three study areas at primary level. A comment should be made on the measure of social class adopted for this study. In households where more than one partner was economically active, the category adopted was that of the partner whose occupation yielded the highest social class rating.[5] Although relatively crude, this method goes some way towards countering the bias of the traditional measure which gives pre-eminence to the male householder. Similarly, in referring to school-leaving age and to qualifications, the value for whichever of the resident parents was highest was selected. The differences in family social class between requesters and non-requesters in both Burns New Town and Maxton City were statistically significant (at the 95 per cent confidence level, x^2). In Burns New Town, requesters were drawn disproportionately from the middle of the social class distribution, while in Maxton City the two extremes were both over-represented. Although the detailed picture is clearly complex, it is important

Table 4.5 Social class distributions of requesters and non-requesters, P1 entry

Social Class (% respondents)	Burns New Town NR	PR**	Maxton City NR	PR	Watt Burgh NR	PR
1	10.4	3.9	2.5	10.1	9.4	8.2
2	27.6	11.5	24.1	24.8	28.0	20.6
3 NON-MANUAL	18.2	34.6	17.7	15.6	11.2	11.4
3 MANUAL	18.9	19.2	29.8	20.2	29.9	26.8
4	5.4	15.3	15.2	14.7	6.6	10.3
5	4.9	3.9	0.6	5.5	3.7	8.3
9*	14.6	3.9	10.1	9.1	11.2	14.4
Number (weighted)	176	27	156	108	792	96

NR= Non-Requesters (attended District School)
PR= Requesters (made a Placing Request)

* Social Class 9= economically inactive
** No response for 7.7 per cent of requesters in Burns New Town

to point out that, in each location, requests were made across the entire social class spectrum. The objective measure of social class was supplemented by parents' own assessment of the class to which they belonged. In Burns New Town, 62 per cent of requesting parents considered themselves to be working class compared to only 46 per cent of those remaining with the district school, while in both Maxton City and Watt Burgh the proportion perceiving themselves as working class was similar in both groups at just over 50 per cent.

Not surprisingly, the distribution of requests according to the income of the main breadwinner was generally similar in form to that of social class. Thus in both Burns New Town and Maxton City, the differences in income between requesters and non-requesters were again statistically significant. Again many of the interesting variations were at school level: the requesters from one of the Watt Burgh schools (School P) for example all had lower incomes than those remaining, while those from one of the Maxton City schools (School M) all had higher incomes. Part of a similar configuration is the type of accommodation occupied by the different groups, statistically significant differences being apparent in both Burns New Town and Watt Burgh. In Burns New Town, those making placing requests were almost exclusively from development corporation housing, the contrast being most marked at one school (School C) where the entire district population were owner–occupiers but nine out of eleven of those requesting in were from development corporation housing. In Maxton City, the variation was less strong and, in terms of total numbers, the movement came almost equally from owner–occupiers and local-authority tenants. The data were also examined to determine whether there was any relationship between movement and the length of residence in an area, with a slight suggestion that in both Maxton City and Watt Burgh those making requests may have spent a shorter time in the locality.

A number of variables were explored relating both to parents' own educational attainment, and to their assessment of the relative importance of getting a 'good education' and obtaining educational qualifications. On parents' leaving age and qualifications, no clear pattern emerged across all three locations. In Burns New Town there was a tendency for requesters to have left school at an earlier age and with lower qualifications; in Maxton City there was a slight tendency in the other direction. On the attitudinal issues, there were interesting variations between the three areas on the general importance which parents gave to the notion of a 'good education' and to educational qualifications, ranging from Burns New Town where concern for both issues was generally high (70 per cent considering qualifications to be extremely important), to Watt Burgh where support was more moderate (50 per cent). In all areas, greater importance was attached to both concerns by those making requests: in Burns New Town 90 per cent of requesters rated a good education as extremely important compared with 80 per cent of non-requesters. In Maxton City comparative figures were 86 per cent and 76 per cent, and in Watt Burgh 72 per cent and 60 per cent.

A number of variables were examined in an attempt to explore the possibility that there may be variations between requesters and non-requesters in the extent to which they adopt a participatory role in the community or in their children's schools. In particular the extent to which parents were members or officials of an organisation or participated in school events or Parent–Teacher associations (PTAs) was examined, but no apparent differences emerged between the two groups save at one or two individual schools. Involvement at a more formal level with the bureaucratic process was analysed to allow exploration of the suggestion that there may be some link between a measure of 'administrative competence' (Nonet, 1969) and the propensity to lodge a placing request. On school issues there appeared to be no relationship between those who had experience of making a complaint and those who made a placing request. On more general complaints (for example to a housing department, a solicitor, the DHSS, or the Inland Revenue), however, there was some evidence in all three areas that requesters were more likely to have pursued one or two complaints in the past. In Maxton City, for example, complaints had been submitted by 68 per cent of requesters compared to 53 per cent of non-requesters, and in Burns New Town the comparative figures were 48 per cent and 28 per cent. There is therefore some support for the suggestion that parents who make placing requests have greater administrative competence than those who do not. However, a certain amount of caution should be exercised in drawing such a conclusion since any individual's propensity to complain depends upon having cause to complain and access to an appropriate channel for complaint, as well as the necessary competence to pursue the complaint.

Questions were asked in the survey about political affiliation and about voting behaviour at the last general election (in 1983). No distinct pattern was readily apparent: amongst requesters Labour supporters were over-represented in both Maxton City and Watt Burgh. Placing-request activity was spread throughout the political spectrum, with individual behaviour reflecting little of party policy. Perhaps not surprisingly, when asked how important they thought it was for children to go to the local primary school, support for the concept was much higher amongst the non-requesters. Thirty-six per cent of non-requesters in Maxton City and 22 per cent in Watt Burgh considered loyalty to the local school to be 'extremely important' compared to only 5 per cent and 6 per cent of requesters.

Various speculations have been voiced as to the extent to which parental-choice legislation may be used differentially for boys and girls. A significant difference by sex was found in Maxton City where the 54 boys for whom placing requests were made came from a total of 158 boys, whereas the 55 girls came from a total of only 109. Thus, placing requests were made for half the girls compared with only a third of the boys. In Watt Burgh, however, the direction was reversed with placing requests submitted on behalf of proportionately more boys than girls. The data was also examined to ascertain the influence (if any) of an older sibling in the household, such a sibling being present in approximately one-half of the families. The evidence suggests that where there was an older sibling a request was less likely to be made. This was particularly the case in Burns New Town where 70 per cent of children for whom requests were made had no older sibling compared with 30 per cent of non-requesters, but the relationship held also in Maxton City and Watt Burgh. For children with an older sibling, when the older sibling went to a non-district school the younger child was likely to follow. In terms of the actual sample, in 60 families, or just under a third of the cases with an older sibling, the older child was at a non-district school. In all but five of these cases a request had been made also for the subject of the survey to attend the same school.

The various relationships described above demonstrate that there can be no ready categorisation of those who made placing requests. Both requesters and non-requesters exhibited a wide range of characteristics, and those seeking to endorse traditional stereotypes as to who makes requests would find little support for their arguments. A similar pattern was found elsewhere in Scotland by Macbeth, Strachan and Macaulay (1986), who concluded that the pattern of placing requests generally reflected the socio-economic characteristics of an area, with a particular propensity to make placing requests among skilled manual workers. As already highlighted, particular locational features of the individual school may be significant. It may be, for example, that the vagaries of a catchment area determine that a particular pocket of, say, local authority housing is in distance terms nearer to a non-district than to the district school and that, for this reason, local authority tenants may be more likely to make placing requests. To categorise such requesters according to a range of socio-economic and other characteristics may be to confound an explanation which is initially straightforward. Alternatively, depending on the relative strengths of 'push' and 'pull' factors for an individual, the appropriate comparisons may be with the district school or with the receiving school.

Parents' Characteristics: Secondary Transfer

Perhaps surprisingly, there were even fewer significant differences at the aggregate level between requesters and non-requesters at secondary transfer. Table 4.6 illustrates the social class breakdown of the two groups in the different study areas, and there were again significant differences (at the 95 per cent confidence level, x^2) between the two groups in Maxton City and in Burns New Town.

Among other potentially distinguishing factors, significant differences

Table 4.6 Social class distribution of requesters and non-requesters, s1 entry

Social Class (% respondents)	Burns City NR	Burns City PR	Burns New Town NR	Burns New Town PR	Maxton Burgh NR	Maxton Burgh PR	Watt Burgh NR	Watt Burgh PR
1	13.8	15.9	1.7	–	6.6	11.5	9.7	17.6
2	34.3	34.3	39.0	42.0	32.2	35.3	24.3	29.4
3 NON-MANUAL	19.5	23.3	21.7	14.0	17.4	22.7	23.3	15.7
3 MANUAL	18.3	13.3	20.4	28.0	30.1	10.1	24.5	19.6
4	3.5	4.6	9.2	2.0	9.2	7.2	5.5	2.0
5	0.9	1.7	2.8	–	3.1	5.5	4.7	9.8
9*	9.7	6.9	5.2	14.0	1.4	7.7	8.0	5.9
Number (weighted)	1074	322	609	47	707	92	853	50

NR= Non-Requesters (attended District School)
PR= Requesters (made a Placing Request)

* Social Class 9= economically inactive

were hard to find. There was some evidence that those making placing requests had stayed at school longer (and in general attained higher qualifications) than non-requesters, and in both Burns City and Maxton Burgh there was a significant difference in political affiliation, a larger proportion of requesters supporting the Conservative Party. Few other differences emerged at the aggregate level. Rather than replicating the primary analysis, we present in Table 4.7 more detail of the social class differentials in Burns City. Although requesters from social classes 1, 2 and 3NM were much more numerous, most especially out of School A and into School D, social class differences were much less marked in proportional terms. Moreover, from School F, for example, a higher proportion of social class 3M, 4, 5 and the economically inactive had made a placing request. These requests were, it appears, as likely to be for a school with a similar social class composition as for a school with a higher one. Some of the reasons which lie behind these movements are set out in Chapter 6.

PARENTS' KNOWLEDGE OF THE 1981 ACT

A prerequisite for the exercise of choice is, of course, knowledge by the parent of the opportunities for exercising such a choice. All those who did not submit a request (both considerers and non-considerers) were therefore asked whether there was anything they could have done if they had wished their child to attend a different state school. Table 4.8 demonstrates that the large majority of such parents were aware of their right to make a placing request, although at primary level the proportion of non-considerers in Maxton City who were uncertain of the situation was over a quarter (19.1 per cent answering 'no' to the question and 8.1

Table 4.7 Social class and school admissions for six schools in Burns City, S1 transfer

School	Admission Status	Social Class	
		1 + 2 + 3NM Number (weighted)	3M + 4 + 5 + 9 Number (weighted)
A	NR	185	0
	RO	87	2
	RI	16	10
B	NR	175	26
	RO	33	5
	RI	14	9
C	NR	67	63
	RO	8	6
	RI	28	19
D	NR	78	37
	RO	5	0
	RI	130	19
E	NR	101	82
	RO	38	12
	RI	15	22
F	NR	105	132
	RO	38	58
	RI	2	0

NR= Non-requesters (attended District School)
RI= Requesters in (made a Placing Request for the school in question)
RO= Requesters out (made a Placing Request for another school)

per cent 'don't know') and at secondary level in Burns New Town it was almost a third (20.1 per cent answering 'no' and 10.6 per cent 'don't know'). The parents who indicated that they were aware of their right of choice were asked to specify what they could have done to get a place at another school. The responses varied, but in the main the variation tended to reflect the actual differences in practice between different regions. At primary level applications in Burns and Watt had to be submitted to the intended school, and in Maxton to the education department. At secondary level requests for alternative schools in Burns were also to go to the education department. When asked where they had learnt of their right of choice, primary parents cited a wide variety of sources, an indicator of the fairly diffuse nature of the pre-school information network. At secondary level the majority of parents had received a letter from the education department or had read of the provisions in a local newspaper. The majority of parents at both stages considered that

Table 4.8 Parental awareness of rights of school choice

'If you had wanted your child to attend a different state school from the district school, is there anything you could have done about it?'

		% Yes	% No	% Don't Know	Number (weighted)
PRIMARY ENTRY					
Burns New Town	NC	83.2	6.5	10.3	147
	C	100.0	–	–	16
Maxton City	NC	72.8	19.1	8.1	132
	C	92.6	–	7.4	27
Watt Burgh	NC	86.6	3.1	10.3	718
	C	100.0	–	–	67
SECONDARY TRANSFER					
Burns City	NC	93.7	2.9	3.4	670
	C	96.3	2.4	1.3	374
Burns New Town	NC	69.3	20.1	10.6	517
	C	100.0	–	–	81
Maxton Burgh	NC	86.4	5.0	8.6	655
	C	100.0	–	–	32
Watt Burgh	NC	77.2	6.9	15.9	710
	C	87.9	–	12.1	132

NC= Non-Considerers (did not consider other schools)
C= Considerers (considered choosing another school)

any application they might have made would have been successful, although secondary parents were a little more hesitant in their assertions, saying that they had 'a good chance' rather than that it was 'almost certain'.

We were interested not only in parents' knowledge of the right to choose, but also in their understanding of their rights should they be refused a place at the preferred school. Table 4.9 shows the response of parents when asked 'can the education department ever refuse parents' requests for a particular school?' It will be seen that there was considerable variation in the responses, both between survey areas and between requesters and non-requesters. A majority, however, were aware that requests could be refused, although at primary level over a third of those who had not made requests were uncertain on this issue. Those who were aware of the authority's power to refuse a placing request were further questioned as to the reasons for which such refusals could be made. By far the largest group of responses, both at primary and secondary level, related .to lack of a place or overcrowding at the desired

Table 4.9 Parental awareness of grounds for refusal

'Under the present law, can the education department ever refuse parents' requests for a particular school?'

		% Yes	% No	% Don't know	Number (weighted)
PRIMARY ENTRY					
Burns New Town	NR	53.4	8.0	38.6	176
	R	80.7	–	19.3	27
Maxton City	NR	34.4	35.6	30.0	156
	R	56.0	22.9	21.1	108
Watt Burgh	NR	43.0	19.6	37.4	792
	R	80.0	13.7	6.3	96
SECONDARY TRANSFER					
Burns City	NR	67.8	19.7	12.5	1 074
	R	81.4	9.3	9.3	322
Burns New Town	NR	41.1	36.0	22.9	609
	R	83.6	8.2	8.2	47
Maxton Burgh	NR	50.7	17.7	31.6	707
	R	80.9	7.4	11.7	92
Watt Burgh	NR	45.1	22.1	32.8	853
	R	80.8	1.9	17.3	50

NR= Non–Requesters (attended District School)
R= Requesters (made Placing Request)

.school. Some parents also mentioned that requests could be turned down if the child exhibited severe behavioural problems. Amongst both requesters and non-requesters at primary level, there was also overwhelming agreement on the reasons for which the education department should be able to refuse parents' requests. These again related to circumstances in which there was overcrowding at the chosen school or in which there was no place for the child in the chosen school. At secondary level, support was strongest for the right to refuse requests when the school would be too crowded to maintain proper discipline.

Parents were questioned in some detail on the circumstances in which they would support the education department refusing a request. A number of situations were outlined and parents were asked to agree or disagree with their validity as grounds for refusing a request. The statements offered were somewhat different for the two levels. At primary entry the majority of parents agreed that placing requests should be refused if additional accommodation would have to be used, to allow the closure of unsuitable accommodation, or if the requested school would be too crowded to maintain discipline. They did not, however, endorse refusal by an authority on the grounds that the district school would give the child a better education, or in order to mix children of different social backgrounds, or to send all the children from one area to the district school. Parents were fairly divided over the validity of attempting to avoid composite classes or excluding a child who might cause trouble though, as on all these factors, there were local variations. At secondary level there was much stronger support for excluding the troublesome child and parents also endorsed refusal if new facilities would have to be built. There was little enthusiasm for attempts to send all the children in the catchment area to the district school or for giving education authorities complete discretion to refuse decisions 'for whatever reason they think is proper'. According to Hirschman (1970), a weak sense of loyalty to the district school by parents in the catchment area suggests that 'exit', in the form of a placing request for another school, will be the preferred response to dissatisfaction and, as we shall see, our survey suggests that this is the case.

Finally, the extent to which parents were aware of the provisions for making an appeal when a placing request had been rejected was explored. When asked 'is there anything the parent can do if he/she still wants a place at the different school?', the majority of responses at secondary level referred to making an appeal, with a second strategy being to contact the education department. Non-considerers, not surprisingly, were less certain of the appeal process. At primary level there was greater variation in the responses between the different areas, more non-requesters in Maxton suggesting contact with the education department rather than a specific appeal. However, as these were initially open-ended responses which were then coded to given categories by the interviewer, there may well have been variations in interpretation between interviewers.

In general therefore there appeared to be a fairly high level of awareness of the various legislative provisions relating to parental choice. Certainly amongst those who made requests there did not appear to be any major areas of misunderstanding. Whether, however, knowledge that procedures are available would necessarily lead to them being utilised if necessary is, of course, a very different question.

THE DECISION-MAKING PROCESS

The process of decision making has generated a vast literature.[6] Despite its limitations, however, one concept which appears of value in the present context is that of 'satisficing' (Simon, 1965). To what extent are parents seeking to maximise various predefined goals in their choice of a school, and to what extent are they seeking a satisfactory alternative which meets certain defined standards? A closely related question is the extent of the search process and the time and energy which are allocated to the exploration of options, i.e. the degree to which choice is 'bounded'. Moreover, to what extent is the prime motivation a 'push' factor, i.e. a desire to avoid the district school, and to what extent is it a 'pull' factor, i.e. a positive attraction towards the requested school? Push factors in particular are likely to be associated with satisficing activity.

For many parents, the pattern of choice behaviour approximated to the satisficing model. It was a matter of finding a satisfactory alternative to the district school rather than making an optimum choice from a large range of possible schools. At secondary level, for example, the majority (62 per cent) considered only one alternative to the district school and a further 27 per cent chose between two alternatives. At primary level this tendency was even more marked: of the 183 requesting and considering parents, 144 (79 per cent) considered only one alternative and a further 32 (17 per cent) only two alternatives. The picture is very much one of choice between one or, at most, two alternatives rather than extensive comparison.

This aspect of the decision-making process was further explored in a series of questions designed to elicit the relative acceptability of the various schools being considered. At secondary level, for example, requesting parents who had considered only one alternative to the district school were asked how they had made their decision. For 52 per cent in Burns and 48 per cent in Maxton, the district school would have been acceptable but the chosen school was better. In Watt, however, 42 per cent considered the district school unacceptable, compared with only a fifth in the other two regions. Twenty-five per cent in Burns, 32 per cent in Maxton and 21 per cent in Watt considered the intended school to be the best school around. When requesting parents had selected be- tween more than one alternative, the majority considered the district school to be unacceptable and, whilst other schools considered would have been acceptable, the school requested was the 'best of the lot'.

All requesters were asked how they would have felt if they had had to send their child to the district school. Over a third (40 per cent in Burns, 44 per cent in Maxton, and 31 per cent in Watt) felt the district school was reasonable but would be much happier if they could opt elsewhere; another third (34 per cent Burns, 37 per cent Maxton, 42 per cent Watt) would have been very unhappy and their children would have attended the district school only if there had been no choice. Six per cent in Burns, 8 per cent in Maxton and 11 per cent in Watt would have sent their child to a private school rather than to the district school and another group (8 per cent in Burns, 4 per cent in Maxton and 9 per cent in Watt) would have moved into another catchment area (six alternatives were offered for this question). Considerers also had their decision making probed in this fashion. Small numbers make the conclusions more tentative. Over- all, however, about one third concluded that, because the district school was acceptable, there was no reason to look hard at other schools; a fifth that, though an alternative would have been acceptable, the district school was the best of the lot and a fifth that, whilst an alternative school might have been better, it was not worth the trouble of making a request. The district school was a satisfactory, if not an optimal, choice. Exploring the concept of choice further, considering and requesting parents were also asked whether they had some notion of an ideal school in mind when making their choice. The majority did not, although 42 per cent in Burns and Maxton and 36 per cent in Watt were working with some ideal notion.

PARENTAL SOURCES OF INFORMATION

To embark on the decision making process, parents obviously require information about the schools which they might wish to consider. Uncertainty prevails both about the extent of parental knowledge of individual schools and about the channels through which parents acquire such knowledge. There have been some attempts, particularly in the field of home–school liaison, to explore the process of information dissemination (Bastiani, 1978; Woods, 1984; Wyn-Thomas, 1985), but parental assessment of many features inevitably remains subjective. Impressions of the school can usually only be gained second-hand, generally from children, and any comparison is, in many cases, with an 'other' which is only hypothetical. If this is true of parents whose child already attends the school, it is of even greater validity for parents whose child has not yet enrolled. Before a child arrives at a specific school (and in the absence of older siblings), it may be difficult to acquire information which can assist in any choice that is being made between schools. Certain measures, school size, facilities or curriculum range, may be fairly readily available and comparable, but for many criteria information will be limited and subjective. Only through a follow-up study once the child has been at the school could there be a comparison of preconceptions with reality.

Exploration of the main sources from which parents obtained the knowledge which informed their decisions depended on a two-stage methodology. Parents were first asked to identify their main sources of information in unrestricted format, and were then asked to rate the importance of each of eleven items on a given list and to select from that list the three sources they considered to be the most important in their own case. Detailed responses varied both by location and by the two methodological strategies, and may have reflected particular policies which operated in different areas. The extent to which the various sources provided information which was accurate is of course unspecified, but nonetheless it is in terms of such sources that parents make their decisions. We will discuss in turn the patterns which emerge at primary and at secondary level.

Information for Primary Entry

Tables 4.10 and 4.11 detail the importance which parents attached to various information sources, first, in Table 4.10, when asked to identify

Table 4.10 Sources of information at P1 entry, open responses

'What would you say were your main sources of information about the primary schools which your child might go to?'

Information Source	Burns New Town % respondents and rank	Maxton City % respondents and rank	Watt Burgh % respondents and rank
Visits/observation	9.8	11.1	14.8
Newspapers	2.6	1.3	1.0
Child has siblings at school	19.7 (3)	18.9 (3)	17.4 (3)
Information booklets	23.6 (2)	7.4	15.4
Neighbours/local people/ other parents	32.5 (1)	33.2 (1)	39.4 (1)
Friends	13.9	22.0 (2)	8.4
Relations	6.5	3.7	3.3
Headteacher	4.0	4.3	1.8
Teachers	5.3	14.6	4.5
'The school'	1.3	2.6	7.0
Nursery school/ playgroup	5.2	3.1	19.2 (2)
Own/spouse's experience through work	6.3	4.7	2.9
Self/spouse/other relation attended	–	5.3	4.6
Education Department	1.3	1.8	4.7
General knowledge/ grapevine	5.9	16.7	12.3
Other	5.0	5.0	6.3
Number of respondents (weighted)	203	264	888
Number of sources (weighted)	259	380	1 412

the sources themselves and second, in Table 4.11, when asked to select the three most important sources from the list of eleven. Emerging clearly from the open-ended responses was the importance of the local network, both specific individuals who acted as informants and the more abstract grapevine, the pool of information which accumulates over time from a variety of non-specific sources and provides the 'stock of knowledge' on which parents base their commonsense understanding. The possible influence of differential local policies is illustrated in, for example, Burns New Town where booklets provided by the school appeared to be a significant source of detailed information, cited by almost a quarter of respondents, while in Watt Burgh there was evidence of close pre-school links, the nursery or playgroup emerging as a major source of information. In distinguishing between requesters and non-

Table 4.11 Sources of information at P1 entry, structured responses

'Which were the three most important sources of information?'

Information Source	Burns New Town % respondents and rank	Maxton City % respondents and rank	Watt Burgh % respondents and rank
1. Visit	71.2 (1)	71.7 (1)	66.1 (1)
2. Newspapers	3.9	4.9	1.8
3. Other children in neighbourhood	14.6	16.3	10.8
4. Own experience of other child(ren) at schools	49.1 (2)	34.7	30.6
5. Information booklets	44.7 (3)	24.3	51.1 (3)
6. Parents of existing/ past pupils	31.1	42.1 (3)	22.9
7. Other friends/ neighbours	10.1	31.4	21.2
8. Primary school teachers/headteachers	44.4	49.3 (2)	57.3 (2)
9. People at work	5.9	0.4 (3)	2.0
10. Nursery school teacher	12.8	16.2	29.0
11. Child minder	0.6	–	0.8
Number of respondents (weighted)	203	264	888
Number of sources (weighted)	582	788	2 600

requesters, the influence of friends appeared particularly strong amongst those who made requests. Friends provided 32 per cent of sources for requesters in Burns New Town compared to only 7.3 per cent for non-requesters, with similar figures in Maxton City of 18.9 per cent and 9.8 per cent and in Watt Burgh of 13.9 per cent and 4.1 per cent. Information booklets, in contrast, seemed to be relied upon much more by those who were not making requests, comprising in Burns New Town 18.5 per cent of sources for non-requesters but mentioned not at all by requesters. It should be noted that the proportion obtaining booklets was considerably lower in Maxton, at 55 per cent, compared to over 80 per cent in both Burns and Watt. An interesting exploration of the content of such booklets immediately prior to their production becoming compulsory was carried out for the Scottish Consumer Council (Atherton, 1982), while the content of current booklets was included in the study by Macbeth, Strachan and Macaulay (1986).

When presented with a structured list from which to select their three most important sources (Table 4.11), visits to the school(s), which had been of little importance in the open-ended question, now featured as a major source of information, cited amongst the top three sources by two-thirds or more of the respondents in all areas, and providing a quarter of the total count of information sources. Perhaps associated with visits, the role of primary school teachers also assumed greater importance, being the second source in both Watt Burgh and Maxton City, and the third in Burns New Town. Parents with children at the school, and other friends and neighbours were accorded less importance than in the unstructured responses, while information booklets were more prominent.

The different responses elicited by the two methods pose interesting questions. To a degree these are methodological[7], but part of the explanation must lie in the fact that when asked for their own sources of information the number of items cited by parents ranged from an average of 1.2 amongst Burns New Town requesters to 1.7 by Maxton City requesters. In the structured questions, on the other hand, parents were asked to select three of the eleven items, allowing for a greater distribution of responses. It is of course also possible that when confronted with a structured list parents recalled the importance of items which did not readily come to mind in the short period allowed for the earlier open-ended response.

Information for Secondary Transfer

A similar approach was used to explore sources of information at secondary level. Using the open-ended strategy, as at primary level, the importance of local informants emerged as the major source in the majority of areas, although information booklets also featured strongly. By comparison, visits and observation received relatively little mention.

As can be seen from Table 4.12, visits and observation achieved much greater prominence using the structured format, a pattern similar to that found at primary level. In both Burns City and Burns New Town they were the most important source of information, in Maxton Burgh they came second and in Watt Burgh third. Information booklets also featured prominently. Thus, a somewhat different picture of reliance on visits and booklets rather than the more subjective accounts of friends or neighbours emerges from this technique. The experience that parents had had with siblings already at the school also featured as a significant source of information. Table 4.12 allows for comparison between requesters and non-requesters in the sources used. In general these appeared broadly similar although some differences were evident. Requesters in Maxton Burgh, for example, attached prime importance to information from primary teachers while non-requesters relied on information booklets; in Burns New Town non-requesters were more likely to rely on their own experience of children already in the system.

Knowledge of the sources of information on which parents rely not only contributes to an understanding of the parental perspective on schooling, but also hints at the particular areas which could be targeted

Table 4.12. Sources of information at s1 transfer, structured responses
'Which were the three most important sources of information?'

Information Source % sources and rank	Burns City NR	Burns City R	Burns New Town NR	Burns New Town R	Maxton Burgh NR	Maxton Burgh R	Watt Burgh NR	Watt Burgh R
1 Visits	19.0 (1)	18.6 (1)	18.8 (1)	20.5 (1)	14.8 (2)	15.0 (2)	14.0 (3)	14.4 (3)
2 Newspapers	1.9	1.3	0.4	0.7	6.5	1.9	3.8	5.4
3 Other children in neighbourhood	3.7	5.2	4.8	6.4	4.3	3.2	8.0	3.8
4 Friends/neighbours	7.2	12.1 (3)	7.3	6.4	9.9	12.9	13.5	16.9 (1)
5 Own experience other child(ren)	13.9 (3)	12.1 (3)	18.1 (2)	11.5	11.3	14.8 (3)	15.1 (2)	11.4
6 Information booklets	16.5 (2)	13.6 (2)	16.2 (3)	14.8 (2)	16.4 (1)	11.6	16.0 (3)	15.3 (2)
7 Parents of existing/past pupils	8.9	9.8	6.2	8.3	8.6	8.0	6.4	11.4
8 Primary teachers	8.9	8.9	5.6	7.9	8.2	16.1 (1)	8.9	6.2
9 Meetings	9.2	8.3	10.9	13.2 (3)	8.0	7.5	4.4	3.8
10 People at work	0.4	2.4	1.1	2.8	0.6	0.9	1.3	2.3
11 Secondary teachers	10.4	7.7	10.6	7.5	11.4 (3)	8.1	8.6	9.1
Number of sources (weighted)	2994	928	1850	257	2326	145	1751	143
Number of respondents (weighted)	1074	322	609	47	707	92	853	50

NR = Non-Requesters (attended District School)
R = Requesters (made Placing Request)

should an authority wish to utilise the most effective channels of communication. An overview would suggest that, at both levels, what at first appeared to be the overwhelming influence of the grapevine among the local population may be modified by the information communicated through visits to the schools, both through observation and through discussion with teachers, and through the pages of the information booklets.

It should, however, not be assumed that parents pore over information booklets, systematically comparing the details of different schools. In Burns only 16 per cent of parents obtained more than one booklet, in Maxton only 2 per cent and in Watt 12 per cent. The proportion looking at three or more booklets was tiny: 4 per cent in Burns and less than 1 per cent in both Maxton and Watt. Of those receiving only one booklet, about three-quarters of parents felt the booklet answered the questions they wanted to know, while 13 per cent admitted to not having read it. Given the debate surrounding the inclusion of examination results in these booklets,[8] parents were asked whether they found the section on results useful. Overall, of those obtaining only one booklet, 35 per cent answered in the affirmative, with 38 per cent saying 'no' and 27.4 per cent being uncertain. From those obtaining more than one booklet, and therefore a higher proportion of choosers, the response was somewhat more positive – 60 per cent finding it useful, 28 per cent not and 12 per cent uncertain. Comparable evidence was obtained in the study by Macbeth, Strachan and Macaulay (1986) who found that examination results influenced half of those making placing requests and one-third of those attending the district school at least 'quite a lot'. They suggest however that information on examination performance may be impressionistic or hearsay rather than the result of rigorous comparison. As Johnson and Ransom (1983) have argued, at the age of secondary transfer, the prospect of assessment by public examination is still several years hence and it is a minority who search and compare according to such criteria.

REASONS FOR REJECTION AND CHOICE

In discussing their reasons for choice, requesting parents were asked the extent to which 'push' factors, the rejection of the district school, had been an important consideration: 'in deciding that your child should go to the intended school was it important to you that your child did not go to the district school?' Table 4.13 shows, at both primary and secondary levels, the numbers who answered 'yes' to this question and it is these parents (see below) who were further asked to give their reasons for rejecting the district school. As can be seen, the relative importance of the push factor varied, but in all areas over half and in the majority of areas over two thirds of requesting parents said it was important to avoid the district school. This factor will of course vary by individual school,

Table 4.13 The extent of rejection of the district school

	Number of requesters (weighted)	Number for whom avoidance of DS was important	%
PRIMARY ENTRY			
Burns New Town	27	21	77.8
Maxton City	108	58	53.7
Watt Burgh	96	60	62.5
TOTAL	231	139	60.2
SECONDARY TRANSFER			
Burns City	322	223	69.3
Burns New Town	47	38	80.9
Maxton Burgh	92	56	60.9
Watt Burgh	50	34	68.0
TOTAL	511	351	68.7

and more detailed analyses in each area reveal that, whereas some schools were strongly rejected, against others there were few complaints. In Watt Burgh, for example, at primary level over half the negative references (32) referred to only two schools (for more detail, see Petch, 1986a).

We have already highlighted the varying weights which parents may attach to the elements of rejection and of choice. A dual strategy was again adopted to ascertain the reasons behind these two elements. First, in an open-ended question, parents were given a full opportunity of stating, undirected, their own explanations. Second, parents were asked to assess the relative importance of each item on a pre-selected list and to select the four most important items from that list. As the issue of choice formed one of the main concerns of the survey, considerable thought was given both to the appropriate strategy for extracting the data and to the choice of factors which should appear in the structured list at each entry stage. The lists were assembled in semi-intuitive fashion, with repeated efforts to restrict them to manageable size. Reference was made to the work then in progress at the National Foundation for Educational Research (Stillman and Maychell, 1986) and Glasgow University (Macbeth, Strachan and Macaulay, 1986) and to a list of factors drawn up for use in research in Belgium by Magiels-Corsus (University of Antwerp). Reference was also made to the reasons which emerged from an analysis of placing request application forms in one of the regions.[9] In compiling a list of choice factors, a comparative format was used with references to, for example, 'a wider range of courses', or the fact that the school was 'easier to get to'. This was considered to reflect more closely the judgments that parents actually make.

Rejection of the District School: Primary Entry

Table 4.14 sets out parents' unstructured accounts of why they rejected the district school. It should be remembered that this table only includes those parents for whom rejection of their district school was an important consideration and that rejection, as highlighted by Johnson and Ransom (1983), may relate to some aspect of the school itself or to characteristics of the children who go there. An average of two reasons was offered by parents, the extent to which the full explanation was explored undoubtedly being influenced by the rigour of the interviewer. It should be noted that the categories presented here are a considerable reduction from the forty-eight initially identified. Inevitably there is a problem of interpretation, particularly when, as here, the parents' responses have already been compressed into a summary note on the questionnaire by the interviewer.

The reasons for rejecting a school were somewhat different in the three survey areas. In Burns New Town, the most frequently cited factor related to the size of the school, but on closer examination, in all but two instances this referred to the gross overcrowding at one school where the use of temporary accommodation had virtually doubled the size of the school. The second most frequently cited factor, that the intended school was nearer than the district school, illustrates a danger that is inherent in discussion of parental choice. There is a tendency to assert that a school which loses pupils is 'bad', whereas one that gains is somehow 'better'. Leaving aside for a moment what in educational terms these particular labels may mean, what is illustrated here is that at least some of the explanation for movement is rather more mundane; in this instance, it is simply a product of the vagaries of the catchment area map. Parents argue that it is more rational to select the nearest school and that the necessity of making a placing request is merely a response to an 'illogical' catchment area.[10] The third explanation offered in Burns New Town, that a child's siblings were at the intended school, is to some extent unhelpful in that it is necessary to know whether this was a result of a positive choice in the past, and, if so, for what reason, or whether it was a consequence of a change in catchment area boundaries or a change of address by the parents.

The number of requesting parents in Burns New Town was of course small and almost half of the factors cited referred to a single school. In Maxton City, however, having siblings at the school was again important, appearing in joint first place. The other two leading factors, on the other hand, were somewhat different: safety problems in getting to the district school and dislike of the 'rough' and 'rowdy' children who, according to the requesting parents, attended the district school. Again more detailed scrutiny reveals that half the safety considerations re-

Table 4.14 Reasons for rejecting the district school at P1 entry, open responses

'Could you tell me the reasons why you did not want to send your child to the district school?'

	Burns New Town % reasons and rank	Maxton City % reasons and rank	Watt Burgh % reasons and rank
Factors relating to size of school or classes	25.6 (1)	3.4	4.2
Accommodation related reasons	9.3	6.9	5.9
DS has composite classes	–	1.7	–
Bad reputation/reports	2.3	6.0	3.4
Poor teaching methods, no individual attention	4.7	1.7	4.2
Poor discipline	–	4.3	1.7
RS is a better school	2.3	8.6	4.2
Don't know much about DS	–	–	2.5
Bad headteacher/deputy	–	–	6.7
Child's siblings at RS	11.6 (3)	13.8 (1=)	9.2 (2)
Child's friends at RS	–	0.9	0.8
Respondent/partner/ relative/friend was at RS	–	5.2	3.4
Safety problems	4.7	13.8 (1=)	5.9
RS is nearer than DS	16.2 (2)	6.0	8.4 (3)
Inconvenient location	4.7	7.8	1.7
DS is in a bad area	2.3	–	1.7
Rowdy, rough children, bad language	7.0	12.1 (3)	17.7 (1)
Child is at RS's nursery	–	–	5.0
General dislike of DS	2.3	0.9	5.0
RS is feeder for desired secondary	–	2.6	0.8
Used to live in area of RS/ moving to RS catchment	2.3	–	4.2
Other	4.7	4.3	3.4
Number of reasons	43	116	119
Number (weighted)	21	58	60

DS= District School
RS= Requested School

ferred to a single school but that dislike of the children at the district school and the language they used extended more widely, embracing six schools within the city. Perhaps of equal interest to the factors which featured most frequently were those which received relatively little attention, since they provide an opportunity to refute some popular myths. Only two parents in Maxton City, for example, rejected schools on the basis of composite classes and throughout the three areas the numbers rejecting on the basis of what might be termed 'educational quality' – bad reputation, poor teaching methods, inadequate discipline – was small. This provides a further caution against too ready an identification of the losing school with poor educational provision.

In Watt Burgh, approaching one-fifth of the reasons offered, mainly in relation to three of the schools, referred to 'rowdy' children or the 'bad language' children used. The other main factors again reflected the fact that siblings were already at the school and its proximity. A consideration not mentioned elsewhere emerged in fourth place, namely rejection on the grounds of a bad head or deputy. Rather than reflecting on a certain individual, these comments related to a total of five schools.

Table 4.15 lists the reasons for rejecting the district school which parents most frequently selected when they were presented with a pre-determined list, the various options being listed on a card handed to parents for the duration of this question. The usual caveats must be entered about the dangers of bias in an ordered list, particularly when, as in this case, it was scanned at fairly high speed.

Some interesting comparisons emerge from the two approaches to data collection. Common to all three survey areas, for example, was an endorsement of item 4 on the Schedule, 'we don't think our child would be happy there', a very general statement within which parents may have embraced the more detailed considerations previously offered. The other factors frequently cited demonstrated a broad agreement with those isolated from the unstructured questioning. In Burns New Town, for example, items 11 and 25 referred to the accommodation problems previously cited and item 2 highlighted the consideration of proximity. In Maxton City, the concern with safety was still dominant (item 9), but closely shadowed by the more general item 3, 'it's an unpopular school'. Together with item 4 these factors may have been selected in preference to the more specific items 2 and 6 which would appear to more closely approximate the concern with 'rough and rowdy children' expressed in response to the open question. In Watt Burgh, as in Burns New Town, the fact that the child would not be happy at the district school emerged as the most commonly cited item, followed, with more certainty than in Maxton City, by item 1, 'the children who go there are not the kind of children that we want our child to mix with'. Seventeen of the twenty-one citations are to the same three schools, with two-thirds of the references on item 4 also to these same schools. Safety problems (item 9) emerged more clearly than in the open responses, particularly in relation to two of the schools.

Once again it is interesting to examine the items which receive little attention. There was, for example, little criticism of teachers or of teach-

Table 4.15. Reasons for rejecting the district school at P1 entry, structured responses (requesters for whom it was important to avoid district school only)

'Looking back over this list, could you tell me what were your four most important reasons for not wanting your child to go to the district school?'

	Burns New Town % reasons and rank	Maxton City % reasons and rank	Watt Burgh % reasons and rank
1 The children who go there are not the kind of children that we want our child to mix with	3.5	5.8	12.7 (2)
2 It is too far away	10.5 (3)	9.5 (4)	9.1 (4)
3 It's an unpopular school, other parents who live around here are sending their children to other schools	3.5	13.7 (2)	1.8
4 We don't think our child would be happy there	17.5 (1)	10.0 (3)	18.1 (1)
5 We are planning to move away from this area	1.8	2.1	1.8
6 Children from the school are badly behaved	3.5	7.9	8.4
7 We don't like the school's teaching methods	3.5		4.2
8 Too much bullying goes on at the school	1.8	1.6	4.8
9 There are safety problems in getting to the school	5.3	14.7 (1)	10.3 (3)
10 People in the family attended the school and we are not happy with it	1.8		3.0
11 The school is in bad accommodation and is poorly equipped	8.7 (4)		0.6
12 We don't like the open-plan layout	1.8	3.1	–
13 It isn't a very caring school	3.5	2.6	3.0
14 The school has a poor reputation for discipline	1.8	6.9	2.4
15 We don't think much of the teachers there	–	1.1	–
16 We don't like the attitude of the school towards uniform	–	4.7	3.0
17 We don't like the way the children at the school speak	3.5	2.1	6.0
18 Parents are not made to feel welcome in the school	–		–
19 The school doesn't give enough attention to the individual child	7.0	2.1	4.8
20 The school doesn't make its pupils work hard enough	3.5	5.3	–
21 The school is under threat of closure	–		–
22 The school doesn't have enough pupils	1.8		–
23 We don't like the school's use of composite classes	–	2.1	–
24 We don't think much of the school's headteacher	3.5	3.1	3.0
25 The classes are too crowded	12.2 (2)	1.6	3.0
Number of reasons	57	190	166
Number (weighted)	21	58	60

ing methods (items 7 and 15) and no sense that parents would not be made to feel welcome (item 18). The use of composite classes was not an issue and even the threat of a school being closed did not appear to worry parents. Indeed, the only school in the survey which was under threat of closure was notable for the high proportion of placing requests – it attracted seventeen against a district population of only five.

Rejection of the District School: Secondary Transfer

Using the unstructured approach at secondary level, parents for whom it was important to avoid the district school, offered over seventy different objections, ranging from complaints about the amount of freedom offered to the children, to dislike of the unwelcoming and uncaring atmosphere within the school. These objections were grouped into a more manageable twenty categories, the relative importance of each varying quite markedly across the four areas. A common complaint (cited most frequently in Burns City and in second place in both Burns New Town and Maxton Burgh) was that the district school had a poor reputation for discipline, providing 13.2 per cent of the 744 total objections. In second place overall, and first in Burns New Town, was the more pragmatic reason of access, the district school being less convenient, or even more distant to get to, than the selected alternative. In third place overall and second in Burns City was rejection of the district school on the grounds that the education provided there was considered to be poor.

As at primary level, however, care should be taken in generalising from the whole sample, with the data being more properly regarded as four case studies. Identifying the factors cited most frequently in the different areas highlights the variation which is found between different localities. In Burns City, as already outlined, the most frequent objections were on grounds of discipline and of poor education. In third place was the concern of parents, which has already been encountered at primary level, that their child would not be happy at the district school. In Burns New Town, the factors of access and of discipline provided a third of the reasons for rejecting of the school's teaching methods and dissatisfaction with the experience of the child's older siblings at the school. The major grounds on which parents rejected schools in the two burghs were completely different, despite the similar size and status of the two towns. In Maxton Burgh the most important reason was the partial explanation that older siblings went elsewhere. A close second was the poor reputation for discipline and in third place the influence of friends and classmates who were going to the intended school. In Watt Burgh, however, the most frequent explanation was that the child did not want to go to the district school, followed by a concern with problems of vandalism and of trouble on the school bus. The third objection related to problems of access and proximity.

In contrast to the open responses, when using the structured list (Table 4.16) parents selected a smaller number of factors across the four

Table 4.16. Reasons for rejecting the district school at s1 transfer, structured responses (requesters for whom it was important to avoid district school only) 'Looking back over this list, could you tell me what were your four most important reasons for not wanting your child to go to the district school?'

	Burns City % reasons and rank	Burns New Town % reasons and rank	Maxton Burgh % reasons and rank	Watt Burgh % reasons and rank
1 The children who go there are not the kind of children that we want our child to mix with	7.0	1.5	6.8 (3=)	9.5 (3=)
2 It is an unpopular school, other parents who live around here are sending their children to other schools	2.0	2.2	–	0.9
3 We don't think our child would be happy there	16.2 (1)	9.5 (3=)	13.1 (2)	17.4 (1)
4 Truancy is a big problem at the school	1.8	5.1	2.8	6.1
5 Children from the school are badly behaved	1.7	–	–	1.7
6 We are planning to move away from this area	3.8	3.6	5.7	7.0
7 We don't like the school's teaching methods	5.2	5.8	3.4	–
8 The school doesn't make its pupils work hard enough	5.4	6.6	5.7	1.7
9 The school is under threat of closure	–	–	–	–
10 Too much bullying goes on at the school	4.8	1.5	1.7	8.7
11 The school has a bad examination record	1.6	10.9 (2)	1.1	2.6
12 The school is hard to get to	4.8	7.3	6.3	4.3
13 Our child doesn't want to go to the school	11.9 (2)	9.5 (3=)	20.4 (1)	15.7 (2)
14 We don't like the school's policy on homework	3.5	1.5	4.0	0.9
15 The school has problems with vandalism, drug use and/or crime	4.6	7.3	3.4	3.5
16 Our child's brothers/sisters (or close relatives) attend(ed) the school and we were not happy with it	1.8	2.9	1.1	3.5
17 The school is in bad accommodation and is poorly equipped	2.5	–	0.6	–
18 The school has a poor reputation for discipline	8.1 (3)	12.4 (1)	5.7	9.5 (3=)
19 The school is too large	–	2.2	6.8 (3=)	2.6
20 It isn't a very caring school	0.5	2.2	0.6	–
21 The school gives its pupils too much freedom	4.4	4.3	1.1	–
22 The school doesn't give enough attention to the less able children	2.0	–	2.3	0.9
23 We are not satisfied with the courses taught there	2.9	–	0.6	0.9
24 We don't think much of the teachers there	0.5	1.5	3.4	0.9
25 We don't like the attitude of the school towards uniform	2.4	–	0.6	–
26 Parents are not made to feel welcome in the school	0.3	–	1.7	1.7
27 The school doesn't give enough attention to the more able children	0.3	2.2	–	–
Number of reasons	765	137	176	115
Number (weighted)	223	38	56	34

areas, although their ranking varied. Overall (first in both Burns City and Watt Burgh, second in Maxton Burgh and third equal in Burns New Town) the most important reason cited for rejecting the district school was that parents did not think their child would be happy there. In second place overall (first place in Maxton Burgh, second in Maxton City and Watt Burgh and third equal in Burns New Town) was the fact that the child did not want to go there, and third in importance (first in Burns New Town, third in Burns City, third equal in Watt Burgh) was a concern that the school had a poor reputation for discipline. Only three other factors were cited within the first three rankings for each area. In Burns New Town the second most important factor was a bad examination record at the school, while in both burghs third equal place was taken by a concern that the children at the district school were not the ones the parents wanted their own to mix with. In Maxton Burgh a specifically local concern, that the school was too large, occupied the remaining third place.

The variations between the two methodologies tended to be in the rank order of the main factors rather than in the introduction of radically different arguments. More important, as at primary level, was the nature of the reasons offered. Only one of those most frequently cited, poor discipline, together with the reference in Burns New Town to the school's bad examination record, referred directly to the quality or content of what is provided by the school. Other reasons either represented factors outwith the educational frame of reference, as with inconvenient location, or only offered a partial explanation, as with 'the child would not be happy' or had asked to go elsewhere.

Choice of the Requested School: Primary Entry

We discussed above the search procedures that parents adopted when they chose an alternative to the district school. In discussing the choice factors which parents cited, it will be shown that amongst many of the rejecting parents the considerations which determine the choice of requested school were closely related to, and indeed were very often the converse of, the factors which had led to rejection of the district school. Again we shall report on the two-stage elaboration of factors and on the responses at both primary and secondary level.

Table 4.17 summarises the responses offered to the open-ended question, and sets out the reasons why parents opted for the requested school rather than for any of the others under consideration. The categories listed are again a reduction from the seventy-five originally identified. That the pattern of choice factors was the obverse of those given for rejecting the district school is readily apparent in Burns New Town. The thirteen parents who made a placing request for one school which opened in 1983 all cited the good accommodation and modern facilities as a reason for doing so. A further eleven comments relating to the same school referred to the small classes and the fact that the specified school

Table 4.17 Reasons for choosing the requested school at P1 entry, open responses

'Now I want to ask you why you are sending your child to the requested school rather than the other schools you considered? Could you tell me the reasons why you chose the requested school?'

	Burns New Town % reasons and rank	Maxton City % reasons and rank	Watt Burgh % reasons and rank
Good headteacher/ teachers	1.3	4.2	3.2
Good relationships, e.g teacher/child, parent/teacher	1.3	1.4	5.7
Good school, good reputation, popular school	12.0 (2)	11.7 (2)	7.8
Aspects of curriculum	2.7	3.1	1.8
Good teaching methods	4.0	3.1	2.8
Impressed by RS/ liked what saw	1.3	3.5	5.7
Non-composite classes	–	1.4	–
Small classes	8.0	–	2.9
Individual attention	2.7	0.3	2.5
RS less crowded than DS	6.7	–	–
Good discipline	4.0	2.8	1.8
Impresssed by children at RS – confident, happy, hardworking	2.7	4.5	5.7
Good accommodation, facilities, surroundings	17.3 (1)	2.8	6.1
Open plan layout	2.7	0.3	1.1
Primary and nursery on same site	1.3	1.0	12.9 (1)
Good area	–	0.7	0.7
Convenient location	9.3	13.4 (1)	5.0
Proximity	8.0	11.0 (3)	9.3 (2=)
Safety	–	7.6	4.3
Neighbours/friends' children go/will be going to RS	–	3.8	1.4
Nursery school friends will be going to RS	1.3	2.4	3.2
Child's siblings at RS	10.7 (3)	10.3	9.3 (2=)
Respondent/partner/friend/ relative was at RS	–	3.8	1.8
Other	2.7	6.9	5.0
Number of reasons	75	290	280
Number (weighted)	27	108	96

DS= District School
RS= Requested School

would be less crowded than the district school. Nearly all these parents had cited overcrowding at the district school as a reason for rejecting it. References to the 'good reputation' of the school provided the second most popular reason for choice in Burns New Town. Siblings and proximity also featured prominently, together with the school being in a convenient location.

In Maxton City, the convenience of the location emerged as the most important determinant of choice, followed in third place by the proximity of the school. The major concerns were therefore unrelated to what was actually provided at the school but reflected rather the idiosyncrasy of the catchment area map or the travel patterns of the parents. Intervening in second place, particularly in relation to two schools, was reference to a 'good school', one with a 'good reputation', a factor cited by 31 per cent of parents. Siblings at the requested school were again given as an explanation for the choice (by 28 per cent of parents) and safety, a factor inevitably compounded with proximity, extended the concern with locational characteristics.

The influence of factors unique to a specific area was illustrated in Watt Burgh where the most frequently quoted reason for choosing a school was that nursery and primary schools were on the same site. This reason was offered in relation to a total of eight schools and reflected a practice common throughout the region. Promotion of a particular policy in a specific region may therefore be a major factor behind the distribution of placing requests. Proximity and siblings each provided twenty-six or 9.3 per cent of the choice factors and only in fourth place was there any consideration of the quality of the school itself with parents again referring to the ubiquitous 'good school'. Over half of these references related to just two schools. Only when account was taken of three categories which all received sixteen references, 'good relationships at the school', 'impressed by the requested school' and 'impressed by the children', did factors specific to the nature of the school itself begin to emerge.

Moving, in Table 4.18, to the selection from a structured list of the four most important determinants of choice, both the generality and the logic of Table 4.15 are maintained. If a school was rejected because the child would not be happy, an alternative was sought where it was thought the child would be happier, hence the importance of item 11 in all three areas. It should be remembered that Tables 4.17 and 4.18 include the views of those for whom avoidance of the district school was not an important consideration (a sizeable number in both Maxton City and Watt Burgh) suggesting that amongst this group also humanistic considerations were of major importance. While the strength of this factor appeared to increase with enhanced numbers, other arguments which were important in Table 4.15 receded, for example, the concern in Watt Burgh about the children their child would have to mix with.

Table 4.18 Reasons for choosing the requested school at P1 entry, structured responses

'Looking back over the list (see below) could you tell me what the four most important reasons were for wanting your child to attend the requested school?'

Reasons (see below)	Burns New Town % reason and rank	Maxton City % reason and rank	Watt Burgh % reason and rank
1.	4.6	5.4	5.0
2.	4.6	5.9	4.4
3.	2.3	1.7	5.0
4.	9.2 (3)	10.3 (1)	8.0 (3=)
5.	–	1.7	1.1
6.	2.3	1.2	1.3
7.	2.3	4.9	3.0
8.	5.7	2.9	3.6
9.	8.1 (4)	8.6 (2=)	8.0 (3=)
10.	6.9	7.8 (4=)	8.8 (2)
11.	16.1 (1)	8.6 (2=)	13.5 (1)
12.	–	2.9	4.7
13.	1.2	1.2	2.8
14.	3.4	4.2	3.3
15.	12.6 (2)	2.4	2.8
16.	3.4	7.8 (4=)	7.2
17.	1.2	0.7	2.5
18.	–	1.7	0.3
19.	–	4.7	3.0
20.	–	–	–
21.	–	1.7	1.1
22.	–	–	1.3
23.	3.4	0.5	1.1
24.	1.2	0.5	1.1
25.	2.3	4.4	1.9
26.	4.6	2.2	3.0
27.	4.6	2.2	1.6
28.	–	3.9	–
29.	–	–	0.6
Number of reasons	87	409	363
Number (weighted)	27	108	96

1. We like the teacher(s) he/she will have
2. The school is better at teaching the basic skills of reading and writing
3. The school has a more friendly atmosphere
4. The school is nearer
5. We prefer the attitude of the school towards uniform
6. The school has a better headteacher
7. The school is more convenient for parent(s) work
8. The school gives more encouragement to the involvement of parents
9. Our child's brothers/sisters attend(ed) the school
10. The school is safer to get to
11. We think our child would be happier there

12. The children who go there are the kind that we want our child to mix with
13. It is a more caring school
14. The school is more convenient for out-of-school arrangements for the child
15. The school is in better accommodation and has good facilities
16. Our child's friends will attend the school
17. The school is smaller
18. I or my spouse/partner or other relatives were there
19. We prefer the style of teaching at the school
20. We prefer the larger classes
21. It is a more popular school, lots of parents from outside the district choose it
22. We prefer the religious education at the school
23. The classes are less crowded
24. The school offers exciting activities to the children
25. The school makes its pupils work harder
26. The school gives more emphasis to the individual child
27. The school has a reputation for better discipline
28. The school does not use composite classes
29. The school has good specialist teachers

In Burns New Town, concern with the happiness of the child was followed by the influence of accommodation, of proximity and of siblings. Proximity moved to first place in Maxton City, while, in second place, the sibling factor vied with the child's happiness. The other main concerns in Maxton City were with safety and with the fact that the child's friends would be attending the requested school. There was some evidence of concern with the teaching the child would receive (items 1, 2, 19 and 25), and at two particular schools some small evidence of selection to avoid composite classes.

The pattern of choice revealed in Watt Burgh was the now familiar one of happiness (item 11), safety (item 10), siblings (item 9) and proximity (item 4). The major significance here was that the factor which was mentioned most frequently in the open question, the location of the nursery on the site of the intended school, was superseded. No provision had been made in the structured list for such an argument and therefore what must be judged a sub-optimal response was achieved. This example highlights well the challenge of the unexpected to the structured questionnaire; in a sense such an instrument can only be constructed if the answers are already known.

The choice factors which parents cite can be compared with the responses offered by parents when asked to select from a list of twelve statements the three they thought most important for when their child left primary school. Most frequently cited was that their child was happy, secondly creative and imaginative, and thirdly obedient and well behaved.

Choice of the Requested School: Secondary Transfer

An emergent pattern is now becoming fairly clear in this discussion of the parameters of choice. Looking first at the evidence of the open response, in first three places overall were the precedent set by older siblings, the choice of a school at a more convenient location and the desire for the child to accompany friends to school. Again it would have been valuable to have known why the friends were going to the requested school or to have enquired why the siblings were enrolled at that school. Was it perhaps the district school at that time, or was the real choice made, as is often maintained, at the transfer of the eldest child? An exploration of the variations between the different areas reveals some determining factors. In Burns City, for example, the convenience of the location ranked first, and the sibling factor third. The second most decisive factor, however, was the availability of a wider range of courses and the provision of specific subjects at the requested school, this factor including a number of parents who selected a particular school because it was known as the school that offered the opportunity to sit 'A' levels (see Chapter 5). Elsewhere, however, this factor featured little. In Burns New Town the most important consideration was proximity, but this was again largely due to the influence of one particular school where the catchment area accorded particularly badly with geographical reality. A number of diverse factors vied for second place, attendance of siblings and the intentions of friends and, of more educational substance, the better examination record, the reputation for better discipline and the more caring, welcoming atmosphere. In Maxton Burgh, the most frequently cited reasons in order were siblings, friends, and better discipline, while in Watt Burgh the preference of the child was pre-eminent, the only area in which it carried such importance.

From the more structured format illustrated in Table 4.19, the pattern which emerges is remarkably uniform. In first three places overall were the judgment that the child would be happier at the chosen school, the avowal by the child that he or she would prefer the requested school, and the assessment that the selected school offered better discipline. This ordering was replicated in both Burns City and Watt Burgh, while in Maxton Burgh it was only disturbed by the ousting of the concern for discipline into fourth place by the desire for the child to attend the same school as friends. In Burns New Town, the child's happiness and the child's preference received equal recognition while in third place ease of access was selected. It is important in interpreting the explanations for choice to appreciate the large number of factors which these parents with children entering secondary school dismissed as of little concern in their own decision making. A group of factors highlighted educational explanations which proponents of the legislation had argued would be important to parents. Item 2, for example, allowed parents to emphasise academic subjects, item 28 to endorse the examination record and item 27 to select the quality of teaching staff. The fact that such concerns were cited as of major importance by only tiny minorities was striking, although perhaps not altogether surprising given the evidence cited

Table 4.19 Reasons for choosing the requested school at S1 transfer, structured responses

'Looking back over the list (see below) could you tell me what the four most important reasons were for wanting your child to attend the requested school?'

Reasons (see below)	Burns City % reasons and rank	Burns New Town % reasons and rank	Maxton Burgh % reasons and rank	Watt Burgh % reasons and rank
1.	1.4	–	1.4	1.1
2.	2.8	3.0	6.6	1.1
3.	2.6	0.6	1.1	1.6
4.	6.4 (4)	3.6	5.5	1.1
5.	2.7	2.4	0.6	3.3
6.	1.1	3.0	2.0	0.5
7.	3.0	2.4	2.9	1.1
8.	1.2	3.6	4.3	3.8
9.	–	–	–	–
10.	1.4	1.2	0.9	0.5
11.	1.7	1.2	1.1	0.5
12.	1.6	–	0.6	0.5
13.	4.2	4.2	7.2 (4=)	6.5
14.	2.4	–	3.1	0.5
15.	0.2	–	0.3	–
16.	5.8	10.3 (3)	3.4	7.6 (4)
17.	9.9 (2)	13.9 (1=)	13.2 (2)	16.9 (2)
18.	15.1 (1)	13.9 (1=)	16.9 (1)	19.7 (1)
19.	3.1	–	1.7	3.3
20.	2.9	2.4	1.1	1.1
21.	0.4	0.6	2.0	–
22.	9.7 (3)	7.8	7.2 (4=)	10.3 (3)
23.	2.2	2.4	–	2.2
24.	2.8	1.2	0.6	2.7
25.	4.4	7.2	8.9 (3)	5.5
26.	–	0.6	–	–
27.	3.7	1.2	1.4	0.5
28.	2.8	9.1 (4)	2.9	1.6
29.	1.4	1.2	2.0	–
30.	1.1	0.6	1.1	0.5
31.	1.6	0.6	–	5.5
32.	0.4	1.8	–	0.5
Number of reasons	1 131	166	349	184
Number (weighted)	322	47	92	50

1. We prefer the school's policy on homework
2. The school places greater emphasis on academic subjects, such as History, Maths and Science
3. We prefer the attitude of the school towards uniform
4. The school makes its pupils work harder

5. The school has a wider range of out–of–school activities, e.g. sports, music and clubs
6. The school assesses pupils more regularly
7. The school offers a wider range of courses
8. The school has a better headteacher
9. The school gives its pupils more freedom
10. The school is more convenient for parent(s) work
11. The school gives more encouragement to the involvement of parents
12. The school is better at helping pupils get jobs
13. Our child's brothers and/or sisters attend(ed) the school
14. The school gives more attention to less able children
15. The school gives more emphasis to practical skills, such as woodwork and domestic science
16. It is easier to get to the school
17. Our child prefers the school
18. We think our child would be happier there
19. The children who go there are the kind that we want our child to mix with
20. It is a more caring school
21. The school gives more attention to the more able children
22. The school has a reputation for better discipline
23. The school is more convenient for out–of–school arrangements for the child
24. The school is in better accommodation and is well equipped
25. Our child's friends will attend the school
26. We prefer the religious education at the school
27. The school has a better teaching staff
28. The school has a better examination record
29. The school is smaller
30. I or my spouse/partner or other relative went there
31. The school emphasises a special subject we want, such as computers or music
32. It is a more popular school, lots of parents from outside the district choose it

earlier on the small numbers who actually compared information on such factors across schools.

CONCLUSIONS

Choice behaviour both at primary and secondary level appears to differ in key respects from that which is often suggested by proponents of parental choice of school. Both those who choose and the factors which they cite in explanation for their choice appear at variance with the assumptions that predominate, and provide little support to exponents of a market ideology. The tentative conclusions from the small study by Elliott et al (1981a) appear therefore to have wider validity, with our findings endorsing the general preference for process rather than product criteria. At least within the state system, the majority of parents who are exercising choice on behalf of their children seem to adopt a humanistic rather than a technological perspective, being less concerned with measurable criteria of product than with the creation of an atmosphere supportive to the child's well-being. Moreover, they appear to base their decisions on limited and possibly inadequate information and tend to be really concerned with the well-being of their own child. The policy-maker may therefore wish to qualify the extent to which encouragement is given to these activities. But it cannot be denied that the reality of behaviour appears to be very different from the parent searching for academic achievement which is commonly portrayed.

A number of qualifications should however be added to this conclusion to avoid too ready a polarisation between the two perspectives. The notion of happiness to which so much reference was made has itself been the object of considerable study (Argyle, 1987). The different ways in which 'happiness' can be assessed and its correlation with factors such as employment, leisure and social relationships can be explored in depth. It may be that in speaking of the happiness of the child, parents have in mind some such complex of factors which in this case may also include assessment of the various details of the educational provision. Parents may, in effect, be using the concept of happiness as some form of shorthand for a more traditional mix of precipitating factors associated with choice behaviour. Indeed there is some evidence to suggest that there may be an association between children's perception of their happiness at school and their educational attainment (Gray, McPherson and Raffe, 1983). The parent may therefore, with varying degrees of awareness, be selecting the appropriate environment knowing that it will be conducive to the achievement of desired educational goals.

It should not be forgotten also that in offering and then selecting their reasons for choice, the mix that parents opt for reflects the particular 'account' which they wish to present of their behaviour. The extent to which this is a deliberately selective construction of reality cannot be known. Given, however, that parents were quite ready to select for example options which spoke of 'not the kind of children that we want our child to mix with', or to speak of 'rough and rowdy children', there is little evidence to suggest that parents felt constrained to volunteer only what might be perceived as acceptable criteria. Greater insight into the complexity and meaning of choice behaviour would, however, have required a less structured and more searching interviewing methodology.

NOTES

1. At secondary level, 206 responses were received from an initial mailing to 701 sets of parents in Burns City (29.4 per cent); while 64 responses were received from a mailing of 233 parents in Burns New Town (27.5 per cent). At primary level, 54 out of 203 parents (26.6 per cent) replied to the first letter in Burns New

Town. The number of responses rose considerably after the second mailing (Table 4.3).

2. Surprisingly little attention has been given to the methodological issue of whether to treat the two parents as a single unit or whether to acknowledge potentially very different responses. The decision was taken in this study to talk to one parent only.

3. Having decided to opt for one parent only, we were concerned to have responses from both mothers and fathers. This was in contrast to, for example, the Plowden Report (Department of Education and Science, 1967) where the large majority of respondents to a survey at primary level were mothers.

4. The very low number of 'considerers' in certain areas, for example in Maxton Burgh at secondary level, and the fact that there was considerable variation between interviewers in the extent to which parents were placed in this category, provide strong evidence for the existence of an interviewer effect and suggest that our estimates of the number of considerers may be unreliable.

5. Many of the perennial worries relating to the measurement of social class are included in the volume edited by Jacoby (1986). The paper by Arber, Dale and Gilbert addresses the particular problems of assessing social class for women.

6. A number of writers, e.g. Smith and May (1980) hold that the traditional distinction between rationalistic and incrementalist models of decision-making is an artificial one.

7. See, for example, Hoinville, Jowell and Associates (1978).

8. The essays by Plewis, Gray, Fogelman, Mortimore and Byford (1981) address the question of how examination results relate to school effectiveness and the extent to which this relationship is understood by parents.

9. It should be recognised that in the completion of an official request form parents may be concerned to present information selectively. Moreover in Burns the form itself directs the parent to 'give details with particular reference to any of the criteria listed on the enclosed *Guidelines on Placing in Schools*'.

10. Garner (1988) uses the addresses of school leavers to define *de facto* catchment areas for secondary schools.

5

RIGHTS OF APPEAL OVER CHOICE OF SCHOOL

Provisions for parents' appeals to local appeal committees and sheriffs are central to the statutory scheme of rights for parents under the 1981 Act. Appeals provide a check on education authorities' determination of placing requests, ensuring children a place in the school their parents request unless one of the statutory grounds of refusal exists. Appeals also affect a number of central concerns of the authority. The outcome of appeals can change the pattern of admissions in the authority, affecting its ability to provide equal educational opportunity in all its schools. In this chapter, we examine the operation of education appeal committees (EACS). We evaluate how well these appeal committees have protected parents' rights of school choice and also consider the effects that appeal decisions have had on the broader concerns of authorities in providing education for all pupils.

THE FUNCTIONS OF APPEALS

The 1981 Act established two levels of appeal for parents whose placing requests are refused by the authority. First, parents can refer the decision of the authority to an appeal committee set up by the authority under the 1981 Act. Secondly, if the appeal committee confirms the refusal by the authority, the parents can appeal to the sheriff whose jurisdiction covers the location of the requested school.

The appeal committee and the sheriff are obliged to uphold the appeal unless they are satisfied that one of the statutory grounds of refusal justifies the refusal of the parents' request. Even where one or more statutory exceptions apply, the sheriff and the appeal committee can confirm the authority's refusal only if they are also satisfied 'that, in all the circumstances, it is appropriate to do so'. In other words, the appeal committee and the sheriff are to decide themselves whether the parents' placing request can or should be refused under the requirements of the 1981 Act, rather than determining whether the authority erred in refusing the parents' request in the first place.

The constitution of appeal committees is governed by provisions in the 1981 Act. The appeal committees are to consist of three, five, or seven members appointed by the authority. The membership of appeal committees is to be drawn from members of the authority or the education committee and others who are parents of school-age children or who have relevant experience in education.

Officers of the education authority, teachers, parents and pupils of affected schools are excluded from serving on appeal committees. Also, members of the authority or of its education committee cannot out-number the other members of the appeal committee by more than one. Finally, the chairman of the appeal committee shall not be a member of the education committee (Schedule A1, Education (Scotland) Act 1981, paras 2–8).

Procedural requirements for appeal committees are set out in the Education (Appeal Committee Procedures) Regulations (1981). The reg-ulations set out requirements for procedures prior to an appeal hearing, focusing primarily on matters of timing and notification of parents. The regulations also specify the order of proceedings at the appeal hearing: the authority presents its case; the parents question the authority; the parents present their case; the authority questions the parents; the authority sums up; and the parents sum up. Both the authority and the parents or their representatives are entitled to call evidence and to question persons giving evidence.

One final provision of the 1981 Act requires that if the appeal com-mittee or the sheriff upholds a parents' appeal, the authority is to review decisions refusing placing requests involving the same stage at the school involved in the appeal. The authority need only 'review' the other refusals. There is no statutory obligation on the authority to change its decisions or to settle the requests consistently with the appeal decision. However, if the authority decides not to reverse its refusal of a placing request, it must inform the parents of this decision and the parents have a new opportunity to refer the authority's decision to an appeal com-mittee and the sheriff.[1]

The statutory scheme of parental choice hinges on the opportunity for parents to question the refusal of their placing request before an appeal committee and, if necessary, before a sheriff. The primary purpose of the 1981 Act was to restrict authorities' ability to refuse parents' school requests. The possibility of an appeal helps to assure that parents' rights of school choice are respected by authorities.

Appeals involving over-subscribed schools

In appeals involving over-subscribed schools, decisions to refuse placing requests are based on limits placed on enrolment at the re-quested school, either on the number of pupils at any stage in the school (based on the number of classes and maximum class-size limits) or on the total number of pupils in the school (based on the school's capacity) (see Chapter 3). Placing requests above the limit are refused on the basis that admitting more children to the school would give rise to one of the statutory grounds of refusal, requiring the employment of another teacher or significant alterations to the school's fabric or facilities or causing serious detriment to order and discipline at the school or the educational well-being of the pupils there.

Appeal committees' and sheriffs' consideration of appeals is set up in the 1981 Act as a two-stage process. In the first stage, the authority must satisfy the appeal committee or the sheriff that grounds of refusal exist. This burden on the authority serves as a check that the authority's admission limits are based on the grounds specified in the 1981 Act. The appeal committee and the sheriff are each required to make an independent determination of whether the authority's use of the school's admission limit to refuse a parents' request is proper. This applies regardless of whether the parent directly challenges that justification. This obligation requires the authority to offer evidence to justify its admission limit. Otherwise, the appeal committee or sheriff would have no basis on which to conclude that the refusals were justified under the 1981 Act. The appeal committee or the sheriff cannot rely wholly on the authority's assertion that the statutory grounds underlie the admission limit.

The second stage of the appeal committee's or the sheriff's consideration is to determine whether refusing the request is appropriate in the particular circumstances of the appeal. The effects of admitting one more child are marginal in most cases. Although these marginal effects may be sufficient to justify refusing most appeals, some appeals may involve considerations that justify making an exception. The family might experience significant hardship or the child might miss special opportunities for which he or she is particularly qualified. The appeal committee or the sheriff can hear the parents' arguments for making an exception in their case and decide the appeal in light of the numbers at the school and the claims made by other parents. The function of appeals here is to identify cases that merit special treatment in ways that are not recognised in the authority's policies (Jowell, 1973; Galligan, 1986).

Appeals involving under-age children

The second type of appeal that frequently arises involves under-age admission requests, that is placing requests on behalf of children under the statutory age of entry. Parents may apply to send their under-age children to school and, since 1984, authorities have treated such applications as placing requests.[2] Placing requests involving under-age children (assuming the school has places) can be refused only if 'the education normally provided at the school is not suited to the age, ability or aptitude of the child' (s. 28A(3)(b)). Authorities differ in their interpretation of this clause. Most authorities consider the exception as a whole (*conjunctively*), holding that ability and aptitude should be considered along with the age of the child. Other authorities consider the terms one by one (*disjunctively*), refusing most under-age requests on the basis of age alone, while granting occasional requests involving children with exceptional ability and aptitude for their age, and children with pressing social needs (see Petch, 1987, for a more extended discussion).

When an authority refuses an under-age placing request, the parents can appeal. The issue that comes before the appeal committee or the sheriff is the same issue decided by the authority: is the education offered at the school 'suited to the age, ability or aptitude of the child'? In applying this standard, the appeal committee or the sheriff must decide whether to view the standard conjunctively, looking at the age, ability and aptitude of the child as a whole, or disjunctively, considering each of the characteristics as sufficient to justify refusing the request.[3] The conjunctive approach requires a more complete evaluation of the child in deciding whether a statutory ground of refusal exists. The appeal hearing would focus on the physical, mental and emotional characteristics of the child and on how the child would fare in school. However, the apparent difference between these two approaches is substantially reduced by the appeal committee's and the sheriff's duties to confirm the authority's refusal only if 'in all the circumstances, it is appropriate to do so'. Even if the appeal committee or the sheriff takes the disjunctive view of the authority's duty, the broad considerations about the child's aptitude and abilities are relevant to the decision of appropriateness.[4] In addition, the appeal committee or the sheriff should take into account other family circumstances, such as the burden of care for the child if he or she is not admitted to school.

The outcomes of appeals can also affect an authority's decision making. Appeal decisions influence the authority's procedures for determining placing requests. Appeal decisions that confirm the authority's decisions reinforce the authority's approach, perhaps leading the authority to expand its interpretation of the grounds of refusal. Reversals on appeal may cause the authority to reconsider its approach to placing requests. If an appeal committee or a sheriff refuses to accept the authority's justification for refusing a request, the authority may have to re-examine its interpretation of the legislation. There are also several practical reasons why an authority may go along with an appeal committee's or a sheriff's interpretation, such as avoiding the time and expense of hearings only to lose or the negative publicity that might result. The prospect of appeals reinforces the authorities' concern to interpret and apply parents' rights correctly in their determination of placing requests (Jowell, 1973; Harlow and Rawlings, 1984).

Appeals also have other, less direct functions. Appeals allow parents to participate in a decision that they see as strongly affecting their children. Parents are given an opportunity to explain their reasons for choosing a particular school and to try to persuade appeal committee members or the sheriff that their child should be able to attend the requested school. Appeal hearings can also provide the authority's officials with an opportunity to let unhappy parents know the reasons for refusing their request as well as to explain what other options are available to them. The officials can also respond to parents' concerns about the district school and inform them about alternative schools. It is important to recognise, however, that the central function of appeals is to reconsider refusals of placing requests to ensure that those decisions are consistent with parents' rights of school choice and that proper account is taken of any particularly strong reasons which parents may have for requesting a particular school. This provides the basis for examining the operation of appeals.

THE OPERATION OF SCHOOL ADMISSION APPEALS

The examination of appeals raises doubts about how well appeals directly perform these functions. Relatively few appeals have been held. Appeal committees have virtually never questioned authorities' admission limits. And only in some authorities have committees tried to balance parents' reasons and circumstances against the authority's concerns. Thus, appeal outcomes have played a minimal role in school admissions. However, the effects of appeals may be indirect. Authorities' anticipation of appeals against refusals may lead them to allow requests that they would have refused in the absence of appeals. The effect of the prospect of appeals is difficult to measure, though in the description of appeals below we can suggest some of the ways that authorities take the prospect of appeals into account.

Appeals have played a limited direct role in school admissions under the 1981 Act. Tables 5.1 to 5.4 provide a statistical summary of the pattern of appeals over the three years 1982–1985 (Scottish Education Department, 1985, 1986 and 1987a).

There have been relatively few appeals compared to the number of placing requests made or the number of children in school. In total, 650 appeals were made in the three-year period. Appeal committees upheld parents in 166[5] of these appeals. In these three years, parents made 59 571 placing requests for non-district schools, so only 1.1 per cent of all placing requests resulted in an appeal and only 0.3 per cent of all requests resulted in an appeal which was upheld. Since the Scottish school population stood at 838 400 in September 1983, less than 0.08 per cent of all Scottish children were the subject of an appeal and less than 0.02 per cent of them obtained a place at the school requested by their parents as the result of an appeal.

The primary reason that appeal rates were so low was that authorities allowed the great majority of placing requests. Thus, parents seldom needed to appeal. Over the three years, 94.1 per cent of all requests were granted without appeal. (Only 4.1 per cent of all requests were actually refused, the remainder being withdrawn by the parents.) Parents appealed in 26.8 per cent of all refusals, so authorities could reasonably expect some challenges when they refused requests.

The aggregate statistics on appeal obscure important differences between different types of requests.[6] Three types of appeals should be

Table 5.1 Placing Requests and Appeals in Scotland, 1982–1983

	Under-age	P1	P2–P7	S1	S2–S6	Total
Requests received	261	4 548	4 892	4 675	2 757	17 133
Requests granted	122	4 514	4 873	4 493	2 714	16 716
(% of requests)	46.7	99.3	99.6	96.1	98.4	97.6
Requests refused	139	34	19	182	43	417
Appeals received	19	11	3	49	9	91
Appeals upheld	2	7	1	17	1	28
Appeals refused	17	4	2	32	8	63
Sheriffs' appeals received	NA	NA	NA	NA	NA	NA
Sheriffs' appeals upheld	–	–	–	–	–	–
Sheriffs' appeals refused	–	–	–	–	–	–

Source: Scottish Education Department (1985), Table 2

mentioned specifically – under-age admissions, primary entry, and secondary transfer. Choice of school was most commonly an issue for parents when children started school and when they transferred to secondary school. (Parents were about six times as likely to request a non-district school at primary entry than at other stages of primary school and nearly ten times as likely to do so at secondary transfer than at other stages of secondary school.) Authorities decided primary entry (excluding under-age requests) and secondary transfer requests according to their schools' admission limits, so when parents appealed they had to challenge the limit or claim that their reasons justified exceptions to the school's limit. Although the proportion of refusals at primary entry was low (1.6 per cent), parents challenged these refusals more frequently (43.7 per cent) than any other kind of refusal. Primary entry appeals also succeeded more often (36.4 per cent) than other types of appeals. On the other hand, secondary transfer requests were refused more often (6.9 per cent) than those at other levels (except for the special case of under-age admissions). Parents frequently challenged refusals at secondary transfer (31.1 per cent), but a lower proportion of appeals succeeded there than at any other level (19.3 per cent).

Finally, under-age admission appeals were a special case. They focused almost exclusively on the child's abilities and the family's circum-

Table 5.2. Placing Requests and Appeals in Scotland, 1983–1984

	Under-age	P1	P2–P7	S1	S2–S6	Total
Requests received	513	5 735	5 537	5 857	2 901	20 543
Requests granted (% of requests)	311 60.6	5 620 98.0	5 359 96.8	5 331 91.0	2 770 95.5	19 391 94.4
Requests refused	165	81	92	434	56	828
Appeals received	35	30	22	141	12	240
Appeals upheld	12	17	6	11	1	47
Appeals refused	21	11	16	124	10	182
Sheriffs' appeals received	2	0	7	21	0	30
Sheriffs' appeals upheld	0	–	7	15	–	22
Sheriffs' appeals refused	1	–	0	4	–	5

Source: Scottish Education Department (1986), Table 2

stances. It was not a matter of how many children should be in school, but whether a particular child should be in school at all. Under-age requests were refused much more often than any other kind of request. Parents appealed against these refusals much less often than against other types of refusals. Yet parents succeeded in under-age appeals about as frequently as they did in other types of appeal. Under-age requests were also growing rapidly (from 513 in 1984 to 1 844 in 1985).

THE EXPERIENCE OF APPEALS

Appeal hearings are the product of a variety of factors: the circumstances of the appeal, the personalities of the parents, education officers, clerks and appeal committee members and the procedures followed in the hearing. Because of the extent of variation in these factors, individual hearings are very different from one another. No single hearing can be described as typical. However, sensitivity to the key issues involved in appeals requires familiarity with appeal proceedings that can come only from a detailed account of such proceedings. For this reason, we present accounts of two days of appeals in a Scottish Region – one day of appeals for admission to an over-subscribed school and one day of under-age admission appeals. The appeals described here illustrate many of the questions that are central to the proper conduct of appeals as well as

Table 5.3. Placing Requests and Appeals in Scotland, 1984–1985

	Under-age	P1	P2–P7	S1	S2–S6	Total
Requests received	1 844	6 390	5 171	5 767	2 623	21 795
Requests granted	1 214	6 133	5 024	5 069	2 533	19 973
(% of requests)	65.8	96.0	97.2	87.9	96.6	91.6
Requests refused	402	155	76	401	48	1 182
Appeals received	47	77	13	157	25	319
Appeals upheld	13	19	2	39	18	91
Appeals refused	29	53	10	112	7	211
Sheriffs' appeals received	2	3	0	26	2	33
Sheriffs' appeals upheld	0	3	–	25	2	30
Sheriffs' appeals refused	1	0	–	0	0	1

Source: Scottish Education Department (1987a), Table 3

many of the difficulties faced by parents, authorities and appeal committees.

One Day of Appeals for Over-Subscribed Schools

In 1985, Burns Region decided to set admission limits on three secondary schools – Dalgleish High School, Rutherford High School and Souness High School – so that over the course of several years these schools could vacate annexes and temporary huts that were in poor condition (see Chapter 3). For each of the schools, the number of district pupils plus the number of placing requests was greater than the admission limit. Burns' admissions policy accorded first priority to district pupils and then gave responsibility for deciding which placing requests would be allowed to the Placing Request Committee (PRC). The Committee admitted all pupils with siblings at the requested schools. It then allowed requests that involved pupils attending feeder primary schools, pupils with medical reasons and travel/safety concerns. For one school (Dalgleish High School), the Committee allowed requests that mentioned 'A' level courses that were only available at that school. For all schools, the final places at the school and all priorities on the waiting list were allocated according to the distance from the pupil's home to the requested school.

Eleven sets of parents appealed (out of 134 requests that were

Table 5.4. Placing Requests and Appeals in Scotland, 1982–1985

	Under-age	P1	P2–P7	S1	S2–S6	Total
Requests received	2618	16673	15660	16299	8821	59471
Requests granted	1647	16267	15256	14893	8017	56080
(% of requests)	62.9	97.6	97.9	91.4	97.0	94.3
Requests refused	706	270	187	1117	147	2523
Appeals received	101	118	39	347	46	650
Appeals upheld	27	43	9	67	20	166
Appeals refused	67	68	28	268	25	454
Sheriffs' appeals received	4	3	7	47	2	63
Sheriffs' appeals upheld	0	3	7	40	2	52
Sheriffs' appeals refused	2	0	0	4	0	6

refused). All eleven appeals were heard by the same appeal committee on the same day. The appeal committee consisted of three members: the *Chair*, a retired headteacher who had chaired almost every appeal committee in the Region; the *Member*, a co-opted member of the Education Committee; and the *Representative*, a person nominated by the local Federation of Parent and Parent-Teacher Associations. There were also two clerks, one senior clerk (*Clerk*), who was responsible for instructing the committee and answering any questions and a junior clerk who handled the papers.

Prior to the appeal hearing, the members of the appeal committee and the parents received papers explaining the details of each appeal. The appeal papers described the authority's decision on the placing requests for each of the schools involved in the appeals. They briefly noted the criteria used by the PRC to allocate places at the school. These sections were written in formal language, using statutory terminology to justify refusing requests, and were identical for all appeals except for details about each school such as the number of places available and the criteria used in deciding admissions. The last section of the report summarised the reasons, if any, the parents had given for making the placing request at the time of making it, as well as citing, for the third time, the statutory reasons for refusing the request. Finally, the papers included a copy of the letter sent to parents informing them that their request had been refused, and a copy of the parents' request for an appeal.

Appeal hearings for each school were arranged consecutively.[7] The parents appealing for a place at each school were escorted in along with the education officials. The Chair briefly introduced the parents to the others seated in the room. The Chair explained the procedures for the hearing and then invited the education official to speak.

The official read a statement of the authority's case. He explained that limits on school admissions generally had to do with maintaining order and discipline, that the limits were based on the design capacity of the school and the physical space there and also on the 'normal maximum class size' as defined in the Conditions of Service for Teaching Staff. He did not explain or justify the basis of the limits any further than that. He made no specific references to conditions at the school in question. He then turned to the decision of the PRC saying that the PRC 'made decisions about placing requests on the information supplied by the parents. While some parents may give better information and some may omit important information, the PRC had to decide on the information at hand'. He went on to consider the appeal committee's duty:

> You may have new information from the parents and it is only reasonable that you might speculate about how the PRC would have decided if they had had this information. However that is not what you are to do. You must decide whether or not the PRC decision was reasonable given the information they had. It is not appropriate for you to agree with the general decision of the PRC but then to uphold appeals because you think they selected the wrong pupils. To do so would be contrary to the wider interests of the children at the schools involved and that is what the PRC was trying to protect when it made its decision.[8]

The parents and the appeal committee were then given the opportunity to ask questions. None of the parents nor the appeal committee members asked any questions about the reasons for the authority's refusals at this time.

The hearing then moved on to consider individual appeals. One set of parents stayed while the others left the room to wait their turn. The official began in each case by questioning the reasons the parents had given for their school request. He made a twofold argument in response to each parents' reasons for their request: he said the school requested by the parents was not uniquely qualified to offer what the parent desired. For instance, one parent wanted her child to receive special music tuition. The official argued that several other schools offered special tuition so that this reason did not justify upholding the appeal. Even when parents based their request on the fact that the child's friends were going to the chosen school, the official responded that it really did not matter because children make new friends at secondary school and which school they went to really did not make a difference. Secondly, the official argued that the parents' reasons did not justify overturning the

PRC because their reasons could easily apply to other children as well. He said that to uphold the appeal on such grounds would be to give the appellant special treatment.

The official also often noted that part of the parents' reasons had to do with dissatisfaction with the district school. He explained that if the appeal was refused, the parents could come to the Education Department to talk about an alternative school which was not over-subscribed. He made it clear to the parents and to the appeal committee that there would be no trouble getting a place at any school with vacant places.

The parents were then asked to state their reasons. Several parents were somewhat awkward about doing so because the official had just gone through their written reasons one by one and argued that they did not justify giving the parents a place. Most parents simply referred to their written submission and listed the reasons, occasionally elaborating on them.

The official and the appeal committee members could then question the parents. At this point, the hearings changed into a general discussion about the parent's school request. The discussions focused on why the parent had requested the school and explored alternative schools which the child could go to if the appeal failed. Appeal committee members initiated such discussions in seven out of ten appeals, inquiring whether parents had considered other schools and determining parents' attitudes toward those schools. The appeal committee members also often explained to the parents why it was necessary to refuse their school request. However, they merely repeated that the authority had set admission limits, that it had refused their request and that there were many other parents in a similar position so that it was not possible to uphold their appeal. Parents often challenged this reasoning. They argued that only a small number of parents had appealed and questioned how the authority could justify denying those few parents a place. The appeal committee members responded by reiterating the importance of fairness to all of the parents who applied, not just to those parents who appealed. They did not try to explain how increasing the number of admissions would cause harm at the requested school. They accepted that the school was already 'full'.

> *Father*: A school the size of Rutherford, surely, they can find four places, not even one child in each class.
> *Member*: Obviously (the parent) is very concerned about getting his child into Rutherford. However, the fact is that four people have appealed, but there are 29 on the waiting list.
> *Father*: Why didn't the other parents appeal?
> *Member*: That's not what matters. Please take very seriously that it is 29 children not four that want into Rutherford. We take it that you absolutely refuse (the district school)...

Representative: Other parents also feel they had a strong case. We can't just look at those who appealed.

Chair: The other parents just realised that they had to accept the authority's decision. That's why they didn't appeal...

In some cases, the official and members of the appeal committee also tried to persuade parents that their impressions of schools were wrong. The official argued that the differences between schools were, with a few exceptions, only small differences in the quality of some teaching, not differences in the courses that were available or large variations in the quality of teaching through the school. Appeal committee members often joined in, saying that often a school's reputation was not accurate.

In three of the appeals to one school (Dalgleish High School) the discussion was focused on the use of requests for 'A' level courses as a criterion in the authority's earlier decisions. (In Burns Region, Dalgleish was the only school that offered a full range of 'A' level courses.)[9] Three parents had mentioned that the availability of 'A' levels was one reason they had requested the school. The discussion during those hearings concentrated on this matter, mostly because it took some time for the committee members to realise that the authority had given some pupils priority because their parents mentioned 'A' levels.

The final stage in each hearing was an opportunity to sum up for the official and then for the parents. In all cases, the official stated that none of the parents' reasons constituted a ground for reversing the decision of the PRC and that to do so would prejudice those on the waiting list who had accepted the authority's decision. Parents usually chose not to sum up since they had so recently been through their case in detail.

After all the appeals for each school were heard, the last set of parents and the education officials left the room. The deliberations of the appeal committee were brief for two of the schools. The Clerk began by reminding the appeal committee that their role was to decide the appeal for a place at the school requested by the parent 'despite all the conversation about alternative schools.' This was the extent of instruction given to members of the appeal committee before they began their deliberations. The committee then quickly refused all six of the appeals, accepting without discussion that the schools were full and could not take more pupils.

Member: With sympathy and accepting the realism with which these parents look at schools, it seems that there is no question but that the authority decided logically and properly. I don't think we can do anything but uphold the authority. I do hope that the parents will be persuaded to put their children elsewhere given their feelings about [the district school].

Representative: The authority clearly acted properly. It's too bad about the third case, since he moved out of the catchment area after being told he could still get his child into Rutherford. (The parent claimed that an official at the Education Department had told him that his child could still attend Rutherford if they moved. The official had responded that the Department is more careful than that in providing information to parents and that the parents' original home had not been in the Rutherford catchment area anyway.) In any case, he can probably afford to move again. Personally, I would have liked to hear a good word about [the district school].

Chair: I agree. We cannot uphold these appeals.

Deliberation about the remaining school's appeals went differently because of the question of 'A' levels and how this had been taken into account in the authority's earlier decisions. After a few comments on how the school was 40 per cent over-subscribed, the discussion immediately focused on the 'A' levels.

Member: I am very unhappy about the PRC's decisions on 11 March when 'A' levels were given priority. (The PRC meeting had been held on the 11 of March.)

Clerk: The 'A' level argument is really just a red herring at s1.

Member: It's a legal point isn't it though? If it was used as a criterion at an early meeting? It puts us in an impossible position . . .

Clerk: I agree it was a bad decision. Every parent could have put it down. Let me raise this problem though. If you uphold appeals, that means that the authority has to review all the other requests to Dalgleish that we turned down. How would they go about that? Anyway, I am not sure you are supposed to be concerned with how the PRC decided.

Member: The criteria used to grant admissions this year are our business. I would recommend that we indicate our grave concern that such a criterion was used and then accept those who have as good a case as the ones admitted already . . .

Representative: I have to object to the use of the 'A' levels so that they are given so much strength that the children are let in. And then the official tells us that 'A' levels are not that important. I agree with [Member]. Those three should be let in . . . And I would never accept [the second parent, who was very aggressive]. I would send him to [two schools that had been heavily criticised by some parents] . . .

Clerk: May I raise a general point? To what extent are you satisfied with the Region's arguments about limits on accommodation?

Member: It doesn't matter. They still have to justify their criteria. We're unhappy with their criteria. The extra pupils are their problem . . .

Chair: There could be a lot of parents who did not appeal who also want 'A' levels.

Member: To some extent, parents who appeal feel more strongly and we can distinguish parents on that ground.

Clerk: So three upheld and two refused. You're upholding the

Region's arguments about accommodation but making three exceptions.

These appeals were typical of the limited number of appeals that had been heard in Burns. Appeal committees did not examine Burns' admission limits. Nor did they evaluate the parents' reasons to see if they merited an exception to the Region's admission limits. Appeal hearings were directed toward persuading the parents that they could not have their choice of school and helping them consider alternatives. The outcomes of appeals illustrated this approach. Of the sixty-one appeals in Burns from 1982 to 1985, only eight were upheld. Three were upheld in the appeal described above. Five others were upheld when the appeal committee objected to the authority's late imposition of an admission limit at a primary school that resulted in five district pupils not getting places. Even in these appeals, appeal committees accepted the authority's admission limits, but held that the errors in the administration of placing requests required that the children be let in.

One day of appeals involving under-age children

Burns' policy toward under-age admission requests was to 'refuse requests unless the child would suffer lasting educational detriment and then only after every alternative had been carefully examined.' At first it had refused to treat under-age requests as placing requests under the 1981 Act. After the sheriffs and the SED held that under-age requests were placing requests, Burns adopted the disjunctive approach to the statutory provision allowing authorities to refuse placing requests when the education offered at the school was not suitable to the 'age, ability or aptitude of the child'.

We describe below two under-age admission appeals which were heard at one sitting of an appeal committee. The committee comprised the *Chair*, the same retired headteacher as in the secondary transfer appeals; two *Councillors* and a co-opted *Member* from the Education Committee; and the *Representative*, a nominee from the local Federation of Parent and Parent–Teacher Associations. The appeal committee was serviced by a Clerk and a member of the Regional Solicitor's Department was also present. The Education Department was represented by two officials, though only one spoke at the hearing.

The set of appeal papers sent to committee members and parents in advance included the order of proceedings adopted by the Region for the conduct of appeal committees, the letter of appeal submitted by the parent(s), a Report by the Director for each case detailing the policy of the Education Committee regarding under-age admissions and outlining the procedure which had been adopted in considering the application before him, copies of the correspondence to parents, and extracts from the minutes of the PRC at which the case had been turned down. The report by the Director incorporated the information advanced by the parents in support of their request and set out the reason(s) for refusal in the particular instance.

After the appeal committee and the clerks were assembled in the hearing room, those attending for the first case (the mother and her brother) were escorted into the room together with the education officials. Members of the appeal committee and the officials were introduced by the Chair.

The official outlined the authority's case, focusing on how Burns' policy was based on age and how 28 February was used as a cut-off date for determining eligibility to enter school, the same date as used by all other Scottish authorities. He referred to the mother's written reasons, arguing that they were domestic and social in nature rather than raising an issue of lasting educational detriment. The official suggested that a nursery place might be available for the child if the mother wanted one.

The mother and her brother then presented their case. The mother had recently separated and it was therefore a traumatic time for the family. The family was currently living with the mother's parents but both mother and grandmother had jobs and caring for the child was therefore a problem. The child's conversational ability was limited and she needed to be in the company of other children to improve her speech. The child's elder sister was already attending P2 in the desired primary school. The child had missed the cut-off date for admission by only a few hours. They stressed that the family had been through a traumatic period and explained that the child had no one to play with until her elder sister returned from school. At present, because she was working full-time, the mother only saw the children in the evening; however, if the child was accepted into school she could get a morning job and see more of both children.

The official and the members of the appeal committee asked questions focused on the child's present education and whether she was ready for school, particularly since her speaking ability was limited.

> *Chair*: Wouldn't it be best to keep her in nursery for a year, let her settle in there?
>
> *Representative*: Children who are young in school are under a great deal of pressure. Clever children can sometimes cope. Don't you think she would be more helped by a more informal, but still structured nursery?
>
> *Mother's brother*: It's a little strange that you are focusing on some trouble with her speaking when there are no professionals here and when you haven't seen her at all.
>
> *Councillor*: Given the problems, would you like to consider a full-time nursery place if she isn't admitted to primary?
>
> *Mother's brother*: It depends on where it is – we can't have the grandmother going just anywhere to collect her.

In his summing up, the official made it clear that admission to school in Burns Region was based on a policy of age-banding. He said that the child was unlikely to suffer lasting educational detriment if she was not admitted to school this year. The family expressed their view that it would help the child a great deal to be in school and pointed out that in England she would have had to be in school.

After the family and officials left the room, the committee quickly agreed to refuse the appeal:

Councillor 2: The only thing to do here is to uphold the decision of the PRC. P1 would have a different finishing time – it would still require the grandmother to make two trips.

Member: I have the feeling the child needs more development, she is not ready yet for primary, nursery would be better for her.

Chair: With the emotional problems she can develop in a less structured environment without the pressure of learning arithmetic and all.

Member: The playgroup is being run by unqualified people, nursery would be structured. All this depends on the mother changing jobs – she won't be able to see them much more anyway...

Councillor 2: It is a family problem rather than an educational one. It demonstrates the need for full-time places, that's the real issue. If nursery places are not available I would be inclined to uphold the appeal.

Chair: All agreed.

The committee then moved on to consideration of the second appeal. The father's letter explained that the family had recently moved from England where his son had been guaranteed a place to start primary shcool in that year, and that with the likelihood of a return to England in the near future he would miss a year's education. The child was 'extremely fluent and intelligent with an extensive vocabulary, able to recognise letters and words, and with a great interest in learning to read and write. To deprive him of this for a further twelve months would be seriously detrimental to him.' The letter of appeal questioned the ability of the committee to decide that primary education was not suited to the age of the child without a personal assessment.

The family (including the child under discussion) and officials were brought in and after introductions the official of the education department again presented the authority's case. The official went through the detailed points of the parents' appeal letter. The official explained that primary education was considered suitable for a prescribed age range. He said the PRC had a wide range of experience and they had considered all the information provided by the parents. The PRC decided on the basis of age, but made some exceptions when children appeared particularly mature. In those cases, they usually asked for assessments. However, because the number of child guidance staff was very limited, no assessment had been requested in this case. The father asked several questions of the official, objecting to the technical language used in correspondence and questioning whether the authority genuinely considered the particular circumstances of children. The father argued that the statute referred to 'age, ability or aptitude'; of these three factors, only one had been considered and the spirit of the Act appeared to be bent by separating them.

The committee asked no questions of the official, and the father then presented the parents' case. He read letters from people who knew the child showing that he was well advanced and increasingly frustrated. He said they had not been aware of the child guidance service but in their original letter had asked for testing and this would have supported their case. The child's mother expressed her concern about the quality of the nursery provision: originally sessions of thirty had catered for those who just missed the age limit whereas now there were sessions of sixty with much younger children. There was only one qualified staff member, students were 'always popping in and out and the head couldn't say how many four-year-olds would be in the afternoon session'. Activities would be lowered to cater for three-year-olds who would distract the staff into caring for them rather than stimulating the four-year-olds. Questions from the appeal committee focused on the child and what the parents would do if their appeal was refused:

Representative: As the representative of parents, I had a child who was five and a half when she started. It means they have a longer time in school, no problems with examinations.

Mother: That presumes we stay in Scotland – if we have to move we'd skip a year. I understand that if we stay in Scotland there might not be a problem . . .

Representative: What aspect of education are you most interested in? Literacy or numeracy?

Mother: Yes, but he is developing an interest in art and showing signs of musical ability. He's shown considerable mathematical ability.

Representative: Have you thought of options?

Mother: Thought of private education – it's too expensive. Interesting to see private schools think three and a half is old enough. I feel I can take him no further. I need the help of a formal teacher.

Member: The collective wisdom of teachers is that age is a very important factor. Teachers strongly oppose early admission. You're not taking account of formal nursery education. Your son may not be able to cope.

Mother: You're generalising, you don't know him.

In his summing up, the official submitted that the nursery school would be providing formal education, that it had an excellent reputation and would be fully staffed with two qualified teachers. He suggested that the authority had looked at the case in the fullest available detail and, while the authority focused on age, it did take exceptions into account.

The father submitted that age was not the right criterion and that he was concerned that no personal contact had been made.

The appeal committee refused the appeal after a short discussion that focused on members' objections to the parents' aggressive style:

Chair: I have experience with the nurseries – they are very good.

Member: Objectionable. He needs a nursery because of the pressure his parents will put on him.

Councillor 1: Decision upheld.

Councillor 2: I have some sympathy for most parents – nothing for them. Children should be protected from parents like that.

The appeal committee, like all others, accepted the authority's interpretation of the phrase 'age, ability or aptitude', and its policies of refusing most under-age requests on grounds of age alone, referring only a handful of cases to child guidance for assessment, and allowing requests only where failure to do so would result in lasting educational detriment. As 'lasting educational detriment' is so hard to prove in the case of a four year-old child, it is perhaps not surprising that no appeal committee has so far upheld an under-age appeal in Burns Region.

APPEALS IN OTHER AUTHORITIES

Appeals differed substantially in other authorities. Appeals come at the end of the school admissions process and their character reflects features of that process. Appeals in two other authorities are described here to give a sense of the different ways appeals can work.(10)

Appeals for over-subscribed schools in McDiarmid Region

In McDiarmid Region, school admissions were determined by the permanent physical capacity of schools. The maximum roll of each school was based on the permanent capacity of the school's buildings. Admission limits were determined by calculating the school's expected roll for s2 through s6 or p2 through p7 and subtracting that from the capacity of the school.

If the number of requests was greater than the number of places left after the district children were accommodated, all requests were sent to the appropriate School Council along with an explanation of how many places were available at the school. The School Council arranged interviews with parents, who were given an opportunity to explain why they wanted their child to attend the requested school. Parents were usually interviewed individually by a sub-committee – even in cases where no vacancies existed after district children were admitted. After the interviews were completed, the School Council met to decide which requests should be allowed and which refused. School Councils often recommended that a few children be admitted above the admission limit. This was especially important at schools with no places for non-district requests. Thus, the role of the School Council was to hear each parent's case sympathetically, to decide which pupils should fill available places at over-subscribed schools, and to find exceptional cases for admission to schools that were filled with district children.

Parents who were refused could appeal. Appeal hearings were organised as the appeals were received. The head clerk tried to schedule appeals to the same school on the same day, but the statutory time limits often made this impossible. Appeal committees consisted of five members – three Regional councillors and two School Council members with no direct interest in the appeals. The members were selected by the head clerk whose main concerns were to pick a chairperson who had experience in appeals and to avoid 'disruptive members' who interfered with the smooth operation of appeals. Members drawn from the School Council were usually teachers.

At the appeal hearing, all appeals for the same school were taken together. The appeal hearing started with an education officer presenting the authority's case for refusing the parents' requests. The authority's case consisted of an explanation of how the school's capacity was calculated, which, according to the clerk, most parents did not understand. The education officer did not describe how more children at the school would affect education at the school or give any details about conditions at the school. Parents were given an opportunity to ask questions, but they seldom asked any.

Each set of parents then gave their reasons for requesting the school. Parents tried to show why their request was special and deserved to be allowed. They often cited family circumstances (siblings at the school, single parents, difficulties with other children, ties to the school), ease of transport to the school, educational reasons (though they were seldom very specific, simply noting that the requested school was better), and medical circumstances. Parents also used this opportunity to raise questions about the authority's claim that the school was full, and commonly argued that the authority would admit more district children: 'Why can't my child fit in when you could fit in another district child?' (McDiarmid had a policy of admitting all district children even if the admission limit was exceeded.)

After all parents' appeals for one school had been heard, the appeal committee adjourned to decide those appeals. (Appeal committees usually heard appeals from more than one school in the course of a night.) Committees focused on single appeals, looking for reasons why requests should be allowed. Questions about schools' capacities were ignored. Committees neither challenged the authority's limit on capacity nor strictly abided by it. They assumed that the authority could and would make room for any additional children they might admit. They examined the parents' reasons, seeing it as the parents' responsibility to explain why they should be granted an exception. Parents' claims involving personal circumstances or medical reasons were usually accepted as long as the committee believed the parents and the parents came in appealing to the committee's sympathy rather than aggressively demanding their rights.

The outcomes of appeals reflected this approach. Committees upheld slightly under one-third of all appeals. The most common pattern for an appeal committee was to uphold one-third of all appeals (one or two appeals out of the five or so to one school). At only four of the thirty-four appeal meetings for which we have records did an appeal committee fail to uphold any appeals. Three of those four meetings involved single appeals. Not all appeals fitted the pattern of granting a few exceptions. At two meetings, committees upheld all parents' appeals, ten in one case and twelve in the other. In these cases, it seems that the committees did not accept the authority's argument that the school was full.

Comparison of the two authorities' experiences with appeals points to two key conclusions about appeals involving over-subscribed schools. First, appeal committees seldom considered the question of whether the authorities' admission limits were justified under the terms of the 1981 Act. Appeal committees were not given the information they would need to make a judgement on the question of whether more children would cause serious detriment to the education provided at the school. The appeal committees appeared to consider questions about admission limits to be irrelevant to their decisions. In Burns, appeal committees assumed admission limits were near-absolute barriers to upholding appeals. In the two cases where they upheld appeals, they did not consider the possible consequences as relevant to their decision: the authority would adapt. In McDiarmid, committees considered exceptions without regard for the admission limit although there appeared to be an implicit assumption that too many exceptions would be wrong.

Secondly, similarities between the authorities' own approaches to admissions and that of their appeal committees are very striking. In McDiarmid both Schools Councils and appeal committees made an effort to identify exceptional cases for admission despite the existence of an admissions limit. In admissions, Burns did not interview parents and took only a cursory look for special circumstances. Instead, its focus was on rapid processing of placing requests within the schools' admission limits. Its appeal committees shared this concern for enforcing the schools admission limits and its lack of interest in special circumstances. The similarities between the authorities and their appeal committees indicated that authorities had not yet developed a clear idea of what appeals were supposed to be. Authorities seemed to consider appeals as an extension of their own admissions process, not as an external check on their admissions decisions. Appeals provided a new statutory mechanism for doing what authorities have had to do all along – deal with parents' complaints about choice of school.

Appeals involving under-age children in Maxton Region

Maxton Region's policy toward under-age admissions had been that children whose fourth birthdays fell after the commencement date (28 February) should not normally be allowed to start school that year. Nursery school or a pre-school playgroup were considered more appropriate for younger children. However, it was accepted that there might be circumstances, e.g. where a given child might be disadvantaged in certain respects, where the admission of an under-age child was appropriate, so long as the school concerned was prepared to accept the child. A special sub-committee, made up of the Convener of the Education Committee, the opposition spokesperson, and one other councillor, interviewed all parents making under-age admission requests. The sub-committee upheld very few requests. In some cases involving children in isolated rural areas where there was no nursery provision, they admitted the child if one of the authority's educational psychologists found that the education normally provided at school would be suitable for the child.

About half of the parents whose requests were turned down have appealed. These parents were often referred to the solicitor, who acted as clerk to the appeal committee, who gave them advice on how to conduct their appeal. As a result, several parents have had their children assessed by an educational psychologist or have approached an experienced teacher to support their case.

The appeals were heard by three person committees: a member of the Education Committee, a Regional councillor who was not a member of the Education Committee, and an outside member drawn from a list nominated by the School Councils. The appeal committees evaluated each appeal on its merits, disregarding Maxton's policy against admitting under-age pupils. In the words of the clerk:

> Although the Regional Council has unanimously (without political division) laid down as a matter of policy that it does not favour early admission . . . it is my view that policy is not taken very much into account by the appeal committee. They are aware of the policy and may regard it as perfectly sensible but as far as they are concerned they are dealing with a single case. Their attitude is 'let's see what it is all about and try to find out why the mother is so anxious to get her child into school this August rather than next'. Remoteness may be a factor, or ill-health. Even if they regard the policy as very sensible, in this case they may find reasonable cause to justify them in departing from it. The committee is independent – it is not some arm of the Regional Council.

The outcomes of appeals reflected this approach. Of seventeen under-age admission appeals decided in 1984–1985, thirteen were upheld. Appeals that were upheld usually involved children whose birthdays fell close to the cut-off date. Children in remote areas and those who had been assessed as able to profit from attending school were also allowed admission.

Comparison of the two authorities leads to similar conclusions. Committees in Burns support the authority's restrictive policy on under-age admissions. Their supportive role combined explaining why the under-age child could not be admitted and counselling the parents to accept a nursery school place for their child. Committees in Maxton, who likewise accepted the authority's general policy, appear to have been willing to consider exceptions to it. Parents were given advice by the clerk about the kinds of arguments which would justify an exception to the general policy. By and large the arguments that persuaded appeal committees were those which the sub-committee was itself prepared to consider. As in the case of appeals for over-subscribed schools, there was a close similarity between the approach of the authority and that of its appeal committee.

EVALUATING APPEALS

Our examination of the operation of school admission appeals reveals that appeals did not adequately serve the functions we identified earlier. Most importantly, appeal committees did not review the admission limits used by the authority or its under-age admission policies and, in some cases, did not consider whether the circumstances of parents' requests justified making an exception and thereby upholding the appeal. A consideration of the operation of the appeal committees, in the light of the functions of school admission appeals described above, shows where committees fall short of what should be expected. Although we focus on appeals for over-subscribed schools, similar conclusions could be drawn from an analysis of appeals involving under-age children.

First, appeal committees often failed to perform their basic responsibility – determining whether an authority's refusal of a placing request was justified in terms of the grounds of refusal specified in the 1981 Act. Appeal committees tended to assume that the decision of the authority was justified. Education officers and the papers supplied to appeal committees described how admission limits were arrived at, but did not present evidence about the circumstances of the school or indicate how education would be affected if more children were admitted. In their deliberations, appeal committees did not discuss whether one of the statutory grounds of refusal applied.

Secondly, appeal committees sometimes did not carry out their second responsibility under the 1981 Act – determining whether refusing the placing request was appropriate in the particular circumstances of the appeal, that is, whether the parents' reasons merited an exception to the school's admission limit. In McDiarmid, the committees routinely examined the parents' reasons and frequently made exceptions. In Burns, however, none of the committees considered upholding a placing request on the strength of the parent's case. Committees sympathetically discussed parents' concerns with them, but the committee did not seem to think they could uphold appeals on those grounds. The only appeals that were upheld involved cases where the committee considered that the authority had done something wrong.

Thirdly, appeal committee members often acted more like officials of the education authority than independent arbiters hearing the parents' appeals against the authority. The mixed role of appeal committees could be seen when members took it upon themselves to explain why the parents were refused their choice of school during the hearing itself, before the committee had had a chance to consider the appeal and reach a decision. In the absence of a clearly defined independent arbiter role, appeal committees took on the role of supporting the authority and the authority's conception of what should happen in appeals, even though independence was essential to the performance of the functions of appeals in the statutory scheme for parental choice.

PARENTS' APPEALS TO THE SHERIFF

If an appeal committee confirms the authority's refusal of a request, the parent can appeal to a sheriff. (See the discussion of the statutory provisions in Chapter 2.) Few parents have appealed to the sheriff. There was a total of sixty-three appeals to the sheriff in 1984 and 1985. Sheriffs upheld fifty-two of these appeals, and refused six, the remaining five cases being withdrawn by the parents.[11] (See Tables 5.2 and 5.3. above) The importance of sheriffs' decisions, however, involves the reasoning of the sheriffs rather than simply the numbers of children and schools affected. The sheriffs' duties in deciding appeals are parallel to those of education authorities and appeal committees. Sheriffs must determine, first, whether a statutory ground of refusal exists in the case of the appellant. If the sheriff is not satisfied that a ground of refusal exists, he must uphold the parents' appeal. Secondly, the sheriff must determine whether it is appropriate, in all the circumstances, to refuse the parents' school request. In considering the statutory grounds of refusal, sheriffs replicate the decision making of the authority (just as appeal committees do). Therefore, authorities and appeal committees should adopt sheriffs' interpretation of the statutory grounds of refusal. Implicitly, this is how sheriffs would rule if parents directly challenged an appeal committee's decision rather than appealing to the sheriff.[12]

Appeals involving over-subscribed schools

In deciding appeals to over-subscribed schools, most sheriffs have adopted one of two different lines of analysis. The 'single child' approach focuses exclusively on the single child involved in the appeal. The 'school-level' approach involves a broader examination of the reasonableness of the school's admission limits given conditions at the school and the number of children applying for admission.

The single-child approach. Most sheriffs' decisions on appeals have adopted the single-child approach.[13] In this approach, the statutory grounds of refusal have been interpreted restrictively. Sheriffs have held that parents' appeals must be upheld unless the authority can show that a ground of refusal exists in the case of the single child involved in the appeal. Appeals have been allowed unless the sheriff was satisfied that the admission of that one child would have required the authority to employ another teacher or to make significant alterations to the school's buildings or facilities or would have caused serious detriment to order and discipline or to the educational well-being of pupils at the school.

In these decisions, sheriffs have distinguished each appeal from the other requests for the specified school that were refused but not appealed. Appeals have been decided in terms of the effects on the school of admitting one more child, not by considering all the other requests that had been refused. One sheriff reasoned:

> [The authority] argued that the effect . . . of me allowing the appeal [would be that it] would review the other unsuccessful cases and would have of necessity to decide them in the same way. Accordingly a question of one child would be converted into a question of several children coming to the school at the one time. In my view this contention is unsound. I can only consider the appeal that is before me. I know nothing of the circumstances of other appeals.
>
> (Mrs M Y v Strathclyde Regional Council (1982))

In addition, these sheriffs have refused to allow existing problems of overcrowding at the school to justify refusals. Existing overcrowding, no matter what the evidence, has not been held to constitute a ground of refusal. The sheriffs have asked the authority to show that admitting one additional child would require it to employ another teacher or incur significant expenditure on accommodation or cause serious detriment to the education of the pupils at the school.

The school-level approach. Some sheriffs have evaluated parents' requests in the context of admissions to the specified school by adopting a school-level approach.[14] In these decisions, sheriffs have looked at conditions in the school. Where the school was overcrowded, so that alterations to the school would have to be carried out in order to maintain 'order and discipline' or to protect the 'educational well-being' of the pupils, the sheriffs have held that statutory grounds of refusal exist. These sheriffs have also taken into account the other parents who requested the same school but were turned down, reasoning that the authority's justification for refusing requests was based on the effect of admitting that group of children of which the appellants' child was one. These sheriffs have rejected the single-child approach, arguing that it makes it virtually impossible to refuse any requests. They have instead examined, often closely, the authority's justification for limiting admissions which has usually consisted of evidence of overcrowding and its detrimental effects on education at the school.

One sheriff explained his reasoning in this way:

Both on the evidence led before me, and as a matter of simple commonsense, it is clear that overcrowding of a classroom must, when it reaches a certain level, be seriously detrimental to the running of, and proper teaching in, that class . . . It is in the interest of sound management of a school that that situation should be prevented from arising, and that cannot be achieved if the number of pupils is allowed to creep up little by little until an unacceptable total is reached. But if . . . each placing request is to be considered in isolation, it is virtually impossible in any one case to say that the pupil's admission will raise a detrimental level of overcrowding to one that is seriously detrimental. This is a difficulty which was clearly felt by [the authority's] witnesses at the hearing, whose concern was not so much about the effect of admitting one extra child, as at the fact that this must ultimately lead to the restoration of Primary 1 to its former level of overcrowding which, in their view, was clearly and seriously detrimental to the educational well-being of the classes as a whole.

For these reasons I am of the opinion that the 1981 Act does not prohibit an education authority from determining the maximum number of pupils in any given class at a level beyond which the class begins to be congested, and that the authority is entitled to invoke the ground that allowing the parents' request would be seriously detrimental to education at the school as a reason for refusing a placing request which would increase a class size beyond that number. *(Forbes v Lothian Regional Council (1982))*

The sheriff then explained that whether the authority's limit was justified was a question of fact on which the evidence should be carefully evaluated.

In this case the sheriff viewed the parents' appeal as a challenge to the authority's admission policy as it was applied to the school they requested. He interpreted the grant of a parental right of school choice as requiring authorities to accord special consideration to parents' requests. He made a careful inquiry into the policy reasons for the authority's decision, hearing evidence on the reasons for limiting class size at the school. Only when he was satisfied that significant collective policy considerations were at stake did he confirm the authority's refusal. He refused to separate the appealing parents' claim from that of other parents in a similar position and based his ruling on policy, not the narrow consideration of the individual claim adopted in the single-child approach.[15]

Comparing the two approaches. Both the single-child and the school-level approaches are plausible readings of the terms of the authorities' duties under the 1981 Act. Choosing between the two requires a careful analysis of their effects on school admissions. Sheriffs who have adopted the single-child approach have argued that each appeal involves only one child so that to consider the general consequences of the approach would be improper. Only one of the sheriffs who have adopted this approach has confronted the inevitable result:

> Looking at these grounds it is difficult at first blush to see how a local authority could ever establish that the addition of one or more pupils would require the local authority to employ another teacher or that one more pupil would give rise to significant expenditure on extending or otherwise altering the accommodation. Again, it is difficult to see how the addition of one more pupil is likely to be seriously detrimental to order and discipline or the educational well-being of the pupils in the school. However, the court and the local authority must deal with the Act in its terms. (*Duggan, Murray and Paul* v *Strathclyde Regional Council* (1983))

This sheriff adopted the single-child approach anyway as he did not recognise that the 1981 Act could be interpreted in any other way. All the sheriffs who have adopted this approach have disregarded the possibility that parents could appeal one by one to the sheriffs who, following the single-child approach, would uphold each appeal in turn.[16]

None of the decisions provided much reason to think that a sheriff properly applying the single-child approach could ever refuse to uphold an appeal. At least one authority (McDiarmid) routinely conceded parents' appeals once they were lodged with the sheriff because it did not believe that sheriffs using the single-child approach would ever refuse an appeal. Parliament provided that each of the statutory grounds of refusal was sufficient to allow authorities to refuse parents' requests, but the single-child approach interpreted those grounds in a way that precluded their use to refuse parents' requests.

The school-level approach allowed the sheriff to view individual parent's rights in the context of all parents' rights and the authority's duty to provide education for all school-age children. Although the three sheriffs who have adopted this approach have all concluded in favour of the authority, none of these outcomes was a foregone conclusion. Under the school-level approach, the sheriff has looked at the actual or potential level of overcrowding, the reasons for imposing a limit on admissions, and the number of other requests which had been refused. The sheriff still had to uphold the appeal unless he was persuaded that overcrowding would result and that this would necessitate either the employment of an extra teacher or give rise to additional expenditure on accommodation or facilities or give rise to serious detriment for the educational well-being of the pupils in the school.

Appeals involving under-age admissions

Sheriffs have played a more direct role in appeals involving under-age admissions. The first issue that sheriffs had to decide was whether a school request on behalf of an under-age child (below the age required by the authority for admission to the school) constituted a placing request under the 1981 Act. If placing requests could only be made on behalf of school-age children, then under-age requests would not be statutory placing requests and therefore authorities would not be bound to allow the request unless a statutory ground of refusal existed and parents would not have rights of appeal to the appeal committee and to the sheriff. Several authorities resisted treating under-age requests as placing requests. However, two sheriffs decided in 1983 that under-age requests did constitute placing requests under the 1981 Act (*Boyne and Boyne* v *Grampian Regional Council* (1983); *Thompson* v *Strathclyde Regional Council* (1983)).

Sheriffs' decisions have not resolved two other key questions. First, there was no definitive interpretation of the phrase 'age, ability, or aptitude', the statutory ground of refusal that applies in under-age admission cases. Most authorities consider the term conjunctively, arguing that age alone is not a ground of refusal and that it must be considered along with ability and aptitude. This was clearly the view adopted by the sheriff in one recent appeal (*Mackay* v *Highland Regional Council* (1985)), but in another appeal the sheriff accepted the view of both parties that the word 'or' implied that the term could be used disjunctively (*Coates and Coates* v *Lothian Regional Council* (1986)).

Secondly, sheriffs have taken different points of view toward the onus of proof in appeals, despite language in the 1981 Act that authorities must satisfy the appeal committee or sheriff that a statutory ground of refusal applies. In one under-age admission appeal, the authority accepted the onus of proof at the hearing (*Thompson* v *Strathclyde Regional Council* (1983)), while in another the parents appear to have undertaken the onus of proof (*Coates and Coates* v *Lothian Regional Council* (1986)). Particularly in these cases, where the issue is whether or not the education provided at the school is suited to the needs of the child, but in other cases too, it is clear that the outcome of the appeal will be affected by where the onus of proof lies.

In sum, appeals to sheriffs have played a small direct role in parental choice, but they could play a much greater role in structuring authorities' and appeal committees' decisions. Sheriffs' decisions have led to under-age requests being treated as placing requests. And, most importantly, their resolution of the single-child and school-level approaches and several substantive issues in under-age appeals could have substantial effects on how authorities decide placing requests. As of 1986, however, these issues had not been resolved.

CONCLUSIONS

Appeal committees and sheriffs were given central roles in parental choice legislation under the 1981 Act. Though relatively few parents have appealed, the importance of appeals does not depend on numbers.

Indeed, appeals might be considered more important because of the low number of appeals – appeals have discouraged authorities from refusing many placing requests. While definitive evidence does not exist, it appears that appeals have been a key factor influencing authorities to allow almost all requests. Authorities concerned to avoid the expense and trouble of appeals have allowed requests even though they considered that the requests should be refused (Tweedie, 1989b). The experience of McDiarmid with appeals to the sheriff sharply illustrates this point. McDiarmid conceded more than forty appeals once they were lodged with the sheriff because the small chance of prevailing did not justify the expense of the appeals.

However, the effect of appeals on authorities' decisions appeared to be blunt. Appeals discouraged refusals of parents' requests generally. They did not appear to influence authorities' interpretations of the 1981 Act or their imposition of admission limits. Appeal committees have generally not evaluated schools' admission limits in deciding appeals. Authorities have not had to justify their admission limits against challenges by parents. The appeal committee either assumed that the limit was justified or that only a few children could be admitted over the limit. Sheriffs, on the other hand, have usually ignored the authorities' justifications for admission limits, instead requiring authorities to show how a single child would cause serious detriment to education at the requested school. Neither the appeal committees nor the sheriffs' approaches provided a review of the schools' admission limits. Appeals did not provide much information to authorities about what justifications for admission limits were appropriate. The only exceptions came in the three sheriffs' decisions that have adopted the school-level approach.

Appeals could play a central role in ensuring that authorities carry out their responsibilities under the 1981 Act, while also allowing authorities to refuse requests where important educational concerns are at stake. Appeals have not played this balanced role so far. The primary effect of appeals has been to discourage refusals, making difficult a balance between the parents' interests and the authorities' concerns. However, this effect of appeals may be fading as most appeals support the authority. If appeals are to promote an appropriate balance between parents' interests and authorities' concerns, appeal committees and sheriffs must become more effective and fairer in their evaluations of the admission limits authorities set for schools.

NOTES

1. The provisions for the constitution and procedures for appeal committees are set out in Chapter 2. See also the text of ss.28E and 28F of the 1981 Act, set out in Appendix B.

2. Authorities, often reluctantly, adopted this approach following the ruling given by the Sheriff Principal in *Boyne amd Boyne* v *Grampian Regional Council* (1983) and the advice contained in SED Circular 1108 (Scottish Education Department, 1984). See Chapter 3.

3. The proper approach depends on whether the 1981 Act is read as extending the substantive rights of parents of under-age children to school entry. The terms of the Act and its legislative history are not explicit. If the Act is seen as extending the rights of parents with pre-school children, then the authority should be adopting the conjunctive approach and the appeal committee or sheriff should also adopt that approach to ensure that the authority is respecting these parents' rights. If the Act is not read in this light, then the disjunctive approach is proper since the authority would not be under any duty to admit under-age children.

4. However, shifting consideration of the child's ability and aptitude to this stage would probably leave the onus of proof on the parents, while under the conjunctive approach, the authority must carry the burden of showing why the education is not suitable for the child.

5. Statistics relating to appeals are not available for 1982.

6. Statistics aggregated for all authorities in Scotland also obscure the importance of large numbers of appeals in particular authorities, while other authorities have few or none. Unfortunately, the SED does not publish appeal statistics for individual authorities. Strathclyde, Lothian, and Grampian Regions have had most of the appeals, though it is not possible to provide precise numbers.

7. The following accounts of appeal hearings are based on notes made while observing the hearings. The excerpts of discussion have been reconstructed from those notes and are not verbatim transcripts.

8. This statement of the appeal committee's responsibility is remarkable for three reasons. First, it is the most detailed and practical explanation the committee members receive concerning how they are to decide. Secondly, the explanation is given by an education officer, one of the parties in the hearing, and the clerk to the committee never comments upon it. Thirdly, and most importantly, it is clearly wrong. The officer's explanation of the committee's responsibility is much too narrow, characterising their role as a deferential review of the PRC's decision rather than as a *de novo* consideration of the parents' request as it is stated in the 1981 Act.

9. Scottish Certificate of Education (SCE) examinations comprised 'O' grades (normally taken after four years of secondary school) and 'Highers' (normally taken at the end of the fifth year). Traditionally pupils entered university after five years of secondary school on the basis of Highers, but as post-compulsory provision expanded in the late 1960s, the SED introduced a sixth-year curriculum leading to a Certificate of Sixth Year Studies (CSYS). This, rather than 'A' levels, is taken in most schools in Scotland. See McPherson and Neave (1976).

10. These accounts are based on interviews with officials respon-

sible for conducting the appeals and an inspection of relevant documents.

11. Statistics on appeals to the sheriff are not available for 1983.

12. The appeal to the sheriff under the 1981 Act is not a review of the authority's or the appeal committee's decision, but is a *de novo* hearing of the parents' placing request. The sheriff does not have the responsibility for determining whether the earlier decisions were correct. However, two sheriffs have said in *dicta* that authorities should use the sheriffs' interpretations in their decision making (Tweedie and Adler, 1986)

13. See, e.g. *Mrs M Y v Strathclyde Regional Council* (1982), *Mrs A B or K v Strathclyde Regional Council* (1982), *Mrs K v Strathclyde Regional Council* (1982), *Duggan, Murray and Paul v Strathclyde Regional Council* (1983), and *Easton v Strathclyde Regional Council* (1984) (Tweedie and Adler, 1986)

14. This approach was adopted in three cases, *Forbes v Lothian Regional Council* (1982), *X v Shetland Islands Council* (1983) and *D v Grampian Regional Council* (1984)

15. Where several appeals have been lodged for the same school, sheriffs have often not appeared to have adopted either approach. Instead they have sought to ascertain whether the grounds of refusal would have existed if all the appeals before them were upheld. In cases involving two or three appeals, the sheriffs' approaches have been very similar to the single-child approach. It is difficult for the authority to pinpoint the educational harms resulting from the admission of two or three children and the sheriffs concerned have refused to consider evidence of overcrowding or the effects of admitting all children whose parents requested the school (e.g. *Kennedy and Kane v Strathclyde Regional Council* (1982)). Sheriffs have also used high standards to determine what constitutes 'serious detriment'. In one case, the sheriff allowed three appeals, holding that the consequential reorganisation of classes would not be seriously detrimental to the educational well-being of pupils at the school, even though the medical room, the stage, and a study room set aside for sixth-year pupils would have to be used for classroom purposes (*Black v Strathclyde Region* (1982))

Only one sheriff's decision has involved more than three appeals: the sheriff heard sixteen appeals together. He did not accept the authority's admission limits because they were based on estimates of the number of returning fifth- and sixth-year pupils used to set admission limits for the school. Moreover, he refused to conclude that teaching science in non-practical classrooms was 'seriously detrimental' as the practice had been tolerated the previous year. He upheld all sixteen appeals (*Weir and Others v Strathclyde Regional Council* (1985))

16. One sheriff adopted the single-child approach and refused the appeal, holding that the admission of one more child would have required the authority to alter its accommodation and facilities to provide an additional class. From the standpoint of the single-child approach, the sheriff's brief note is not persuasive. Thus, although the authority claimed that it would have to form a new class, the question of accommodating one more child in one of the existing classrooms does not seem to have been raised (*Easton v Strathclyde Regional Council* (1984)). Other

sheriffs who have adopted the single-child approach have rejected similar arguments that an authority's policies would require it to employ an additional teacher or add an extra classroom (e.g. *Duggan, Murray and Paul* v *Strathclyde Regional Council* (1982)).

6

THE IMPACT OF PARENTAL CHOICE ON SCHOOL ADMISSIONS

In this chapter, we first consider the take-up of placing requests throughout Scotland and subsequently analyse in detail their impact on admissions to primary and secondary schools in two Scottish cities.

THE TAKE-UP OF PLACING REQUESTS[1]

In the first four years following the implementation of the Scottish legislation, the number of placing requests doubled from 10 456 in 1982 to 21 795 in 1985 (see Table 6.1). Of the placing requests, 96.3 per cent were for children of school age and 3.7 per cent were for under-age children, the latter increasing from 261 (1.5 per cent of the total) in 1983 (no statistics are available for 1982) to 1 844 (8.8 per cent of the total) in 1985. Among children of school age, more than half the requests (56.5 per cent) were for primary school while fewer than half (43.5 per cent) were for secondary school. After increasing steadily from 1982 to 1984, the number of placing requests for primary schools levelled off in 1985 while the number for secondary schools actually fell somewhat. However, as a percentage of the declining school population, placing requests for both primary and secondary schools continued to increase.

Over the four years 1982–1985, 97.7 per cent of requests for primary school and 94.2 per cent of requests for secondary school were granted,

Table 6.1. Number of placing requests received* and percentage granted**, 1982–1985

		1982	1983	1984	1985	Total	
Under-age	No. received	–	261	513	1 844	2 618	(3.7%)
	% granted	–	47.5	63.0	66.5	63.9	
Primary	No. received	5 746	9 440	11 272	11 561	38 019	(54.4%)
	% granted	96.9	98.5	97.7	96.7	97.7	
Secondary	No. received	4 710	7 432	8 758	8 390	29 290	(41.9%)
	% granted	96.3	97.8	92.8	91.6	94.2	
All placing	No. received	10 456	17 133	20 564	21 795	69 968	
requests	% granted	96.6	97.8	94.7	92.2	95.0	

* From 1983 onwards, the number received includes requests which were subsequently withdrawn
** Granted initially or on appeal
Source: Scottish Education Department (1987a) Table 1

either at the initial stage or, subsequently, on appeal to an appeal committee or the sheriff. However, there were downward trends in the success rates between 1983 (when 98.5 per cent of primary school requests and 97.8 per cent of secondary school requests were granted) and 1985 (when the corresponding figures were 96.7 per cent and 91.6 per cent), reflecting the growing practice of a number of authorities of restricting admissions to schools which would otherwise have been over-subscribed. In contrast to these very high success rates, the success rates for under-age placing requests, which ranged from 47.5 per cent in 1983 to 66.5 per cent in 1985, were substantially lower.

At both primary and secondary levels, the majority of requests have been for children entering the first year of school (see Table 6.2). In 1985, 55.3 per cent of primary school requests were for Primary 1 (P1) while 68.7 per cent of secondary school requests were for Secondary 1 (S1). For pupils starting their primary or secondary schooling, 9.6 per cent and 8.7 per cent respectively had made a placing request that year. At later stages the placing-request rates were much lower, averaging 1.4 per cent for P2–P7 and 0.9 per cent for S2–S6.

National figures, such as these, mask considerable regional and local variations. The more urbanised education authorities, where many schools are situated relatively close to one another and where several schools are within reasonable travelling distance for many pupils, have considerably higher placing-request rates than the largely rural authorities. In 1985, four largely urban authorities had placing-request rates (for P1 and S1) of between 10 per cent and 15 per cent while five predominantly rural authorities had rates of 3 per cent or less.

Within regions, the same relationships are to be found and placing-request rates are highest in the cities and lowest in the rural areas. It

Table 6.2. First-year placing requests as a proportion of totals for primary and secondary schools*, 1982–1985

	1982	1983	1984	1985	Total
Primaries					
% P1	NA	48.2	50.9	55.3	51.7
% P2–P7	NA	51.8	49.1	44.7	48.3
Secondaries					
% S1	NA	62.9	66.9	68.7	66.3
% S2–S6	NA	37.1	33.1	31.3	33.7

* Placing requests for under-age children not included
Sources: Scottish Education Department (1985) Table 2
       Scottish Education Department (1986) Table 2
       Scottish Education Department (1987a) Table 3

follows from this that placing-request rates in the cities are higher than those for the regions in which those cities are located. Thus, for example, in 1985, 22.1 per cent of pupils entering the first year of primary school and 22.7 per cent of pupils entering the first year of secondary school in Maxton City had made placing requests, compared with rates of 12.1 per cent and 6.5 per cent elsewhere in Maxton Region. Likewise, in Burns City, 19.1 per cent of pupils entering P1 and 19.2 per cent of pupils entering S1 had made placing requests compared with rates of 6.9 per cent and 5.9 per cent for P1 and S1 admissions elsewhere in Burns Region.

ANALYSING MOVES BETWEEN SCHOOLS

In order to examine the impact of parental choice on admissions to primary and secondary schools, we conducted a detailed analysis of moves between schools in Burns and Maxton Cities. Placing-request rates in these two authorities were among the highest in Scotland. However, in other respects, as we have explained in Chapter 3, they embody some important historical and contextual differences. For many years prior to the implementation of the 1981 Act, Maxton Region had operated a very flexible allocation and transfer policy. As a result, the legislation made little immediate difference to regional policy. By contrast, Burns Region, was strongly committed to the development of links between schools and their local areas. Children were allocated to their local (catchment-area) school and requests for an alternative school were usually turned down unless the child in question already had a sibling at the school or there were documented medical reasons to support the request.

Instead of examining flows between schools throughout these two regions, we focused on flows between schools in the two cities in which the incidence of placing requests was highest. For similar reasons, we focused on admissions to the first year of primary school and the first year of secondary school.

Our data comprise placing-request data and other administrative data made available to us by the two education authorities, survey data obtained from the 1981 School Leavers Survey carried out by the Centre for Educational Sociology (CES) at Edinburgh University, and catchment-area data derived from the 1981 Census. In each case, the analysis is based entirely on aggregate data and considerable care must be taken in making inferences which apply to individual pupils (Borgatta and Jackson, 1980). The results are not only of interest in themselves but also provide a context for interpreting data derived from the two parents' surveys discussed in Chapter 4.

In analysing these data, we have attempted to bear in mind some of the arguments (outlined in Chapter 2) which were advanced by supporters and opponents of the 1981 legislation. Advocates of the legislation pointed to the fact that 'good' schools would grow while critics pointed to the fact that the loss of pupils would accentuate the problems faced by schools in 'poor' areas. Supporters of the legislation argued that it would provide a means for some children, at least, to escape from schools in deprived areas while opponents predicted that the main beneficiaries would be middle-class parents who would use it to obtain the schooling they wanted for their children. However, it is important to note that all these views implied that the legislation could have quite a substantial effect on the social and educational composition of school intakes.

PRIMARY SCHOOLS IN THE TWO CITIES

Burns City has 82 non-denominational primary schools with more than 3 000 pupils entering P1 in each year. Maxton City, by comparison, has 38 non-denominational primary schools and an annual intake of about 1 500 pupils into P1. In each city there is a small Catholic sector: this comprises 15 primary schools in Burns City and 14 in Maxton City. In each of the four years since the legislation was introduced, the proportion of P1 parents who made a placing request in Maxton City was higher than in Burns City (Table 6.3). Among the non-denominational schools in Burns City, the proportion of P1 pupils making placing requests increased steadily from 13.1 per cent in 1982 to 19.2 per cent in 1985. In Maxton City, the proportion increased from 17.5 per cent in 1982 to 24.7 per cent in 1983 and then levelled off. These increases are in line with trends for the rest of Scotland. The proportion of placing requests for Catholic

Table 6.3. Placing requests for P1 entry, 1982–1985

| | Non-denominational schools | | | | Catholic schools | | | |
| | Burns City | | Maxton City | | Burns City | | Maxton City | |
	Number	%	Number	%	Number	%	Number	%
1982	408	13.1	280	17.5	23	8.1	22	5.8
1983	443	14.4	377	24.7	25	8.6	42	11.4
1984	604	16.8	371	23.5	30	8.6	34	11.1
1985	688	19.2	402	24.6	51	17.4	34	10.0

Sources: Data provided by Burns and Maxton Region Education Departments. The percentage figures represent the ratio of placing requests to the size of the P1 intake in each sector in the two cities. The number of placing requests and the size of the P1 intake both include small numbers of pupils from outwith the two cities.

Note: The figures for non-denominational schools in Burns City differ slightly from those recorded in Table 3.5. This is both because the data in this table refer to all the non-denominational primary schools in Burns City Division while those in Table 3.5 refer only to schools within the old city boundary and because of the different basis for comparison.

schools was considerably lower, probably because catchment areas for Catholic primary schools are much larger and the schools therefore further apart. The Catholic sector is, in any case, quite small in both cities and will not be considered further. In Maxton City, no P1 placing requests were refused over the period 1982–1985, although some schools exceeded their nominal capacities. In Burns City, 35 P1 placing requests (1.6 per cent of the total) were refused over the four-year period, and in addition nine children who registered late were refused admission to their catchment-area school.

In both cases, schools that lost pupils and schools that gained pupils were to be found in all areas of the city. A few schools made substantial gains while others made substantial losses. However, substantial losses and gains were more common in Maxton City than in Burns City. Thus, while one primary school out of the 82 primary schools in Burns City lost more than half its catchment area population, the figure for Maxton City was two out of 38. More strikingly, seven out of the 38 primary schools in Maxton City gained more than half their first year pupils from outside their catchment areas, compared with three out of 82 primary schools in Burns City.

MOVEMENT BETWEEN PRIMARY SCHOOLS

Complete data for movements between schools in the two cities were available for 1984 only. However, by a happy coincidence, this was the year in which we carried out our parents' survey. Preliminary analyses showed that most of the P1 requests were for a school close to the catchment-area school. To capture this, every pair of adjacent schools was identified (without reference to placing request data) by the following operational definition: two schools were defined as 'adjacent' if their catchment areas had a common boundary running through a residential area. Thus, schools with contiguous catchment areas which were separated, for example, by a park or a golf course were not held to be adjacent. Of placing requests in Burns City, 83 per cent were to an adjacent school and in Maxton City, 85 per cent. Thus, it made a good deal of sense initially to focus on moves between adjacent schools. This made it possible to examine the influences on choice of school by calculating the probability of moving from each school to every adjacent school and relating this probability to the characteristics of the schools concerned and their catchment areas.

Network diagrams for Burns City (Figure 6.1) and Maxton City (Figure 6.2) show every possible adjacent boundary and the movements in both directions across that boundary. Several features are immediately apparent for both cities. There are very few pairs of schools between which pupils moved in both directions. The movements between schools took place among sub-systems or groups of schools, which appear to correspond to neighbourhoods within the city. For Burns City, in particular,

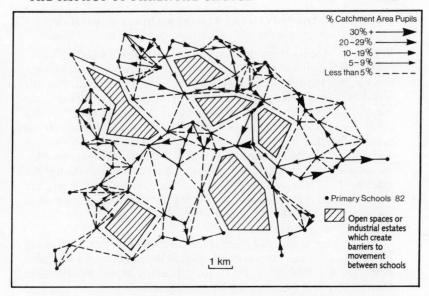

Figure 6.1.   Mapping of placing requests across adjacent boundaries between
primary schools in Burns City, 1984.

which has more parks and open spaces than Maxton City, these neighbourhoods are a consequence partly of past planning decisions and
partly of the physical geography of the city. We will see below that they
also correspond to areas that are relatively homogeneous in their social
composition.

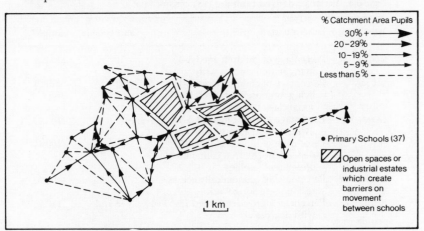

Figure 6.2.   Mapping of placing requests across adjacent boundaries between
primary schools in Maxton City, 1984.

EXPLAINING THE MOVEMENT BETWEEN ADJACENT PRIMARY SCHOOLS

In order to identify those differences between schools and their catchment areas which best predict movement between two adjacent primary schools, two sources of data for classifying schools were used. The first was data from the 1981 Population Census, aggregated to school catchment areas using the Small Area Statistics Package SASPAC (SASPAC, 1983). We selected a total of six variables from the 1981 Census on the grounds that they had all been used in other pieces of social research and had some plausible relationship to parental choice. Wherever possible we obtained information from the Census that related to children in the catchment area, for example the local authority tenure variable refers to the percentage of children aged 5–15 in the catchment area living in local authority housing. Details of the six variables derived from the Census data are given in Table 6.4.

In both cities residential segregation resulted in distributions of the census variables that were skewed towards the two extremes (for more detail, see Raab and Adler, 1987). Thus, 16 of the 38 primary schools in Maxton City and 24 out of the 82 primary schools in Burns City had catchment areas in which 80–100 per cent of the children lived in council housing. In Burns City, which had a smaller percentage of local authority housing overall, 40 schools had catchment areas that contained 0–20 per cent local authority housing. There was a smaller proportion of such schools in Maxton City, but in neither city were there many schools with

Table 6.4. Variables derived from the 1981 census data

Mnemonic	Description	Census table	Sample*
NOCAR	Percentage of children aged 5–15 living in households with no car	31	(100%)
SOC12	Percentage of children aged 0–15 living in households with head in social class 1 and 2	52	(10%)
LATEN	Percentage of children aged 5–15 living in local authority housing	29	(100%)
SINGP	Percentage of households with dependent children containing one-parent families	31	(100%)
UNEMP	Percentage of economically active residents seeking work	20	(100%)
HIGHE	Percentage of residents aged 18–59/64 with degrees etc	48 and 52	(10%)

* Some of the census data are only coded for a 10 per cent random sample of households.

catchment areas that contained a roughly equal mix of public and private housing.[2]

Not surprisingly, a similar picture emerges for social class.[3] In Burns City there were a number of schools with catchment areas containing 70–80 per cent social class 1 and 2 households (which, in terms of national figures, is a very high percentage), while 20 schools out of the 82 had catchment areas containing almost no social class 1 and 2 households. In Maxton City, there were also a very large number of catchment areas containing almost no social class 1 and 2 households and rather fewer at the other end of the scale, since Maxton City is a more working-class city than Burns City.

In each city the Census variables were very highly correlated with one another. The correlations ranged from 0.60 to 0.92 in absolute value, with roughly half the correlations exceeding 0.80 for each city. Principal component analysis gave very similar results in the two cities identifying two principal components with very similar weightings in the two cities. The first principal component had the highest weightings from three variables – unemployment (UNEMP), single parents (SINGP) and families with no car (NOCAR) – the third of which is frequently used as a surrogate for low income. The second one had the highest weightings for percentage of children in social class 1 and 2 households (SOC12) and for percentage with higher education (HIGHE). These two components explained 92 per cent and 95 per cent of the total variance in Burns City and Maxton City respectively. Thus, in the analyses reported below we have replaced UNEMP, SINGP and NOCAR with a composite variable SEP (socio-economic problems) which combines these three variables with equal weight and, to aid interpretation, was scaled to range from 0 to 100 in each city. Similarly SOC12 and HIGHE were replaced by a composite variable SOCED (social class and education) which again was scaled from 0 to 100 in each city. As the remaining variable (LATEN) did not load strongly on either component, it was entered separately.

In addition to Census data, we collected data from the local authority on characteristics of the schools. In this respect we were much less well served than at secondary level where considerably more data were available. However, at the primary school level, we were able to collect the following data: the date on which the school was built, the percentage of pupils in composite classes, the percentage receiving free meals (which was similar to some of the Census variables and had a correlation of 0.90 with the socio-economic problem component), the pupil/staff ratio (which in Burns City also correlated very highly with socio-economic deprivation because the percentage of free meals was used to allocate extra teachers to deprived areas), the growth rate (calculated as the ratio of P1 pupils to P7 pupils), the roll of the school and the capacity of the buildings.[4]

The Census and school variables were used as predictors of movement between schools in a logistic regression of movement across adjacent boundaries (McCullagh and Nelder, 1962). Using this model, the odds of moving between two schools with identical school and Census variables are obviously the same in both directions. However, a difference in school and/or Census variables will create different odds for each direction of movement. For example, if the odds of moving between two identical schools are 1:30, i.e. 1 to 30,[5] and if the differences between the schools increase the odds in one direction by a factor of (say) 5 to 1:6, then the odds of movement in the opposite direction will be reduced to 1:150. Using this model, we can identify the variables that best predict movement in the two cities by a regression in which the proportion of movement across every possible adjacent boundary is the dependent variable. There were 362 such directions of movement in Burns City and 162 in Maxton City.[6]

The results of predicting movement using one variable at a time are given in Table 6.5., where they are expressed in terms of the maximum increase in odds of movement for each variable. For example, taking the percentage of children in local authority housing (LATEN) in Burns City, the pair of adjacent schools with the largest difference in local authority tenure differed by 97 per cent. This was a reflection of the very pronounced degree of residential segregation in the city. The fitted model predicts that the odds of moving from the schools where most of the children lived in local authority housing to the school in which fewest of them did will increase by a factor of 3.1 compared to the odds of movement between schools with identical percentages of children in local authority housing, i.e. that the odds will increase from 1:29 to 1:9. Similarly the model predicts that the odds of moving in the other direction will decrease by a factor of 3.1, i.e. from 1:29 to 1:90.

In both cities school roll (ROLL), pupil:staff ratio (PSR) and growth rate (GROWTH) are the best predictors of placing requests, with movement being towards larger, growing schools with high pupil:staff ratios. However, all three of these variables, as well as the percentage of pupils in composite classes (COMPOS), may have been influenced by earlier movement into the schools. Thus by 'explaining' movement in terms of these variables, we may, in effect, be 'explaining' movement in 1984 in terms of movement in previous years. This interpretation is supported by the results of using the P1 catchment area population (CAP) as a measure of size instead of school roll. In both cities (Table 6.5), CAP is only a very weak predictor of the odds of making a placing request. Of course, the importance of ROLL, PSR and GROWTH may well be manifestations of a 'bandwagon effect' in which the extent of movement in a given year is influenced by the extent of movement in previous years (Simon, 1957). The other non-growth related variables which influence movement have very similar effects in the two cities. The composite measure of socioeconomic problems (SEP) is the next best predictor of movement in both

Table 6.5. Influence of school and census variables on odds of making a placing request for a primary school in Burns and Maxton Cities

Variable	Burns City			Maxton City		
	Coefficient**	Maximum difference	Odds change for largest difference***	Coefficient**	Maximum difference	Odds change for largest difference***
*School**						
ROLL	.004	433.	5.0	.007	293.	7.7
PSR	.197	9.0	5.5	.164	7.	3.0
GROWTH	.940	1.6	4.6	1.31	1.	3.7
COMPOS	−.017	82.	4.0	−.005	54.	1.3
CAP	.005	75.	1.5	.007	47.	1.4
FRMLS	−.022	63.	3.9	−.008	52.	1.5
DATE	−.060	6.	1.4	−.001	130.	1.2
Census						
SEP	−.019	76.	4.3	−.014	66.	2.5
SOCED	.015	80.	3.1	.001	94.	1.1
LATEN	−.011	98.	3.1	−.003	82.	1.3

* The meanings of the mnemonics used for school variables are as follows: ROLL – school roll; PSR – pupil:staff ratio; GROWTH – P1 pupils:P7 pupils; COMPOS – percentage of pupils in composite classes; CAP – P1 pupils in catchment areas; FRMLS – percentage of pupils eligible for free meals; DATE – age of school, measured on a 7-point scale in Burns City and in years in Maxton City. All the data was provided by the two Education Authorities.

** This is the coefficient in the regression of log (odds of making a placing request) against each of the variables listed in the table. A + sign indicates that higher values of the variable are associated with more placing requests; a − sign indicates the opposite.

*** This is the increase in the odds of movement across the adjacent boundary corresponding to the largest difference in the value of each variable. The odds of making a placing request between two adjacent schools which did not differ on any variable were 1:29 in Burns City and 1:21 in Maxton City.

cities, followed by free school meals (FRMLS) which, as we noted above, was highly correlated with SEP.

There were also some differences between the cities. In Burns City there was some tendency for pupils to move away from areas of local authority housing (LATEN) and towards higher social class 1 and 2/higher education (SOCED) areas, whereas in Maxton City these two variables had almost no influence on movement. In general, the social variables (FRMLS, SEP, SOCED and LATEN) had a stronger influence on movement in Burns City than in Maxton City. In neither city, however, were the influences on movement particularly strong and examination of the data showed examples of movements between schools which could not be predicted from differences in the social variables. The shorter odds for Maxton City (1:21) compared with Burns City (1:29) of movement between schools when there were no differences between them reflect the higher background level of movement in Maxton City.

As well as looking at the predictors of movement individually, we examined their joint effect in a step-wise analysis. Variables associated with growth in previous years (ROLL, PSR and GROWTH) were excluded and a step-wise regression performed for each city using the remaining variables. In both cities, the first variable to enter the regression was SEP (with a negative coefficient) and this reduced the effect of all the other variables. In Burns City, the next variable to enter was SOCED (with a positive coefficient) after which no other variables predicted movement. In Maxton City, the same variable entered at the second step but with a negative coefficient. Thus, in both cities, movement was away from schools serving areas where the unemployment rate was high and there were large numbers of low income and single parent households. However, allowing for this, movement in Burns City but not in Maxton City was into more 'middle-class' areas, i.e. into areas containing more social class 1 and 2 parents and adults with higher education. This reflects the fact that there was some movement from schools with 'working-class' (low SOCED) catchment areas to schools with 'middle-class' catchment areas in Burns City but not in Maxton City where schools in the more advantaged (high SEP) working-class (low SOCED) areas gained most pupils.[7]

Given the polarisation of the school catchment areas by housing tenure and social class, it seems at first surprising that these variables did not have more effect on movement. To understand why this is so we must return to our network diagrams and consider the social geography of the two cities. Figures 6.3 and 6.4 display the six Census variables for the schools in the two cities, using a star for each school. Each 'arm' represents a census variable. To take one example, the arm pointing upwards refers to the rate of unemployment. The school with the lowest unemployment rate in the city will be marked in the centre for unemployment; the school with the highest unemployment rate will be

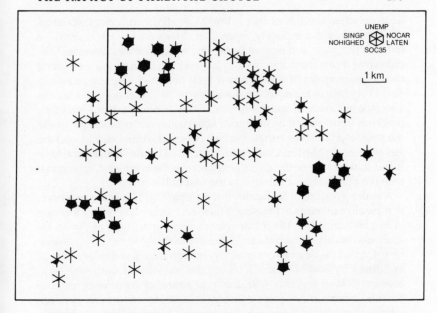

Figure 6.3. Characteristics of primary school catchment areas in Burns City
(Inset shows area featured in Figure 6.6).

marked at the extremity. Note that the scoring of the social class and
higher education variables has been reversed so as to be positively
correlated with the other variables. The school with highest values on all
six indicators (unemployment, single parents, no car, local authority
tenure, social class 3–5, no higher education) would appear as a 'closed'

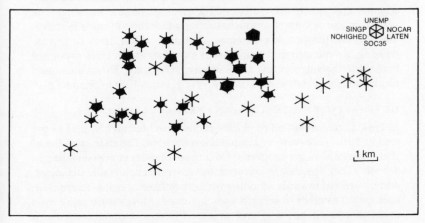

Figure 6.4. Characteristics of primary school catchment areas in Maxton City
(Inset shows area featured in Figure 6.5).

hexagon while the school that is lowest on all the indicators would be represented by a completely 'open' star. Many such schools are to be found in the south and west of Burns City which contains many middle-class areas. From the maps, one can also pick out the housing estates and their characteristics. There are two very deprived housing estates in Burns City, one in the north-west and one to the east of the city. One can also pick out areas of council housing with fewer social and economic problems (represented by hexagons squashed down on the top), where the three top variables (single parents, unemployment and no car) are less extreme. In Maxton City, deprived areas of council housing are to be found to the north of the city, particularly in the north-east, in contrast with the more affluent suburbs to the east of the city.

A striking feature of both cities is the extent to which primary schools that are alike in terms of housing tenure and social class cluster together in neighbourhoods. This result accords with an analysis of the socio–economic status of secondary school pupils (Willms, 1986) which revealed that the degrees of social segregation among secondary schools in Burns City and Maxton City were the second and third highest in Scotland. Taken together with the local nature of movement between schools, it explains why there is very little tendency to move between schools that differ in terms of housing tenure and social class. In Maxton City, in particular, the pattern of movements is almost entirely within areas that are homogeneous with respect to housing tenure and social class. Within neighbourhoods, there is movement away from areas with more to areas with fewer socio–economic problems. Sub-systems of movement occur both in middle-class and working-class areas in Maxton City, but the system with the largest total movement is the area of council housing to the north-east of the city. This is illustrated in Figure 6.5 where it is clear that movement, is taking place within the housing scheme, and not to the surrounding areas of private housing. The pattern in Burns City is somewhat different. Although there is movement within the housing schemes, and also within areas of private housing, we can also find examples of movement from areas of council housing to the surrounding areas of private housing. This is illustrated for the housing estates in the north-west of Burns City in Figure 6.6.

MOVES BETWEEN NON-ADJACENT PRIMARY SCHOOLS

In 1984, 15 per cent of all P1 placing requests in Maxton City and 17 per cent in Burns City were to a non-adjacent school. The characteristics of these moves were very different from those of moves between adjacent schools. They frequently involved travel over considerable distances, and movement towards schools with very different catchment areas. In each city, a number of schools were involved. Moves were away from areas of council housing and areas with socio-economic problems towards areas containing more social class 1 and 2 households and more

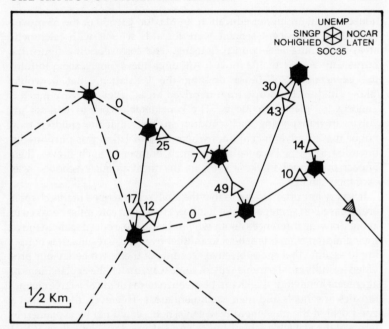

Figure 6.5. Detailed mapping of placing requests between primary schools in North-East Maxton City (percentage of catchment area pupils).

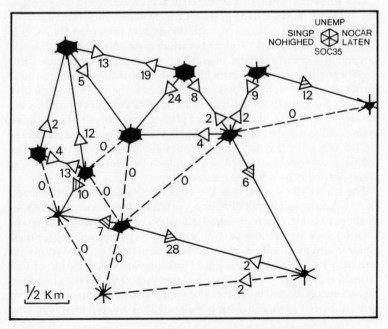

Figure 6.6. Detailed mapping of placing requests between primary schools in North-West Burns City (percentage of catchment area pupils).

households with higher education. In Maxton City 50 of the 55 moves between non-adjacent schools were towards schools with catchment areas containing less council housing. The corresponding figure for Burns City was 81 of 102 moves. Although these moves seem to fulfil the expectations of those drafting the legislation, that it would 'allow children to escape from deprived areas', they are very much a minority of placing requests. The considerable cost to parents involved in transporting such children suggests that the children may not be the 'disadvantaged' ones whom the legislation was purportedly intended to help. Because of the small number of such moves their impact on school intakes, even in the most popular schools, was extremely small.

It is very important to stress that the analyses described in this chapter are all based on aggregate data. It follows that great care must be taken to avoid drawing inferences about why individual parents decide to move their children from one school to another from these results. It is tempting to assume that the subjective accounts of their own behaviour provided by individual parents will, in some way, match the explanations of aggregate behaviour which can be given in terms of the objective characteristics of schools and their catchment areas. However, the fact that a good deal of the movement between schools could not be explained in terms of the available school and catchment area variables suggests that the match may not be a very good one.

Our survey data did, of course, relate to individuals and it is interesting to reflect on the extent to which conclusions which can be drawn from the survey are consistent with the account presented above. Our sample of primary school parents included parents who lived in the catchment areas of a cluster of eight primary schools in Maxton City, together with parents from outwith the area who made a placing request for any of these eight schools. In three cases, the number of placing requests for the school exceeded the number of district pupils; conversely, in one case, the number of placing requests out of the school exceeded the number of district pupils who remained. The cluster included two schools which gained a substantial number of pupils from 'non-adjacent' moves as well as a number of schools where gains and losses were due to 'adjacent moves'.

The survey did not provide any evidence that, even at a local level, there were any significant differences in terms of social class, household income, housing tenure, political affiliation or any other variable (see Chapter 4) between those parents who made a placing request for their children and those who did not. Just over 50 per cent of the Maxton City parents who made a placing request for a primary school (56 out of 109) claimed that it was important to them that their child did not attend the district school, two schools (both of which lost substantial numbers of pupils) being particularly unpopular with parents. However, the reasons they gave for rejecting the district school and selecting an alternative were entirely consistent with the importance which our aggregate-level analysis attached to local moves. Thus, the most frequently cited reasons for rejecting a primary school were the safety problems associated with getting to and from the school in question while the most frequently cited reasons for choosing a primary school was its convenient location (open-ended) and the fact that it was the nearest school (structured response). Where the administrative boundaries of school catchment areas made little sense, parents have, in effect, used their rights under the 1981 Act to modify the catchment-area boundaries. This was clearly the case for one conveniently located primary school with a very small catchment area which continued to attract large numbers of placing requests despite being under threat of closure (Adler and Bondi, 1988). By contrast, the reasons parents gave for choosing another school, which benefited from a large number of non-adjacent moves, most often referred to the reputation and popularity of the school and to the happiness of their child. This suggests that the reasons for adjacent and non-adjacent moves may be rather different.

Our survey provided some support for the existence of 'bandwagon effects' (see above). Thus, among the structured responses, the second most frequently cited reason parents gave for not wanting their child to attend the district school was that the school was 'unpopular, with other parents sending their children to other schools'. This criticism was particularly directed at two schools which had experienced large net outflows in previous years. On the other hand, very few parents cited the school's 'popularity, with many parents from outside the district choosing it' as a reason for sending their child there. Thus, the survey suggested that an awareness of other parents' behaviour served to amplify losses but not gains.

Finally, our survey results were consistent with another of our aggregate-level findings. In answer to an open-ended question, the third most frequently cited reason (after safety problems and siblings already at another school) for avoiding the local school was that the children who went there were 'rough and rowdy' and 'used bad language'. Although there was little support for the structured response that 'parents did not want their children to mix with the kind of children who went to the district school', the open-ended response may well reflect the higher incidence of socio-economic problems (SEP) among schools which have lost pupils through parental choice. Overall, however, the large number of reasons cited by parents, few of which had any correlates in our aggregate-level analysis, is consistent with the fact that we were only able to explain a relatively small proportion of the total amount of movement.

SECONDARY SCHOOLS IN THE TWO CITIES

Burns City contains twenty non-denominational and three Catholic secondary schools.[8] Maxton City, on the other hand, has ten non-denominational and three Catholic secondaries.[9] In both cities, there was a substantial decline in secondary school rolls between 1982 and 1985. The S1 rolls fell over the four years from 5 032 to 3 878 in Burns City, and from 2 605 to 2 100 in Maxton City.

In each of the four years since the legislation was introduced, the proportion of S1 parents who made a placing request in Maxton City was higher than in Burns City (see Table 6.6).

Among the non-denominational schools in Burns City, the proportion of S1 pupils who were the subject of a placing request increased from 13.2 per cent in 1982 to 20.0 per cent in 1985. In Maxton City, the proportion increased from 14.0 per cent to 23.7 per cent over the same period. These increases are broadly in line with trends for the rest of Scotland. Among the much smaller number of Catholic schools, the proportion of S1 pupils who were the subject of a placing request also increased. However, in both cities, this proportion was substantially lower than the corresponding proportion for non-denominational schools. For this reason, and because there was relatively little movement into or out of the Catholic sector, placing requests among the Catholic secondary schools in the two cities will not be considered further.

In Maxton City, no S1 placing requests were refused over the period

Table 6.6. Placing requests for S1 transfer, 1982–1985

| | Non-denominational schools | | | | Catholic schools | | | |
| | Burns City | | Maxton City | | Burns City | | Maxton City | |
	Number	%	Number	%	Number	%	Number	%
1982	589	13.2	291	14.0	43	7.3	47	8.9
1983	654	15.6	336	16.6	43	10.9	50	9.9
1984	825	20.6	413	21.8	60	12.4	51	12.0
1985	695	20.0	402	23.7	58	14.7	72	15.2

Sources: Data provided by Burns and Maxton Region Education Departments. The percentage figures represent the ratio of placing requests to the size of the S1 intake in each sector in the two cities. The number of placing requests and the size of the S1 intake both include small numbers of pupils from outwith the two cities.

Note: The figures for non-denominational schools in Burns City differ slightly from those recorded in Table 3.4. This is both because the data in this table refer to all the non-denominational secondary schools in the Burns City Division while those in Table 3.4 refer only to schools within the old city boundary and because of the different basis for comparison.

1982–1985. In Burns City there were no refusals until 1985. However, in that year, 66 requests for s1 (9.9 per cent of those submitted) were refused after intake limits were imposed on three of the most over-subscribed schools. It will be recalled (see Chapter 3) that intake limits were imposed following a series of reviews of secondary school provision in the city and a decision by Burns Regional Council to reduce the number of surplus secondary-school places by phasing out the use of annexes and temporary accommodation. As it happens, two of the most over-subscribed schools had annexes while the third used a considerable amount of temporary accommodation.

In both cities, some schools made substantial gains while others made substantial losses. Thus, average gains and average losses of fifty pupils or more per year were by no means uncommon. Three (out of twenty) secondary schools in Burns City and two (out of ten) in Maxton City lost more than 25 per cent of their catchment-area population over the period 1982–1985. Likewise, three secondary schools in Burns City and two in Maxton City gained more than 25 per cent of their first-year pupils from outside their catchment areas. By and large the schools which gained most pupils lost very few, while the schools which lost large numbers made few gains. Thus, in Burns City, the school which gained most pupils in proportional terms over the period 1982–1985 drew 42.1 per cent of its s1 intake from outside its catchment area but only lost 8.5 per cent of its catchment-area population to other schools, whereas the school which lost most pupils saw 42.9 per cent of its catchment-area pupils go to other schools and drew a mere 4.1 per cent of its s1 intake from outside its catchment area. Exactly the same pattern was found in Maxton City.

In Maxton City, three schools increased their share of the gains from 53.3 per cent of all requests in the city in 1982 to 71.9 per cent in 1985, while five other schools increased their share of the losses from 68.2 per cent in 1982 to 73.5 per cent in 1985. Over the period 1982–1984, the picture in Burns City was very similar. Four schools increased their share of the gains from 35.3 per cent to 55.4 per cent while four other schools increased their share of the losses from 33.7 per cent to 51.2 per cent. Thus, in both cities, the flows into and out of certain schools were cumulative, providing the strongest evidence so far for the existence of 'bandwagon effects' (Simon, 1957). However, the imposition in 1985 of intake limits on three of the four 'most popular' schools in Burns City reduced the proportion of placing requests for these schools to 43.7 per cent of the total number of requests made and to 36.9 per cent of those granted. One very interesting effect of imposing intake limits on some of the schools which gained most pupils was to reduce the outflows from some of the schools which lost most pupils. Thus, the proportion of the total number of losses suffered by the four 'least popular' schools fell from 51.2 per cent in 1984 to 44.7 per cent of requests made and 44.3 per cent of requests granted in 1985.

The trends described above are illustrated in Figures 6.7 and 6.8. Here the measures are (for gains) the average ratio of placing requests for the schools to the size of the s1 intake and (for losses) the average ratio of placing requests for other schools to the s1 catchment-area population. For Burns City schools, separate calculations for requests made and requests granted in 1985 were undertaken.

In the case of Maxton City, one of the gaining schools has been distinguished from two others while two of the losing schools are distinguished from three others. In the case of Burns City the gaining school which did not have an intake limit imposed in 1985 has been distinguished from the three which did. It might appear that the slight rise in requests for the other sixteen schools in Burns City was the result of a redistribution of the placing requests for the schools with restricted intakes. However, detailed examination of the 1984 and 1985 placing requests from the fourteen schools which lost substantial numbers of pupils in 1984 does not support this view. In only three out of the fourteen schools considered was there any evidence of parents switching from the intake-limited schools to other schools, and the number of placing requests for such schools in 1985 was much less than the number of requests in 1984 for schools whose intakes were restricted the following year. Although survey evidence (see Chapter 4) showed that 69 per cent of s1 parents who made a placing request considered it important to

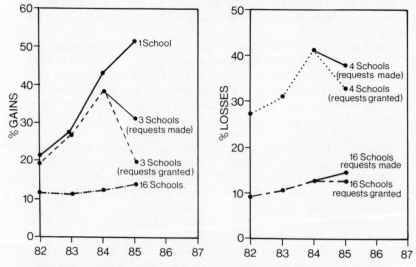

Figure 6.7. Placing request gains (as a proportion of first year intakes) and losses (as a proportion of catchment area populations) for secondary schools in Burns City, 1982–1985.

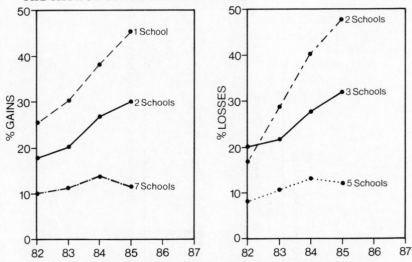

Figure 6.8. Placing request gains (as a proportion of first year intakes) and losses (as a proportion of catchment area populations) for secondary schools in Maxton City, 1982–1985.

avoid the catchment-area secondary school, the finding of an acceptable alternative was also an important consideration. Thus the drop in the ratio of placing requests for other schools to the catchment area population in the schools which lost most pupils indicates that the imposition of limits on over-subscribed schools did afford some measure of protection to the most under-subscribed schools. However, it also suggests that some of the parents of children at these schools were inhibited from making placing requests and, as a result, continued to send their children to their catchment-area school. The gaps (in Figure 6.7) between the percentage of requests made and the percentage granted in 1985 represent the proportions of parents whose children were prevented from attending the schools they had initially requested.

In addition to analysing gains and losses separately, we can analyse their joint effects on the intakes of individual schools. In Tables 6.7 to 6.9 we set out the gains and losses experienced by secondary schools in Burns City.[10] In Burns City, three schools (Dalgleish High School, Rutherford High School and Souness High School, referred to here as D, R and S) were clearly over-subscribed (Table 6.7). They all experienced substantial net gains, which increased over the period 1982–1984. They also exceeded the region's staffing and building use plans and, by a much larger margin, the intake limits which were set in 1985 to enable the region to remove distant and often unsuitable annexes and temporary accommodation (see Chapter 3). By contrast, five schools (G, J, L, N

Table 6.7. Placing requests and s1 intakes for secondary schools in Burns City, 1982–1985 (over-subscribed schools)

School		1982 Choice	1982 Intake	1983 Choice	1983 Intake	1984 Choice	1984 Intake	1985 Choice	1985 Intake
D	Gains	+53	211	+74	217	+171	291	+77	191
	Losses	−14		−14		−6		−17	
R	Gains	+36	355	+76	386	+80	356	+41	297
	Losses	−12		−12		−9		−8	
S	Gains	+41	224	+80	259	+100	263	+20	196
	Losses	−4		−1		−5		−7	

Note: The Region refused 38 requests for School D, 19 requests for School R, and 14 requests for School S in 1985. These requests are not included in the totals for the schools.

and O) were equally clearly under-enrolled. They all experienced sub-stantial net losses which, when combined with declining age cohorts, resulted in very small s1 intakes that fell considerably short of the point, which Burns Region had set at 150 pupils, where the size of the intake began to create serious curricular and staffing problems. In 1984 and again in 1985, two of the schools had s1 intakes of less than 100 pupils while the other three schools were clearly heading in that direction. On the other hand, twelve schools were neither over-subscribed nor under-enrolled and can be said to have had s1 intakes that fell within the 'acceptable' range (Table 6.9). Although some of these schools (e.g. C and I) experienced large net gains while others (in particular F) experi-enced large net losses, fairly small gains were offset by fairly small losses.

The gains and losses experienced by secondary schools in Maxton City are set out in Tables 6.10 to 6.12. Two schools (B* and C*) were clearly over-subscribed (Table 6.10). School B* would have been seriously over-crowded without the use of an annexe and substantial temporary accom-modation. Moreover, its s1 intakes are substantially greater than those which have been fixed for the replacement school which Maxton Region is committed to building (see Chapter 3). School C* is regarded as over-subscribed in terms of its very large s1 intake, although pupils can be accommodated through the use of an annexe. Both these schools made increasing net gains over the four-year period. By contrast three schools (A*, F* and I*) experienced increasing net losses over the period and, by 1985, were clearly under-enrolled (Table 6.11). In each case, parental choice exacerbated the problems of small catchment-area popu-lations. By 1985, two of the schools (A* and I*) had s1 intakes of less than 100 pupils while the third school (F*) had only slightly more than this. These five schools can be contrasted with five others whose s1 intakes fell within the 'acceptable' range (Table 6.12). However, two of these five schools (D* and E*) were losing pupils and could easily become under-enrolled. On the other hand, parental choice eased the problems of one school (J*).

EXPLAINING THE MOVEMENT BETWEEN SECONDARY SCHOOLS

A detailed breakdown of placing requests by catchment-area school and requested school was available in both cities for 1984 only, and our attempt to explain the detailed pattern of moves between schools is therefore based on 1984 data. It should be noted that, in 1984, the pattern of placing requests in Burns City was not yet influenced by the intake limits which were subsequently imposed on three schools.

The most obvious influence on movement between schools was the proximity of the various secondary schools to the homes of the pupils. From the point of view of an individual family, the appropriate measure would have been the extra distance which the child would have had to travel to attend the requested school rather than the catchment-area

Table 6.8. Placing requests and s1 intakes for secondary schools in Burns City, 1982–1985 (under-enrolled schools)

School		1982		1983		1984		1985	
		Choice	Intake	Choice	Intake	Choice	Intake	Choice	Intake
G	Gains	+4	164	+5	124	+1	100	+7	89
	Losses	−49		−76		−107		−83	
J	Gains	+6	171	+5	118	+1	98	+0	106
	Losses	−51		−84		−97		−50	
L	Gains	+15	188	+26	175	+23	138	+21	122
	Losses	−19		−44		−45		−46	
N	Gains	+16	119	+24	114	+23	89	+10	83
	Losses	−19		−16		−29		−47	
O	Gains	+17	171	+8	161	+6	123	+6	116
	Losses	−15		−27		−23		−35	

Note: 22 requests from these five schools were refused in 1985

School		1982 Choice	1982 Intake	1983 Choice	1983 Intake	1984 Choice	1984 Intake	1985 Choice	1985 Intake
A	Gains	+35	231	+37	223	+26	177	+58	222
	Losses	−40		−41		−100		−49	
B	Gains	+25	305	+47	273	+30	207	+14	151
	Losses	−31		−18		−25		−34	
C	Gains	+45	203	+37	206	+57	193	+42	196
	Losses	−12		−24		−22		−19	
E	Gains	+48	265	+40	217	+52	226	+39	239
	Losses	−26		−27		−31		−18	
F	Gains	+2	267	+4	235	+3	218	+6	175
	Losses	−92		−92		−111		−84	
H	Gains	–	–	+6	126	+14	169	+14	159
	Losses	–		−1		−0		−0	
I	Gains	+46	225	+63	236	+100	224	+95	187
	Losses	−23		−30		−42		−15	
K	Gains	+26	289	+14	270	+25	271	+27	249
	Losses	−22		−22		−26		−8	
M	Gains	+9	289	+6	200	+15	230	+15	180
	Losses	−16		−30		−19		−11	
P	Gains	+43	250	+40	217	+52	226	+56	192
	Losses	−9		−20		−23		−26	
Q	Gains	+22	250	+40	217	+52	226	+39	239
	Losses	−25		−9		−20		−16	
T	Gains	+19	180	+22	167	+22	152	+29	150
	Losses	−35		−41		−57		−29	

Note: School H opened in 1983

school. However, this would have been very time consuming to calculate and, as our analysis is of aggregate data, we have used an average measure of the extra distance which all the pupils in the catchment area would have had to travel if they had attended another school. The extra distance was calculated as the distance between the centroid of the grid co-ordinates of the feeder primary schools associated with each secondary school and the requested school, minus the distance between the centroid and the catchment area school.[11] There were two cases (one in each city) where this distance was negative, indicating that the requested school was closer to the primary schools associated with the catchment-area school than the catchment-area school itself.

Various approximations are involved in using this measure of extra distance.[12] Nevertheless, as we show below, our derived measure of extra distance was a good predictor of movement between schools.

Allowing for the influence of distance, what differences between schools best predict movement? To answer this question, two sources of data for classifying schools were available. The first was the 1981 Population Census, and we selected the same six variables that we used in the analysis of movement between adjacent primary schools (see Table 6.4 above). In both cities, residential segregation resulted in distributions of the Census variables that were skewed towards the two extremes. The range, i.e. the difference between the highest and the lowest value of each of the six variables was substantial and was, in most cases, only slightly less than the corresponding range for primary-school catchment areas (for more detail, see Adler and Raab, 1988). Such segregation occurs because, in both cities, secondary-school catchment areas are built up from contiguous primary-school catchment areas with similar social characteristics.

A comparison of the two cities reveals that the only significant differences in their secondary-school catchment areas relate to social class and higher education. Whereas none of the secondary-school catchment areas in Maxton City contained more than 40 per cent of adults in Social Class 1 and 2 occupations, there were several schools in Burns City which were located in predominantly middle-class catchment areas with SOC12 in the range 40–65 per cent. Likewise the proportion of adults who had received higher education was substantially greater in Burns City than in Maxton City. Both these differences, like the corresponding differences between primary-school catchment areas, reflect the fact that Maxton City is a more working-class city than Burns City.

In each city the secondary-school catchment area Census variables were even more highly correlated with one another than the corresponding primary-school catchment area Census variables: The correlations ranged from 0.72 to 0.99 in absolute value, with roughly half the correlations exceeding 0.85 in absolute value. As in our analysis of P1 placing requests, we replaced UNEMP, SINGP and NOCAR with a composite vari-

Table 6.10. Placing requests and s1 intakes for secondary schools in Maxton City, 1982–1985 (over-subscribed schools)

| School | | 1982 | | 1983 | | 1984 | | 1985 | |
		Choice	Intake	Choice	Intake	Choice	Intake	Choice	Intake
B*	Gains	+27	139	+48	171	+58	175	+66	193
	Losses	−18		−19		−24		−16	
C*	Gains	+83	330	+111	372	+145	374	+165	366
	Losses	−28		−35		−30		−28	

Table 6.11. Placing requests and s1 intakes for secondary schools in Maxton City, 1982–1985 (under-enrolled schools)

School		1982 Choice	1982 Intake	1983 Choice	1983 Intake	1984 Choice	1984 Intake	1985 Choice	1985 Intake
A*	Gains	+6	167	+12	140	+9	116	+11	81
	Losses	−34		−56		−69		−66	
F*	Gains	+14	158	+19	147	+10	114	+8	109
	Losses	−35		−46		−49		−49	
I*	Gains	+29	156	+30	149	+30	122	+18	92
	Losses	−23		−45		−62		−67	

able SEP (socio-economic problems) which combines these three variables with equal weight and, for ease of interpretation, was scaled to
range from 0 to 100 in each city. Similarly SOC12 and HIGHE were replaced
by a composite variable SOCED which was also scaled from 0 to 100 in each
city while LATEN was entered separately.

Our second source of data was information on the schools and their
pupils. Here we were much better served than in our analysis of P1
placing requests and a total of ten variables was available for each
secondary school. Thus, for each city, we had data on the number of
requests to transfer from each secondary school to every other secondary
school in the city. The movements between schools were modelled in
terms of (i) our extra distance measure for each possible direction of
movement and (ii) the differences in school and Census variables between the requested school and the catchment-area school. Once again,
the formal technique used in the analysis was logistic regression, with
the proportion of the catchment-area pupils making a request as the
dependent variable.

As we have already explained, logistic regression has a simple interpretation in terms of the odds of movement. In this case the odds of
movement decrease as extra distance increases. For example, increasing
the distance between two identical schools by 1km might reduce the
odds of making a placing request to 1:30, i.e. 1 to 30. These odds are then
modified by differences between the schools. For example, if the differences favoured the requested school by a factor of 5, the odds would
increase from 1:30 to 1:6 but if the differences were in the opposite
direction the odds would be reduced by a factor of 5 to 1:150.

The logistic model has the following formal structure:

log odds of making a placing request = $a + b$ (extra distance
measure) + c_1 (difference$_1$) + c_2 (difference$_2$) + ...

where a, b, c_1, c_2 are the fitted coefficients and difference$_i$ is the difference
between the value of the ith school or census variable for the requested
school and its value for the catchment-area school.

THE EFFECT OF DISTANCE

As we explained, our measure of extra distance was much the strongest
predictor of movement between schools in both cities. Several different
analyses were performed to find the best way to model the relationship
between the odds of movement and this extra distance. The measure of
extra distance which gave the best fit in the regression equation was:

log (extra distance + constant)

The constant term is required in the argument of the logarithm because
of the negative distances mentioned above. Different constants gave the
best fit in the two cities – 1km. for Maxton City and 2km. for Burns City –
but the results were not sensitive to slight changes in this specification.
The effect of using the logarithm of extra distance is to give greater

Table 6.12. Placing requests and s1 intakes for secondary schools in Maxton City, 1982–1985 (acceptable range schools)

School		1982		1983		1984		1985	
		Choice	Intake	Choice	Intake	Choice	Intake	Choice	Intake
D*	Gains	+23	220	+22	194	+29	179	+19	151
	Losses	−32		−39		−65		−60	
E*	Gains	+10	190	+8	200	+23	198	+11	142
	Losses	−63		−51		−50		−58	
G*	Gains	+17	265	+14	214	+27	220	+14	196
	Losses	−2		−3		−5		−7	
H*	Gains	+45	262	+36	246	+52	233	+58	216
	Losses	−31		−45		−53		−49	
J*	Gains	+37	191	+36	196	+30	155	+26	140
	Losses	−10		−11		−8		−8	

weight to short distances – on a logarithmic scale 2km. and 3km. are much further apart than are 12km. and 13km. This scaling is appropriate because most moves are to nearby schools, and small differences in distance are more important in such moves than in moves across the city.

The fit of the relationship between extra distance and the odds of making a request in Burns and Maxton Cities is illustrated in Figure 6.9. A value of, for example, 0.04 on the y axis represents an odds of making a placing request of 4:100. The exponential curves show that the odds of making a placing request decline rapidly as distance increases. The decline is particularly marked in Burns City and suggests that movement between schools in Burns City is even more local than between schools in Maxton City. At a distance of 4km (2.5 miles), the odds of movement between two otherwise identical schools were almost 2:100 in Maxton City but only 1:100 in Burns City.

THE INFLUENCE OF SCHOOLS AND THEIR CATCHMENT AREAS

The influence of schools and their catchment areas on movement was explained by adding school variables and Census variables to the model along with log distance. If a difference in one of these variables increased the odds by a factor of, say, two, this would mean that the relationship of

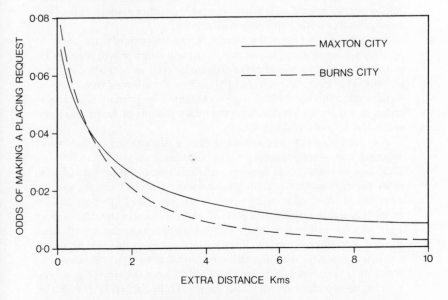

Figure 6.9. Effect of extra distance on the odds of making a placing request in Burns and Maxton Cities.

the odds of making a placing request to distance would be the one shown in Figure 6.7, but multiplied by a factor of two throughout.

The influence of school and census variables (taken one variable at a time) is summarised in Table 6.13. Overall the similarity between the two cities is quite remarkable. With the exception of TRUANCY (a measure of self-reported truancy obtained from the CES School Leavers Survey), the directions of the relationships between all the other schools and Census variables and the odds of making a placing request are the same in both cities. Moreover, the relationships are all in the expected direction – towards schools with higher attainment measures, higher social-class schools, previously selective schools and larger schools; and away from schools serving local authority housing schemes and with catchment areas characterised by a high incidence of unemployed and low income households. Furthermore, the strength of the relationships between the school and Census variables and the odds of making a placing request (measured by the size of the coefficient in the regression equations for the two cities) are, in many cases, uncannily similar.

The three measures of school attainment (TOTSCEP and S5:S4 in particular) are the greatest single influences on movement and have very similar coefficients in the two cities. However, they appear to have more influence in Burns City where there is a greater variation between schools in the level of measured attainment. This can be seen from the larger values of the maximum difference between any two schools in Burns City on almost every variable, and is also apparent in other assessments of the average size of school attainment differences.

Comparisons between the effects of placing requests on entry to primary school (Table 6.5) and transfer to secondary school (Table 6.13) is difficult in that no measures of attainment were available for primary schools. However, the effects of the Census variables were broadly similar, although the odds change for Maxton City primary schools was rather less than for Maxton City secondary schools or for primary and secondary schools in Burns City.

In order to look at the joint effect of several variables on the rate of requests, a step-wise regression was performed. As before, and for the same reasons, ROLL was omitted. After distance, the first variable to enter the regression equation was the same in both cities (S5:S4), the direction of movement being towards schools with higher staying-on rates. When this variable was entered, the influence of the other school attainment measures was much reduced in both cities, and in both cities the direction of influence of all the social class measures was reversed, i.e. it was towards schools with lower social class characteristics. The social class variables which were selected to enter the step-wise regression in the two cities are set out in Table 6.14. In Table 6.14, we also set out the regression coefficients for a multiple regression model containing distance, S5:S4 and SOC12P. Although this was not the model selected by

Table 6.13. Influence of school and census variables on odds of making a placing request for a secondary school in Burns and Maxton Cities

Variable	Burns City			Maxton City		
	Coefficient**	Maximum difference	Odds change for largest difference***	Coefficient**	Maximum difference	Odds change for largest difference***
*School**						
TOTSCEP	0.966	2.6	12.6	0.819	1.7	3.9
S5:S4	0.051	48.	11.2	0.050	38.	6.7
S6:S5	0.034	58.	7.3	0.034	47.	4.8
ROLL	0.002	1163.	8.1	0.002	1089.	6.4
CAP	0.004	233.	2.7	0.002	124.	2.5
SES	1.38	1.46	7.5	1.13	1.1	3.6
FRMLS	−0.043	45.	7.0	−0.015	33.	1.6
SOC12P	0.029	44.	3.7	0.019	50.	2.6
TRUANCY	0.036	4.6	1.6	0.044	11.	1.6
HISTORY	0.404	4.0	5.0	0.254	3.	2.1
Census						
SEP	−0.025	64.	4.9	−0.016	65.	2.1
SOCED	0.012	102.	3.3	0.022	63.	4.0
LATEN	−0.016	89.	4.1	−0.017	90.	4.4

* The meanings of the mnemonics used for school variables are as follows: TOTSCEP – total SCE passes per pupil in the year group[13]; S5:S4 – S5 staying-on rate; S6:S5 – S6 staying-on rate; ROLL – school roll; CAP – S1 pupils in catchment area; SES – composite measure of socio-economic status[14]; FRMLS – percentage of pupils eligible for free meals; SOC12P – percentage pupils in social classes 1 and 2; TRUANCY – % self-reported truancy; HISTORY – history of the school[15]. TOTSCEP, SES, SOC12P and TRUANCY were derived from the CES School-Leavers Survey; the other data was provided by the two education authorities.

** This is the coefficient in the regression of log (odds of making a placing request) for a model containing distance and each of the variables in the table. A + sign indicates that higher values of the variable are associated with more placing requests; a − sign indicates the opposite.

*** This is the increase in the odds of movement between schools which are a given distance apart corresponding to the largest difference in the value of each variable.

Table 6.14. Step-wise regression analyses

Variables entering the regression

	Burns City	Maxton City
STEP 1	Distance	Distance
STEP 2	S5:S4	S5:S4
STEP 3	SOCED	SOC12P

Regression coefficients for model with distance, S5:S4, SOC12P

	Burns City	Maxton City
S5:S4	0.082	0.115
SOC12P	−0.031	−0.049

the step-wise procedure for Burns City, it had a predictive ability which was very close to the model (which included SOCED instead of SOC12P) which was selected by the step-wise procedure. Various other regression models were explored in particular models which used TOTSCEP (the standardised measure of SCE passes) in place of S5:S4 and SES (the standardised measure of socio-economic status) in place of SOC12P. However, the predictive ability of these alternative models was substantially lower and, although the regression coefficients for SOC12P or SES were substantially reduced when TOTSCEP was entered into the regression, the direction of the relationship was not always reversed.

It is clear that the results outlined are not particularly robust. Nevertheless, they can be interpreted as follows. For a pair of schools which are a given distance apart, movement between the schools will be increased in the direction of the school with the higher S5 staying-on rate. The odds will be increased by a factor of two for an 8 per cent increase in staying-on rates in Burns City, or a 6 per cent increase in Maxton City. However, if we compare two schools with the same S5 staying-on rates, then movement between these schools will be increased in the direction of the school which achieves this staying on rate with a lower proportion of social class 1 and 2 parents. This is despite the fact that movement between two schools is, on average, from schools with a lower proportion of social class 1 and 2 parents to schools with a higher proportion of such parents.

Thus, in Burns and Maxton Cities, there is some evidence to suggest that one effect of the Parents' Charter was the migration of pupils from 'less effective' to 'more effective' secondary schools, i.e. from schools in which attainment measures are lower to schools with similar social class intakes in which attainment measures are higher (McPherson and

Willms, 1986).[16] It does not, of course, follow from this that parents chose to send their children to these schools because they were more effective. Indeed, the evidence presented in Chapter 4 suggests that parents did not select secondary schools in terms of their superior attainment measures, let alone their greater effectiveness. The reasons parents gave for rejecting their local catchment-area school (where they did so) and for choosing the school which their child attended, referred most frequently to concerns with where the child would be happiest, to the child's own preferences, and to the state of discipline at the school. In fact, parents made very few references to examination results, other educational outcomes, or the quality or content of what was provided at the schools in question. If parents were aware of an instrumental connection between happiness, their child's preferences and discipline on the one hand and school effectiveness on the other, they were most reluctant to express it.

To understand these results we must again consider the social geography of the two cities. Figures 6.10 and 6.11 display the six census variables for secondary schools in the two cities in the form of a star for each school. In most cases, the centre of the star represents the geographical location of the school.

Inspection of the two city maps will reveal a number of reasonably full hexagons and a number of fairly empty ones. The extremes are not quite

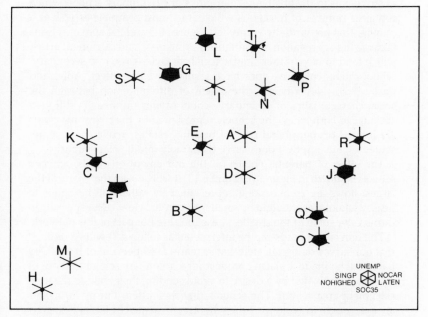

Figure 6.10. Characteristics of secondary school catchment areas in Burns City.

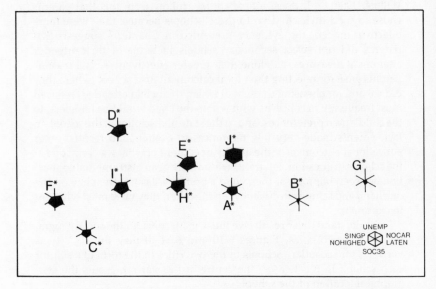

Figure 6.11. Characteristics of secondary school catchment areas in Maxton City.

as striking as in the analogous mappings of city primary schools which contain a number of hexagons which are almost complete as well as a number that are virtually empty (cf. Figures 6.3 and 6.4 above). This is because the aggregation of contiguous primary-school catchment areas, which tend to have rather similar social characteristics, into secondary-school catchment areas does have a small levelling effect (Adler and Raab, 1988). Nevertheless, the extent of differentiation between the social characteristics of secondary-school catchment areas is still very striking. In both cities, the schools represented by the fullest hexagons are located on peripheral council housing estates, while those represented by the emptiest ones serve the largely middle-class suburbs.

The effect of parental choice on the movement of pupils between schools is shown in Figures 6.12 and 6.13. It will be seen that many of the largest flows are from schools represented by rather full hexagons to nearby schools represented by smaller hexagons. However, especially in Burns City, some of the smallest hexagons are not part of this network.

The movement maps can be interpreted as follows. It will be recalled that our survey data indicated that as many as 69 per cent of Burns City parents who made a placing request for a secondary school (223 out of 322) were motivated by a desire to avoid sending their child to the local catchment-area school. The schools that they often, but by no means always, sought to avoid were the schools represented by larger hexagons which have catchment areas comprising local-authority housing

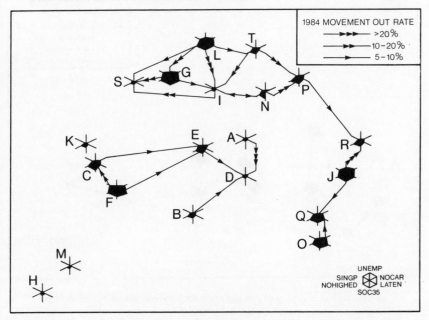

Figure 6.12. Mapping of placing requests between secondary schools in Burns City, 1984.

schemes. It will also be recalled that the best single predictor of movement from one school to another was the distance between the two schools. Thus, very few parents made placing requests for schools where substantial extra travelling was involved. In looking around for an alternative school, the old senior secondaries (or, at least, some of them) were often very conveniently situated. Being centrally located, they were more accessible than some of the newer suburban schools. Quite aside from whatever lingering prestige may still have been attached to such schools, they were often in a better location to attract pupils from adjacent schools than were the suburban schools, in spite of the fact that the latter may have had 'better' catchment areas. Many of these schools not only had 'good' examination results and high staying-on rates; they were also 'effective' schools in that, on average, they did better than other schools with similar pupil characteristics.

The above interpretation should not be pushed too far. Where two of the old senior secondaries were situated close to one another, one often benefited at the expense of the other. Moreover, there were one or two cases where schools did not lose pupils although our model predicted that they would do so. Nevertheless, much of the movement between schools can be explained in terms of the social geography of school catchment areas, the histories of individual schools and the fact that most parents were unwilling to consider schools which involved much

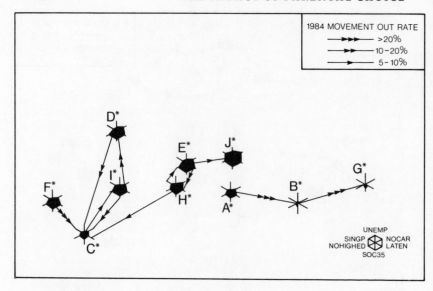

Figure 6.13.   Mapping of placing requests between secondary schools in
Maxton City, 1984.

additional travelling. In both cities, these factors combined to produce a
small number of highly sought-after schools and a corresponding
number of extremely unpopular schools. Burns Region sought to prevent the emergence of overcrowding at three of the most popular schools
by imposing intake limits and, in so doing, stemmed the outflow from
several other schools. However, in both cities, a number of schools
serving some of the least prosperous housing schemes were left very
exposed. Two such schools in Burns City and two in Maxton City had s1
intakes of 100 or less in 1985. It would be quite remarkable if they were
able to offer a range of opportunities comparable to those provided by
larger schools in more favourable circumstances.

As with primary school parents, we can contrast the account outlined
above with conclusions which can be drawn from our survey data. Our
sample of secondary school parents included parents who lived in the
catchment areas of a cluster of six secondary schools in Burns City,
together with parents from outwith the area who made a placing request
for any of these six schools. These six schools included one very 'popular' school (School D) which attracted a net inflow of 165 placing requests
in 1984 and was subject to an intake limit in 1985, as well as one rather
'unpopular' school (School F) which experienced a net outflow of 108
placing requests in 1984. School D, serves a largely middle-class catchment area in the centre of the city and is represented by an open-star on
Figure 6.10 while School F is situated on a peripheral housing scheme

characterised by high levels of social deprivation and is represented by a rather full hexagon. The cluster of schools also contained one school (School A) which was very poorly located in terms of its catchment area in that the main buildings and the annexe were both located in School D's catchment area.

The social class of the parents who made placing requests into and out of the six schools in the cluster has already been described in Chapter 4. At none of the six schools were there any discernable social class differences between parents who made a placing request and parents who sent their children to the district school. Moreover, those who made placing requests tended to send their children to schools with similar social class intakes. Thus the major flows were from School F to School C and from School A to School D. Within the survey area, there was little evidence of those moves from schools with lower social class intakes to schools with higher social class intakes which were so evident in other parts of the city.

A detailed study of the reasons parents gave for their choice of school reveals a strong rejection of School F on the grounds that discipline was poor, there was too much freedom and informality within the school, teaching methods were unpopular and pupils were not made to work hard enough. Conversely, parents who chose School C in preference to School F most frequently did so on grounds of its 'better discipline'. However, for most of them it was also the nearest alternative. The popularity of School D is attributable to two very different considerations. Some parents, particularly from School A, reported that they had chosen it because it was more conveniently situated,[17] while other parents appear to have chosen it on the grounds that they regarded it as a good school with a caring atmosphere where their child would be happier. In addition, parents claimed that the school offered a wider range of courses, including English 'A' levels in place of Scottish Sixth Year Studies (see Chapter 5). However, it is worth noting that few parents chose the schools because they thought it had a better examination record. Likewise, there was no discernable evidence that parents rejected the district school because they thought it had a poor examination record.

As in the case of our primary school survey, the reasons given by individual secondary school parents were, on the whole, compatible with the conclusions of the aggregate-level analysis described in this chapter, even if they only rarely provided direct confirmation for them. The survey provided considerable support for the importance of proximity, especially in the case of one school which was situated in the catchment area of another, since many of the parents who opted for this school cited its location as a reason for so doing. Individual secondary school parents did not refer to gains or losses of pupils from the schools in question or to the schools which would be attended by their children's

friends with the same frequency as their primary school counterparts
and the survey therefore provided little direct support for the 'bandwagon effects' described in this chapter. Although poor discipline and
unspecified references to a poor education were cited as reasons for
rejecting one school and the wider range of courses on offer as a reason
for selecting another, there were very few references to examination
results or other outcome measures. Thus, it would appear that movement towards high attaining schools is a consequence of choice on other
grounds. However, as with our survey of primary school parents, the
large number of idiosyncratic reasons for choice, which have no correlates among the variables used in our aggregate-level analysis, best
explains why the latter can only explain a relatively small proportion of
the total amount of movement.

CONCLUSIONS

A number of conclusions can be drawn from these aggregate results.
Although Maxton City is a more working-class city than Burns City, a
higher proportion of parents in Maxton than in Burns has used the
legislation to make placing requests for primary schools and for secondary schools. In both cities, there were more placing requests for non-
denominational primary and secondary schools than for the much
smaller number of Catholic schools. And in both cities, the proportion of
parents who made a placing request for primary and secondary schools,
in the Catholic as well as the non-denominational sectors, increased
quite substantially over the period 1982–1985. Thus, by 1985, some 20 per
cent of pupils entering the first year of primary school and the first year of
secondary did so after making a placing request. Finally, over the period
1982–1985, there was considerable evidence of 'bandwagon effects'. As
far as primary school intakes are concerned, three main conclusions can
be drawn from this analysis. First, there has been considerable movement into and out of primary schools throughout the two cities and, as a
result, some primary school rolls have altered substantially, albeit not as
much as some secondary school rolls (see below). By and large, schools
either gained or lost pupils and there were relatively few schools in
which gains have been offset by losses.

Secondly, those parents who have used the legislation cannot all have
been middle class since substantial inter-school movement has taken
place in areas of the two cities where no middle-class people live. This
conclusion is consistent with the results of our survey of primary school
parents (see Chapter 4) which made it clear that placing requests have
been made by parents across the entire social class spectrum and not
predominantly by a middle class minority.

Thirdly, most of the moves have been to an adjacent primary school
and have taken place within relatively homogeneous areas. In Burns
City, but not in Maxton City, there has been some movement from areas

of council housing to more middle-class areas and, in both cities, parents have moved their children away from schools with catchment areas that contain more socio–economic problems to schools with catchment areas that contain fewer. These results are again consistent with our survey data which suggested that about 54 per cent of Maxton City parents who made a placing request for their child to enter P1 were concerned to avoid sending their child to the local (catchment area) school. In doing so, some parents referred to the 'rough and rowdy' children who went to the district school (this was particularly marked in the case of two schools) and, in selecting another school, they most often referred to proximity and safety considerations.

The above results notwithstanding, the extent of unexplained movement is considerable and suggests that there are other factors that we have been unable to measure that affect the decision to make a placing request. Among the possible reasons are the following: (i) merely considering adjacent boundaries may not be enough to explain geographical reasons for making placing requests – e.g. schools which do not involve crossing busy roads or are near shops and local facilities may be more attractive; (ii) at primary school level, the available school variables are very limited and tell us little about the schools' characteristics or achievements – better school variables, if they were available, might enable us to make better predictions; (iii) even if we had better school variables, the flows across adjacent boundaries might still not bear a simple relationship to any of the measurable aspects of the schools or their catchment areas. This would be the case if movement was influenced by (non-generalisable) local considerations.

As far as secondary school intakes are concerned, four main conclusions can be drawn. First, some schools in both cities made substantial gains while others suffered considerable losses. Over the period 1982–1985, a small number of schools in each city gained an increasing proportion of pupils who were the subject of placing requests while another small group lost an increasing proportion of such pupils. By and large, the schools which gained large numbers of pupils made few compensating losses while the schools which lost large numbers of pupils made few compensating gains. However, the imposition of intake limits on three of the 'most popular' secondary schools in Burns City in 1984 did result in a reduction in the number of requests for these schools in the following year. This, in turn, helped to stem the outflow of pupils from a number of the 'least popular' schools.

Secondly, distance was the best predictor of movement, few placing requests being made for secondary schools when much additional travelling was involved (this applied even more in Burns City than in Maxton City). Considered one at a time, school attainment measures were most highly correlated with movement (again this was particularly so in Burns City where there was a greater variation between schools in the level of measured attainment). For schools which were a given distance apart, the odds of movement increased in the direction of the school with the higher s5 staying-on rate. However, when two schools with the same s5 staying-on rate were compared, the odds of movement increased in the direction of the school with the smaller proportion of social class 1 and 2 parents.

Thirdly, most of the schools which lost large numbers of pupils were situated in the least prosperous housing schemes while most of the schools which gained substantial numbers were located in mixed inner-city areas. Thus, unlike moves between primary schools which mainly take place within relatively homogeneous areas, moves between secondary schools frequently involve transfers between catchment areas with different social characteristics. Moreover, in both cities, the schools which gained most pupils were all previously selective schools (although not all previously selective schools made substantial gains).

Fourthly, large outflows have, in a few cases, combined with declining school rolls and a small catchment area to produce very small intakes. Coupled with low staying-on rates and poor examination results, this can only exacerbate the problems faced by these schools. All in all, the evidence in Burns and Maxton Cities suggests that the Parents' Charter is leading to the emergence of a number of highly sought-after and a number of very unpopular secondary schools and thus to increased inequalities in educational provision.

Comparing placing requests for secondary schools with those for primary schools, the extensive network of moves and the predominance of moves to nearby schools was evident in both cases. Other evidence (see Macbeth, Strachan and Macaulay, 1986 and Chapter 4) has established that placing requests have been made by parents from across the entire social class spectrum and not merely by a middle-class minority. The pattern of requests for primary and secondary schools in the two cities, which includes substantial numbers of requests from areas containing very few middle-class families, are consistent with these findings. But, while most of the primary school requests involved moves between adjacent schools in relatively homogeneous areas, most of the secondary school requests were to nearby schools in rather different catchment areas. Thus, although we must exercise great care in making inferences from aggregate data, it seems likely that placing requests for secondary schools have had a greater effect on the social composition of school intakes than placing requests for primary schools have had. This is especially so where there were large outflows to nearby schools from those secondary schools which serve local-authority housing schemes. Comparing the two cities, the similarities between them were quite remarkable. There were similar trends in the two cities, the sâme type of schools lost and gained pupils, and the same factors influenced movement. Although there were fewer differences between individual schools and their catchment areas in Maxton City than in Burns City, parents who made placing requests in Maxton City selected schools that involved travelling greater distances than did parents in Burns City.

NOTES

1. The data in this section are based on official statistics, the major source being the SED's Statistical Bulletin (Scottish Education Department, 1987a).

2. Using individual level data from the 1981 CES School Leavers Survey linked to enumeration district data from the 1981 Population Census, Garner (1988) has shown that, after controlling for individual home variables and schooling, neighbourhood deprivation has a strong and independent effect on educational attainment.

3. Willms (1986) has shown that most of the variation in the socio-economic composition of schools in Scotland is due to the unequal distribution of pupils in the top two of the Registrar General's social class categories. The percentage of children in Social Class 1 and 2 households was selected in preference to other measures of social class for this reason.

4. On checking, the measurement of capacity was found to be inaccurate in many cases and was therefore excluded from the analysis.

5. If the odds of making a placing request are 1:30, i.e. 1 to 30, this means that there will be one placing request for every 30 pupils who attend their local catchment-area school.

6. The computations were performed by the computer package BMDP using the program PLR (Dixon, 1983), although the accompanying significance levels were not correct because individual parents do not decide to move school independently of other parents. Thus the assumption of independent events implicit in the statistical model is not justified. The approach we adopted is very similar to one used by Flowerdew and Aitken (1982) to predict migration patterns between areas, and they are likewise cautious about how to interpret the associated significance levels. Flowerdew and Aitken use a Poisson model which is appropriate since their migration rates are small enough to have little impact on the population of the areas from which movement is taking place. Our logistic model is more suitable for larger percentage movements. The use of the logistic model, however, introduces a further complication. Should one consider the whole catchment-area population as the denominator in the calculation of the percentage movement to one particular school, or should children who have moved to other schools be excluded from the calculations? The latter approach would be equivalent to the competing risk models which are employed in survival analysis. There are pros and cons for each choice, but we selected the first option and have used the total catchment-area population as the denominator. This might have led to

inappropriate results if almost all the pupils in one school selected other schools, but this was not the case in either city.

7. It should be noted that the interpretation of multivariate analysis is complicated by the correlations between the predictors
and the influence of all the predictors on movement is fairly
weak.

8. There were actually twenty-one non-denominational secondary
schools in the (former) City Division of Burns Region Education
Department. However, one of these is situated several miles
outside the city boundary and there were very few transfers
between it and any of the other schools in the city. It has
therefore not been included in the analysis.

9. The (former) City Division of Maxton Region Education Department also contains a two-year non-denominational secondary
school. This was not included in the analysis because it is
located some distance from the city and because nearly all the
few transfers at s1 were to the school that pupils would, in any
case, have transferred to at s3.

10. The gains and losses do not include a small number of moves
into and out of the Region or into and out of the private sector.
The 1985 figures refer to the number of placing requests granted
and thus to the achieved s1 roll of the school.

11. In both cities, one or two primary schools had 'split' catchment
areas and at one or two other primary schools pupils could
choose between two secondary schools. In the first case, each
part of the primary school catchment area was separately allocated to the appropriate secondary school; in the second case,
the primary school catchment area was allocated to the secondary school chosen which the majority of pupils attended. The
analysis took account of several changes in transfer policy over
the four year period.

12. The use of the centroid of each set of primary schools as a
measure of location was obviously an approximation. As the set
of primary schools associated with each of the secondary
schools formed a single contiguous area in all but one case (in
Burns City), this approximation is a reasonable one. In addition,
the use of distance measured, as the crow flies, from the centroid of the grid co-ordinates may not be a particularly good
measure of the extra distance which is actually involved. More
realistic considerations would involve assessing the extra distance in terms of the routes to school which pupils actually take.
Although it was beyond our resources to do this for every
possible pairing of schools (there were $20 \times 19 = 380$ possible
pairings in Burns City and $10 \times 9 = 90$ in Maxton City), we
accept that we have not modelled distance in an ideal fashion.

13. TOTSCEP is a standardised measure (mean = 0, s.d. = 1) of
overall attainment in Scottish Certificate of Education (SCE) examinations, initially scored on a 0–14 scale and averaged over all
the pupils in a year group. A more detailed description of this
variable can be found in McPherson and Willms (1986).

14. SES is a standardised measure (mean = 0, s.d. = 1) of socio-
economic status, which is itself a weighted composite of father's
occupation, mother's education and number of siblings. A more
detailed description of this variable can also be found in
McPherson and Willms (1986).

15. HISTORY was scored as follows: schools which used to be fee-paying senior-secondaries were given a score of 5, other senior-secondaries were scored 4, post-reorganisation comprehensives 3, pre-reorganisation comprehensives 2, and schools which used to be junior-secondaries 1. Senior-secondaries offered courses leading to national certification at 17 or 18; junior-secondaries terminated at 15 or 16 and did not offer national credentials. Most senior-secondaries had selective intakes and, in this sense, they resembled the English grammar schools while the junior-secondaries resembled the English secondary moderns. Under the Education (Scotland) Act 1945, fees were not abolished and some senior-secondaries (those with highest status) continued to charge fees.

16. There are two different conceptions of school effectiveness. The first concerns all the benefits accruing to a pupil as a result of attending a particular school, and therefore includes the 'contextual effect' of the social composition of fellow pupils. The second conception concerns the boost associated with attendance at a particular school once the contextual effect has been discounted and may be associated with what teachers do (although this was not measured in this study). The first conception can often be measured without bias in an aggregate or school-level only model while opinion suggests that the second conception cannot be measured without bias in this manner. It is clear that the second conception is the one which is being employed here but, both for the reason referred to above, the results were not particularly robust and because inferences drawn from the analysis of data for two cities in one year need to be treated with caution, our conclusions concerning effectiveness are presented rather tentatively.

17. Since the two schools are only a couple of minutes walk from each other, this reason should, perhaps not be taken too seriously. However, parents may have been reacting to the fact that their children would actually have walked past School D on their way to School A.

7

ASSESSING THE SIGNIFICANCE OF THE 1981 ACT

The contrast, outlined in Chapter 2, between the relatively weak form of parental rights of school choice which applied under the 1980 Act in England and Wales and the relatively strong form which applied under the 1981 Act in Scotland persisted for several years. However, in May 1987, Kenneth Baker, the Secretary of State for Education and Science, announced that, if the Conservatives won the forthcoming general election, they planned to introduce a new Education Act which would strengthen the rights of parents in England and Wales and further reduce the powers of local education authorities. In the increasingly ideological climate of the times, the balance between the concerns of education authorities and those of parents in respect of school admissions was still seen to lean too heavily towards the former. After their victory in the 1987 general election, the Conservatives duly introduced their Education Reform Bill. Reflecting the breakdown in trust between central government, local authorities and the teaching profession, which was becoming increasingly more apparent, the Education Reform Act 1988 was, of necessity, nearly twice the length of the 1944 Act.

THE EDUCATION REFORM ACT 1988

Few other pieces of legislation have attempted so ambitiously to re-design a major public service from top to bottom[1] or faced such bitter and widespread professional opposition (Wilbey and Crequer, 1988). The Secretary of State saw the Act as an attempt to raise standards by freeing schools from bureaucratic and professional straitjackets, and creating a service that was responsive to consumer preferences. On the other hand, many of his critics, pointing to the 415 new powers which the Act conferred on the Secretary of State, saw it as an irreversible shift of power towards the centre, and as the biggest single attack on local democracy this century. Other critics, pointing to the increased role of market forces within the public sector, feared that it would lead to a retreat from the post-war commitment to equality of educational opportunity, and that it might even pave the way for a privatised education service.

As far as school admissions were concerned, the 1988 Act sought to prevent local education authorities from setting maximum admission limits below the physical capacity of the school and from refusing to admit children when there was room for them in the school. It will be recalled (see Chapter 2) that, in England, the broad and general exceptions to the duty of an education authority to comply with parental preferences, which applied (under s.6(3) of the 1980 Act) when compliance with parents requests' would 'prejudice the provision of efficient education or the efficient use of resources' enabled an authority to justify a refusal by referring to conditions at schools other than the one requested by the parents or to conditions in their schools generally. By contrast, in Scotland, where the grounds of refusal were more narrowly defined (under s.28A(3) of the 1981 Act) an authority could only refer to conditions at the school requested by the parents.

The 1988 Act equates 'physical capacity' with 'the standard number' and stipulates that 'the authority . . . shall not fix as the number of pupils in any relevant age group it is intended to admit to the school in any school year a number which is less than the relevant standard number' (Education Reform Act 1988, s.26(1)). The relevant standard number is defined as either the number of pupils admitted to the school in 1979, when school rolls were substantially higher than they were a decade later, or the number admitted in the preceding year, whichever is the greater (s.27(1)). However, if as a result of a reduction in the availability of accommodation at the school, the LEA takes the view that the standard number is too high, it may refer the matter to the Secretary of State who is alone empowered (under ss.27(4) and (5)) to reduce it.

To the extent that the 1988 Act imposes numerical limits on school admissions, and sets these limits at levels which, in the context of declining school rolls, will rarely be attained, it represents a significant step towards 'open enrolment'. Moreover, it has led to a situation in which parental rights of school choice in England and Wales now correspond quite closely with those which have existed in Scotland for some time, in so far as the 1981 Act sets out a number of grounds for refusing admissions but likewise makes it very difficult for an education authority to justify imposing limits on enrolments. One result of the strengthening of the parental choice provisions in the 1988 Act is that our case study of the implementation and impact of the 1981 Act in Scotland is of considerably greater salience for England and Wales than it would otherwise have been.

ASSESSING THE ARGUMENTS OF SUPPORTERS AND CRITICS

One way of assessing the significance of the parental choice provisions in the Education (Scotland) Act 1981 is to examine the arguments put forward by supporters and critics of the legislation (outlined in Chapter 2) in the light of our evaluation of its implementation and impact (as set out in Chapters 3–6). Some of the arguments advanced by different parties merely reflected a preference for individualistic or collective values, but others involved claims which can be assessed in the light of empirical evidence. The latter are our main concern here.

Supporters of the 1981 Act argued that the legislation would prove to be very popular with parents, while critics asserted either that it was unnecessary (since most education authorities already operated flexible admissions policies) or that it would raise expectations which could not be realised. The statistics on the take-up of placing requests can be used to assess these claims. The number of parents making requests increased from 10 456 in 1982 to 21 795 in 1985, and to 23 075 in 1987 (Scottish Education Department 1987b). Not only were there substantially more requests for out-of-area admissions after the enactment of the 1981 Act (see Chapter 3) but the number has continued to rise. By 1985, 9.6 per cent of pupils entering the first year of primary school and 8.7 per cent of those entering the first year of secondary school had been the subject of a placing request and, by 1987, the proportions had increased to 10.5 per cent and 9.9 per cent. Although these proportions are quite substantial, the fact remains that nine children out of ten continued to attend their district school. Since, in some areas, it is simply not practicable for parents to send their children anywhere else but to the local school, it is not surprising to find that there were considerable variations between and within education authorities and that the proportion of placing requests was highest in cities, where rates of 20–25 per cent among non-denominational schools were not uncommon, and lowest in rural areas, where the rates rarely exceeded 2–3 per cent. Thus, while the legislation has proved to be rather popular in the cities and, to a lesser extent, in other urban areas, it has made little impact elsewhere.

Supporters of the 1981 Act also argued that, with falling school rolls, most schools would be able to accommodate the extra pupils whose parents might wish them to go there. Although this has been true on the whole, and the success rate remains very high, there has been a continuing downward trend in the number of placing requests which have been granted. Of placing requests for primary schools, 97.7 per cent were granted in the four-year period 1982–1985 but, in spite of falling school rolls, this fell to 96.7 per cent in 1987. The corresponding figures for secondary schools were 94.2 per cent for 1982–1985 and 92.4 per cent for 1987 (Scottish Education Department, 1987b). Thus, although most placing requests could be accommodated, a small but growing proportion could not.

One of the main arguments advanced by critics of the 1981 Act was that it would mainly benefit middle class children. On the other hand, supporters of the legislation stressed that it would be of particular benefit to bright children in deprived areas. Our survey data (see Chapter 4) provides no support for the first of these claims, while evidence for the second is, at best, equivocal. Thus, we were unable to detect any overall relationship between social class and the take-up of placing requests, which were made by parents from right across the social class spectrum. The same applies to other socio–economic characteristics and, in this respect, our conclusions confirm those of Macbeth, Strachan and Macaulay (1986). The absence of any overall relationship with social class at the individual level does, of course, mask some fairly strong social class relationships at the aggregate or school level. At primary school level, the schools which have lost most pupils have been those with catchment areas containing a high incidence of social problems. At secondary school level, they have been schools serving inner-city housing schemes where the incidence of multiple deprivation has likewise been high. Although children who have opted out of schools serving these communities may have benefited, those who have remained with the district school may have had to pay a heavy price if they and their schools have become even more stigmatised than they were previously.

Another argument advanced by critics of the 1981 Act was that it would weaken the links between school and community and lead to increased social segregation. Referring to the first part of the argument, the evidence suggests that the links between school and community may have been altered rather than weakened by the legislation. At primary school level, our survey data (see Chapter 4) indicate that requesting parents attached great importance to the location of the school and to safe access for their children. The importance of proximity was confirmed by our analysis of aggregate placing request data (see Chapter 6) which showed that 83 per cent and 85 per cent of placing requests for primary schools in Burns City and Maxton City were to an adjacent school. It was equally confirmed by the finding that, at secondary school level, distance was the best predictor of movement and that few placing requests involved much extra travelling. Although we have not analysed the data in detail, there is evidence to suggest that, at transfer to secondary school, there has been considerable variation in the incidence of placing requests between the different primary schools in the catchment area of a given secondary school. Thus, while some primary schools have remained 'loyal' to their district secondary school, others have produced most of the 'exodus' to other schools. To the extent that this is the case, parents may have confounded supporters as well as critics of the legislation by redefining school catchment areas and thus altering the link between schools and the communities which they serve. However, although this would suggest that the first part of the critics' case is probably false, the second part is almost certainly true. At both primary and secondary level, the loss of some pupils has, in the case of some under-enrolled schools, left other pupils in a very exposed postion. Thus, while the 1981 Act has led to the integration of some pupils from areas of multiple deprivation into schools with adjacent catchment areas, it has probably increased the segregation of those who remained at the district school.

Another related argument advanced by critics of the 1981 Act was that it would lead to a situation in which some schools were seriously over-subscribed while others were chronically under-enrolled and that this, together with the cost of implementing the statutory provisions, would result in an inefficient use of scarce financial resources. If the authorities had taken no remedial action, there would have been some overcrowding at primary school level. Burns dealt with this by imposing admission limits in an *ad hoc* fashion when, in the view of the Education Department, the school could not accommodate additional pupils.[2] One consequence in Burns has been that latecomers to the catchment area have sometimes been refused admission to their district primary school. On one early occasion, Watt imposed an intake limit (see Chapter 3) and Maxton has now followed suit, although it has identified the schools in advance.[3] At the secondary level, some schools in Burns City and Maxton City were seriously over-subscribed. Burns dealt with this problem by vacating annexes and temporary accommodation and by imposing admission limits on the schools concerned, but Maxton has not done anything about this problem. Where Burns and Maxton have imposed intake limits, these have, on the whole, been upheld on appeal although, with one exception, these limits have not been tested in front of the sheriff. In the light of sheriffs' decisions elsewhere (see Chapter 5) this must be regarded as fortunate from the regions' point of view. As a result, it can be argued that, with the possible exception of two secondary schools in Maxton Region (B* and C*, see Chapter 6), by 1985 there were no over-subscribed schools in the three authorities we studied, merely schools that were full to capacity. However, this was clearly not the case in McDiarmid Region where many of the schools involved in appeals to the sheriff were seriously overcrowded.

Burns and Maxton Regions contained a growing number of chronically under-enrolled secondary schools (in 1985, two out of twenty secondary schools in Burns City and two out of ten in Maxton City had intakes of less than 100; by 1988 the combined number had risen to eight) about which they could do very little. This was, of course, partly the result of falling school rolls, but in every case, parental choice was the precipitating factor. The existence of these under-enrolled schools will certainly have generated some additional costs for the authorities concerned. This is because small schools and small classes both entail higher spending on pupils; the former because the per capita costs of buildings and facilities are relatively higher, the latter because teacher:pupil ratios are relatively lower (see Chapter 1). Because the effects of small intakes on school rolls are cumulative, the additional costs associated with under-enrolment are likely to increase over time.

A counter-argument advanced by supporters of the legislation was that it would make schools more responsive to parents. Although we do not have any evidence, e.g. about the response of schools or education authorities to the loss (or gain) of pupils, that bears directly on this claim, several pieces of indirect evidence suggest that this may be very difficult to achieve in practice. In our survey (see Chapter 4), 60 per cent of requesting parents whose children were about to enter primary school and 69 per cent of those whose children were about to transfer to secondary school, said that it was important for them that their children did not attend the catchment-area school. However, some of the most commonly cited reasons, e.g. safety (for primary entry), proximity and the type of children who go to the school, are not reasons to which a school can respond. Moreover, the existence of 'bandwagon effects' (see Chapter 6), which are in part attributable to earlier inflows or outflows of older siblings, can be very hard to redress. These difficulties are captured very well in the reported comments of the Headteacher of the most under-enrolled secondary school in Burns Region and an Assistant Rector of School C*, the most over-subscribed secondary school in Maxton Region.

I had an outstanding staff, highly motivated. We were a model of primary-secondary liaison. We had primary teachers and children attending our music and art classes. We went into local primary schools and put on exhibitions and did reprographics for them. We operated an 'open door' policy and had 60 adults attending our classes. We started a homework policy. We used local papers to spread good news about the school. You'd have thought being a football manager would have helped, wouldn't you? It didn't help any [Headteacher of School G in Burns Region whose first year intake fell from 164 in 1982 to 80 in 1985 and to 58 in 1988].

This school is far too large. It's an embarrassment to us. Make no mistake. I discourage parents from sending their children here . . . It is very rare for parents from other catchment areas to come and look at the school before asking to send their children here. If they do, the janitor shows them round [Assistant Rector of School C* in Maxton Region whose first year intake rose from 330 in 1982 to 366 in 1985. Although it fell back somewhat to 299 in 1988, this must be seen in the context of declining school rolls].

The difficulties experienced by under-enrolled and over-subscribed schools call for different explanations. In *Exit, Voice and Loyalty*, Hirschman (1970) argued that 'customers' can express their dissatisfaction with an organisation in one of two ways: by leaving it for another (the 'exit' option) or by trying to change it for the better (the 'voice' option).[4] His analysis was intended to have general application but is clearly very pertinent to parental choice of school. This is because parental choice legislation was intended to facilitate exit, in the expectation that an outflow of pupils from a school would encourage it to take stock of its performance and do whatever is necessary to regain the confidence of parents who do send or could send their children to the school in question. However, exit may make it more difficult for schools to improve. If parents who might have worked to improve a flagging school leave it instead, this may deprive the school of the possible benefits of voice. Moreover, because smaller intakes mean fewer staff and less resources, schools that start to lose pupils may find it very hard to recover.

Although we do not have any direct evidence for this, one explanation for the enduring popularity of a small number of over-subscribed schools, particularly at secondary level, is that, in choosing a school, overcrowding does not appear to be a particularly salient consideration for parents. However, neither this explanation nor the previous one should be pushed too far. Some recently-appointed headteachers of under-enrolled secondary schools in Maxton City have managed to halt (and, in some cases, reverse) the decline in intake numbers[5] while the number of pupils admitted to School C* (referred to above) did eventually decline after reaching a peak of 383 in 1986.[6]

Supporters of the 1981 Act claimed that it would enable 'good' schools to expand and force 'bad' schools to improve or lead to their eventual closure. What constituted a 'good' or a 'bad' school was rarely specified but was regarded as self-evident, at least for parents. Thus, popular schools were 'good' schools, while unpopular schools were 'bad' schools. Moreover, by allowing popular schools to expand and unpopular schools to contract, there would be an overall improvement in standards. Although some schools have expanded while others have contracted, no schools in our three study Regions closed as a result of parental choice and there is, as yet, no evidence that the legislation has contributed to an overall improvement in standards. Our attempt to model the choice process (see Chapter 4) produced little evidence of parents seeking to identify the best available school for their children. However, to the extent that choice involves satisficing (Simon, 1965) rather than maximising, the logic of the quasi-market would still apply, albeit with much less precision. For parents who considered alternatives to the district school, the number of schools considered was very small and the factors which parents referred to were frequently geographical and social rather than educational. Thus, most choosing parents considered only one alternative to the district school and very few considered more than two. In so doing, proximity was clearly a very important consideration. So too were safety (for primary schools) and the kind of children who went to the school. In fact, the emphasis which parents placed on the happiness of their child and the child's own preferences (at secondary school level) may well have had more to do with social considerations such as these than with educational ones. However, although there was little evidence of parents assessing schools in terms of measurable educational outcomes or, even, in terms of the nature and quality of teaching at the school, our analysis of aggregate data (in Chapter 6) showed that, at secondary level, pupils transferred from schools with poorer examination results and lower staying-on rates to schools with better examination results and higher staying-on rates. Although the gaining schools had better results than the losing schools, it does not follow that they were better schools or that the pupils who transferred to them will necessarily do better as a result of doing so. A complete evaluation of the suggestion (in Chapter 6) that schools which gained pupils were 'more effective' schools in either of the senses referred to above[7] is an extremely complex task which we were unable to pursue.

This discussion leads naturally into the final set of arguments put forward by critics of the legislation, namely that it would lead to increased inequalities in educational opportunity and to the re-emergence of a 'two-tier' system. Once again, the evidence is derived from our analysis of placing requests for secondary schools in Burns City and Maxton City. In both cities, placing requests exaggerated the problems of schools which lost pupils. Almost without exception, they were situated in the least prosperous housing schemes while schools which gained pupils were located in mixed inner-city areas. The former were either purpose-built comprehensive schools or had previously been non-selective (junior secondary) schools while the latter had usually been selective (senior secondary) schools. In terms of educational resources and educational opportunities, the problems faced by schools which lost pupils are clearly much the greater. In both cities, placing requests had, in a few cases, combined with falling school rolls and small catchment areas to produce intakes which were scarcely viable. Combined with low staying-on rates and poor examination results, such schools could not possibly provide the same set of curricular choices or educational opportunities as schools with larger intakes. Thus, the legislation has quite clearly led to a widening of educational inequalities and to the re-emergence of a 'two-tier' system of secondary schooling in the big cities. However, the two-tier system is unlike that described in Chapter 1 in that the lower tier now caters for a minority of working-class pupils, whereas, prior to reorganisation, it catered for a majority of them. However, the existence of a small number of what are, in effect, junior secondary schools located in the most deprived areas of the large cities and serving some, but by no means all, the children in those areas poses some very difficult issues of policy for the education authorities concerned.

Just as many of the arguments outlined above rest on different value preferences, so too does any assessment of them. Some people will welcome any move towards an individual client orientation while others will regret any departure from a collective welfare orientation. Likewise, some people care more about aggregate welfare, e.g. about the proportion of the population at school which acquires educational qualifications, while others care more about distribution, e.g. about equality of educational opportunity. And, in any case, while some people may describe a bottle as 'half-full', others will describe the same bottle as 'half-empty'. Thus, it is impossible to produce an assessment of the parental choice provisions in the 1981 Act which everyone will accept. Moreover, a final assessment of some of the arguments calls for more empirical evidence than is currently available.[8] Nevertheless, it is clear that some of the claims made by supporters of the legislation have been borne out by events while others have not. Likewise, some of the critics' arguments have been validated while others have not. By way of conclusion, we now return to two of the main themes outlined in Chapter 1.

INDIVIDUAL CHOICE AND COLLECTIVE WELFARE

The 1981 Act has resulted in the shift away from some of the central concerns of a collective welfare orientation towards those associated with an individual client orientation. In particular, the parental choice provisions embodied in Sections 28A–28F, have led to a shift away from an authority-wide approach towards a child-centred approach to school admissions. The encouragement given to individual choice, the matching of pupils with the schools selected by their parents and the introduction of quasi-market forces into education have imposed constraints on authorities' attempts to achieve an academic and social mix, set upper and (more crucially) lower bounds on school intakes and school rolls, achieve an efficient use of scarce resources, and promote equality of educational opportunity. It is not our intention here to suggest that education authorities were necessarily particularly good at achieving any of the objectives mentioned above. Our intention is, rather, to point out that the 1981 Act will make it much more difficult for education authorities to achieve such objectives in the future and to make clear that the introduction of quasi-market forces will not necessarily be to everyone's advantage.

Comprehensive schooling in Britain has not had a very good press. Few of the recent evaluations have identified gains from reorganisation that were either socially or educationally significant. Indeed, for many commentators of varying political, social and educational opinions, the comprehensive school has come to symbolise the supposed failure of the social–democratic reformism of British educational policy since the 1944 Act (see, for example, Cox and Marks, 1980; Centre for Contemporary Cultural Studies, 1981; Hargreaves, 1982). Indeed, much of the recent debate about standards, accountability and the effectiveness of schooling can be read as a criticism of comprehensive schools and policies, as can a number of legislative changes culminating in the Education Reform Act 1988. However, as McPherson and Willms (1987) point out, negative conclusions about the potential and performance of comprehensive schooling were somewhat premature in the sense that a majority of

British secondary schools only became fully comprehensive in the mid-1970s and there had not been any attempts to evaluate anything approaching a fully comprehensive system. Moreover, their recent evaluation of the later stages of comprehensive reorganisation in Scotland produced a much more positive assessment in that inequalities in attainment associated with socio–economic status declined, while overall standards of attainment rose. However, in anticipating the long-term effects of parental choice, the assisted places scheme and the proposals for opting out, they concluded that the early 1980s may come to be seen as 'the high point of egalitarian reform', and anticipated that the effects of recent government policies would inhibit, or even reverse, the processes of equalisation and improvement.

If McPherson and Willms are correct, the shift away from an authority-wide towards a child-centred approach to school admissions will not only lead to increased educational inequalities but also to a decline in educational standards. Moreover, their study suggests that, contrary to much received opinion, these two outcomes are not just contingently related. There is already evidence in the cities of increased inequalities although there is, as yet, no evidence of the effects of the 1981 Act on standards of attainment. Such evidence is, however, crucial to an evaluation of the long-term effects of the 1981 Act.[9]

The 1981 Act gave individual parents the opportunity to choose the schools they wished their children to attend. However, the aggregate of such choices may well not represent outcomes which individual parents would have chosen. Thus parents might well not have chosen situations in which some schools are overcrowded or full to capacity and require to use distant annexes or temporary accommodation, while other schools are critically under-enrolled and face reductions in staffing and restrictions in the curriculum. Such outcomes are due to what Hirsch (1977) called 'the tyranny of small decisions' and result from the promotion of 'positional competition'[10]. The logic is as follows: some parents choose to make a placing request for a particular school but, to the extent that other parents also do so, that school may be over-subscribed and thus less desirable; other parents opt for their catchment-area school but, to the extent that others do not, that school may be under-enrolled and likewise less desirable. Now assume (this is probably a reasonable assumption) that an under-enrolled school is a worse prospect than an over-subscribed one; more parents may make placing requests (on the assumption that other parents will do so) and the effect is greater under-enrolment than would otherwise have been the case. The experience of Burns Region which imposed intake limits on several of its over-subscribed secondary schools (see Chapters 3 and 6) offers some reassurance in that this partially stemmed the outflow from a number of under-enrolled schools. However, these limits have not been tested by an appeal to the sheriff and the experience of McDiarmid Region (see

Chapter 5) suggests that they might not be sustained if they were. Moreover, there were special circumstances (i.e. annexes and temporary accommodation which could be taken out of use) which would not generally apply to over-subscribed schools. Thus Hirsch's argument that 'the positional sector is a misleading guide to what individuals would demand if they could see and act on the results of their combined choices' still applies.

CLIENTS' RIGHTS AND AGENCY DISCRETION

The 1981 Act also resulted in a shift away from agency discretion towards individual rights. This had considerable implications for the agency since, as we argued in Chapter 1, individual rights impose duties on administrative agencies and shape case-level decision making. We look first at the effects of these on parents, and then at their effects on education authorities before, finally, asking whether they have achieved the right balance between them.

About 10 per cent of parents in Scotland currently make placing requests for entry to primary school and for transfer to secondary school. Although there is some (not very strong) evidence (see Chapter 4) that those who made placing requests were more 'administratively competent' than those who did not, the large majority of those who did not make placing requests knew that they could have done so. The number of parents who have made placing requests represents a considerable increase over the number who requested out-of-area admissions before the 1981 Act came into effect, and almost all these placing requests have been granted. Thus, few parents have had to use the new appeal procedures. Those who have done have not been greatly aided by these procedures – appeal committees have rarely upheld parents' appeals although sheriffs have done so more often in the few appeals that they have heard.

All three of the education authorities we looked at continued to use the same initial allocation procedures as they had before the 1981 Act came into effect, the main changes being the greatly increased number of requests, particularly in the larger cities, and, the standards used in case-level decision making. Almost all these requests were granted and education authorities were thus less able to determine the overall pattern of admissions to schools. One result of this was that the use of distant annexes and temporary accommodation was often prolonged while other schools were left empty. It was due both to the restrictive language of the 1981 Act and to the existence of appeals which discouraged education authorities from adopting broad interpretations of the statutory exceptions to their duties to comply with parents' requests and forced them to allow requests, even where they would have preferred to refuse them. However, the appeal procedure has not provided a very effective review of the decisions taken by education authorities. This is because appeal committees lacked the necessary independence and competence to perform this task properly and because most of the sheriffs have adopted the 'single child' approach and individualised the issues brought before them (see Chapter 5). Thus, for different reasons, the actual decisions of appeal committees and sheriffs have made little impact on case-level decision making – appeal committees have generally been supportive of the authorities and where, as in McDiarmid Region, sheriffs have routinely upheld parents appeals, the authorities have generally conceded in those cases but carried on regardless in others.

In an important article, McAuslan (1983) argues that the period since 1979 has seen an attempt to reverse the 'onward march of the processes of collective consumption' and a return to more market-orientated processes. This has led to a new set of conflicts which, for the most part, have not really been concerned with individual grievances against administration, but have involved clashes of policy between different agencies of the state. But the judges' 'preference for individualising issues and so seeing all issues brought before them in terms of the individual with a grievance against the bureaucracy' and 'their general preference – their ideological preference – for the individual as opposed to the collective' has prevented them from grasping what is really at issue. Thus, instead of acting as a check on government, a task which administrative law has never performed very effectively, they actively facilitate the government's attack on collective consumption, and do so in a highly partisan way. Our critique of sheriffs provides strong support for McAuslan's analysis but actually goes further.

In the South Glamorgan case (R v *South Glamorgan Appeal Committee ex parte Evans* (1984)), the only case of judicial review to reach the courts so far, the Divisional Court held that (English) appeal committees were required to adopt a two-stage consideration of appeals under the 1980 Act (see Chapter 2). First, the appeal committee had to decide whether the admission of the child would have prejudiced efficient education at the school. If the appeal committee found that no prejudice would result, it was to allow the appeal but, if it concluded that the admission of the child would cause prejudice, it was then required to move on to the second stage, namely that of determining whether the prejudice caused was 'sufficient to outweigh the parental factors'.

Although the approach advocated in the South Glamorgan case individualises the issue by seeing it in terms of a parent with a grievance against an authority, it does have some merit in that it calls for an attempt to balance the concerns of the parent against the policies of the authority (Tweedie, 1989a). The 1981 Act likewise calls for a two-stage consideration of appeals (Tweedie, Adler and Petch, 1986). In appeals involving over-subscribed schools, (Scottish) appeal committees and sheriffs should, following McAuslan, first determine whether admission limits are set in such a way that breaching them would satisfy one of the statutory exceptions to the authority's duty to comply with placing requests under the 1981 Act. Where the authority is unable to show that this would be the case, it would have to allow the appeal but where the authority is able to show that one of the statutory exceptions would apply, appeal committees and sheriffs would then decide whether the circumstances of the parents' case merited making an exception to the admission limit.

If appeal committees and sheriffs should attempt to balance parents' claims against authorities' policies, so too should case-level decision makers. However, this still falls short of the ideal in that it assumes that the available places in the school were appropriately allocated in the first place. This is very questionable, since the hostility of the client autonomy version of the individual client orientation to trade-offs between parents and the indifference of the collective welfare orientation to the identities of the individual children who attend particular schools (see Chapter 1) has, in many cases, resulted in the adoption of very simple adminis-trative procedures for determining priorities in the case of over-sub-scribed schools. Each of the three education authorities we studied gave priority to children in the school's catchment area. Burns adopted a set of guidelines containing nine factors which could be taken into consider-ation but refused to place them in rank order. In practice, priority has usually been given to the presence of older children at the school; validated medical reasons sometimes secured preferential treatment, as did membership of a single parent family; and, finally, distance from the school was often used to give priority to some claims over others. Watt actually guaranteed a place in the district school to all children in the district (even to the point of reserving places for new housing de-velopments within the catchment area). However, it did not identify any other criteria which were to be taken into account and, in the only case where a school was held to be over-subscribed, priority was eventually determined by lottery. After admitting children in the catchment area, Maxton gave priority to children with siblings at the requested school and then used distance from the school to determine which children should be given priority when there were not enough places for all of them.

This has given rise to something of a paradox. Although the 1981 Act sought to make school admissions responsive to parental choice, and parental choice has certainly prevailed when there has been space in the requested school, education authorities have applied somewhat arbi-trary administrative criteria which have had little to do with reasons for choice, or have failed to put forward any criteria at all, for giving priority to the claims of some parents over others when the school has been full. Case-level decision makers have been unwilling to assess the merits of parents' claims in hard cases, i.e. when parents' choices came up against intake limits, while appeal committees and sheriffs, by their unwillingness to consider the merits of parents' claims, have conferred approval on the authorities' practices.

The parental choice provisions in the 1981 Act clearly gave parents rights of school choice for their children. The fact that the right in question is a right to choose should not necessarily be taken to entail support for a 'choice theory' of rights or lead to an acceptance of the assumptions on which choice theories are based, in particular the belief that choice is paramount and that there can only be arbitrary ways of deciding between competing rights claims. This does not follow since an interest theory of rights can easily embrace parents' rights of school choice by including parents' interests in choosing schools for their children among a range of relevant interests which it seeks to protect. In addition to a parent's right to choose, the right of the child to an 'adequate and efficient provision of schooling', the rights of other children and the rights of other parents would all need to be considered. Since rights only become problematic in conditions of scarcity, theories (such as the 'interest theory' of rights), which give some guidance about the appropriate distribution of scarce resources, are to be preferred to other theories (such as the 'choice theory' of rights), which provide no basis for interpersonal comparisons. To subsume parental rights of school choice within an interest theory permits us to see how they should be balanced (and against what) in cases of competition.

Unlike the Scottish legislation, the English legislation specifically provides for parents to give reasons for their preferences (see Chapter 2). In practice, Scottish education authorities have allowed parents to give reasons for their requests, although they have frequently ignored most of them and decided between competing claims in terms of one or more administrative criteria. Parents who have appealed have usually explained their reasons at length, although the decisions of appeal committees and sheriffs have rarely taken these reasons into account. This may well be because they lack a criterion for assessing the merits of parents' claims. In our view, the adoption of a child-centred orientation, which focuses on the interests of the children concerned, would provide such a criterion. Moreover, it would give at least limited recognition to the interest-based right of children to attend schools for which they are particularly suited. When a parent requests a particular school, the authority would have to consider the implications of granting or withholding the request for the child, and would have to balance this request with the requests of other parents and its concern with the well-being of other children. Case-level decision makers would still only be able to refuse requests for one of the reasons set out in the legislation. But, having decided how many pupils could be admitted to an over-subscribed school, they would make more of an effort to examine parents' reasons and children's circumstances in determining, first, which children should be admitted and, secondly, whether an exception should be made to the school's intake limit.

THE RIGHT BALANCE

We cannot conclude that the 1981 Act has achieved the right balance between individual and collective concerns. For education authorities, the shift towards an individual client orientation threatens the achievement of too many of the goals associated with a collective welfare orientation. Although the prospect of appeals has encouraged education authorities to adopt narrow interpretations of the statutory grounds for refusing placing requests, appeal committee decisions have not provided a very effective check on local authorities' implementation of the legislation. The same is true, for different reasons, for sheriffs. Appeal committees and sheriffs have rarely questioned whether the imposition of intake limits could be justified under the Act or, where they can be justified, sought to ensure that parents' concerns are properly balanced against each other and those of the authority.

Our conclusions would not be so negative if the 1981 Act had struck a rather different balance between individual parents and education authorities which, for example, would have enabled the latter to give some measure of protection to under-enrolled schools. But it would also have been less negative if education authorities had, within the limits imposed by the legislation, sought more vigorously to promote collective concerns; if appeal committees and sheriffs had exercised their roles rather differently by acting as a more effective check on local authority decision making and ensuring a better balance between the concerns of individual parents, the interests of individual children and the policies of education authorities; and, finally, if parents had based their choices on a better understanding of educational processes and educational outcomes and been less influenced by social considerations and by anticipating the outcomes of other parents' decisions. However, legislation must be judged by its impact on the real world and, on this criterion, our assessment of the 1981 Act must embrace the actual responses of education authorities, appeal committees, sheriffs and parents. Although it remains to be seen whether the Education Reform Act 1988 produces a better balance in England and Wales, the prospects are not particularly auspicious.

NOTES

1. As far as schools were concerned, the Education Reform Act 1988 introduced a national curriculum; clarified and safe-

guarded the position of religious education; altered the provisions of the 1980 Act to allow parents to enrol their children at any school that had the physical capacity for them; allowed schools to opt out of local authority control and become grant-maintained schools, funded directly by the DES; allowed the Secretary of State to enter into an agreement with 'any person' to establish a city technology college; abolished the Inner London Education Authority (ILEA) and transferred its powers to the thirteen Inner London boroughs; specified that primary and secondary schools with more than 200 pupils should receive a budget from the LEA which they would be free to spend as they wished, and greatly increased the powers of school governors; and defined the occasions when schools could charge parents for 'extras'. Through parallel legislation, many of these provisions will also apply to Scotland. Under the School Boards (Scotland) Act 1988, (Scottish) School Boards will have similar powers to those of (English) School Governors. Moreover, although Scottish Office Ministers initially regarded opting out and city technology colleges as 'inappropriate for Scotland' the provisions of the Self-Governing Schools etc (Scotland) Act 1989 enable Scottish schools to opt out of local authority control and provide for the establishment of technology academies in Scotland.

2. In Burns City, children were refused admission to three primary schools in 1983, to one primary school in 1984 and to three primary schools in 1985. In 1988, children were refused admission to nine primary schools.

3. In Maxton City, intake limits were imposed on one primary school in 1985, on two primary schools in 1986, on three primary schools in 1987 and on five primary schools in 1988.

4. 'Loyalty' is not an option but is, rather, a variable which is introduced to explain why some 'customers' choose one option rather than the other.

5. School F* is perhaps the best example. S1 intakes declined from 158 in 1982 to 109 in 1985 (see Table 6.11). In 1986, they fell again (to 91) but, after the appointment of a new headteacher, they rose to 105 in 1987 and 114 in 1988. The appointment of a new headteacher to School A* likewise stemmed the decline in S1 intakes (which had fallen from 167 in 1982 to 81 in 1985) but, although these increased to 98 (in 1986) and 138 (in 1987), they fell back to 99 in 1988. In other schools, e.g. School I*, S1 intakes continued to fall in spite of the appointment of a new headteacher. The S1 intake for this school was only 33 in 1988.

6. The S1 intake at School C* fell from 383 (in 1986) to 326 (in 1987) and 299 (in 1988).

7. For an account of the two different conceptions of school effectiveness, see Chapter 6, Note 16.

8. The following pieces of research would be particularly useful: a follow-up study of parents designed, *inter alia*, to ascertain whether, with the benefit of hindsight, they think they made the right choice; a follow-up study of pupils which would attempt to compare the educational attainment of placing request pupils with those of pupils who attended their district school and also to assess whether changes in school intakes had any effect on attainment; a study of the relationship between school

popularity and school effectiveness; a study of the ways in which schools respond to gains and, in particular, losses of pupils; and an investigation of the effects of parental choice on the morale of teachers and pupils and the breadth of the curriculum. See also Adler (1986b).

9. Through the inclusion of a question relating to placing requests on the 1988 School-Leavers Survey, the Centre for Educational Sociology at Edinburgh University hopes to be able to provide some answers to these questions.

10. Hirsch (1977) defines this as follows:

By positional competition is meant competition that is fundamentally for a higher place within some explicit or implicit hierarchy and that thereby yields gains for some only by dint of losses for others. Positional competition, in the language of game theory, is a zero-sum game: what winners win, losers lose. The contrast is with competition that improves performance or enjoyment all round, so that winners gain more than losers lose, and all may come out winners – a positive sum game [p.52].

See also Schelling (1978).

BIBLIOGRAPHY

Adler, M. (1986a) 'Review of R. Cranston: Legal Foundations of the Welfare State', *Journal of Law and Society*, Vol.13, No.1, 147–51.

—(1986b) 'Parental Choice in Education: a Position Paper', unpublished paper prepared for the Scottish Education Department.

—and Asquith, S. (1981) 'Discretion and Power' in M. Adler and S. Asquith (eds) *Discretion and Welfare*, London, Heinemann, 9–32.

—and Bondi, L. (1988) 'Delegation and Community Participation: an Alternative Approach to the Problems Created by Falling School Rolls' in L. Bondi and M. Matthews (eds) *Education and Society: Studies in the Politics, Sociology and Geography of Education*, London and New York, Routledge, 52–82.

—Petch, A. and Tweedie, J (1987) 'The Origins and Impact of theParents' Charter' in D. McCrone (ed) *Scottish Government Yearbook 1987*, Edinburgh, Unit for the Study of Government in Scotland, 289–330.

—and Raab, G. (1988) 'Exit, Choice and Loyalty: the Impact of Parental Choice on Admissions to Secondary Schools', *Journal of Education Policy*, Vol.3, No.2, 155–79.

Adler, R. (1985) *Taking Juvenile Justice Seriously*, Edinburgh, Scottish Academic Press.

Alexander, D. (1984) 'Public Sector Housing in Scotland' in D. McCrone (ed) *Scottish Government Yearbook 1985*, Edinburgh, Unit for the Study of Government in Scotland, 152–70.

Arber, S., Dale, A. and Gilbert, G.N. (1986) 'The Limitations of Existing Social Class Classifications for Women' in A. Jacoby (ed) *The Measurement of Social Class*, London, Social Research Association, 48–93.

Argyle, M. (1987) *The Psychology of Happiness*, London, Methuen.

Atherton, G. (1982) *The Book of the School*, Glasgow, Scottish Consumer Council.

—(1987) *The Law of the School: A Parent's Guide to Education Law in Scotland*, Edinburgh, HMSO Books.

Audit Commission (1986) *Towards Better Management of Secondary Education*, London, HMSO.

Baldwin, R. and Hawkins, K (1984) 'Discretionary Justice : Davis Reconsidered', *Public Law*, Winter, 570–99.

—and McCrudden, C. (1987) *Regulation and Public Law*, London, Weidenfeld and Nicholson.

Bankowski, Z. and Nelken, D. (1981) 'Discretion as a Social Problem' in M. Adler and S. Asquith (eds) *Discretion and Welfare*, London, Heinemann, 247–68.

Banting, K. (1979) *Poverty, Politics and Policy*, London, Macmillan.

Bastiani, J. (ed) (1978) *Written Communication between Home and School*, Nottingham, University of Nottingham School of Education.

Beales, A., Blaug, M., Veale, D., West, E. and Boyson, R. (1970) *Education: a Framework for Choice*, London, Institute for Economic Affairs.

Benn, C. and Simon, B. (1972) *Half Way There: Report on the British Comprehensive School Reform*, Harmondsworth, Penguin Books (Second edition).

Birkenshaw, P. (1985) *Grievances, Remedies and the State*, London, Sweet and Maxwell.

Bondi, L. (1989) 'Selecting Schools for Closure: Theory and Practice in 'Rational' Planning'. *Journal of Education Policy*, Vol.4, No. 2, 85–102.

Borgatta, A. and Jackson, D. (1980) *Aggregate Data Analysis: an Interpretation*, London, Sage Publications.

Briault, E. and Smith, R. (1980) *Falling Rolls in Secondary Schools*, Windsor, National Foundation for Educational Research – in two parts.

Buck, T. (1985) 'Schools Admission Appeals', *Journal of Social Welfare Law*, July, 227–51.

Bull, D. (1980a) 'The Anti-Discretion Movement in Britain: Fact or Phantom?' *Journal of Social Welfare Law*, March, 65–83.

—(1980b) 'School Admissions: a New Appeals Procedure', *Journal of Social Welfare Law*, July, 209–33.

—(1985) 'Monitoring Education Appeals: Local Ombudsmen Lead the Way', *Journal of Social Welfare Law*, July, 189–226.

Campbell, T. (1983) *The Left and Rights*, London, Routledge and Kegan Paul.

Central Policy Review Staff (1977) *Population and the Social Services*, London, HMSO.

Centre for Contemporary Cultural Studies (1981) *Unpopular Education: Schooling and Social Democracy in England since 1944*, London, Hutchinson.

Coleman, J.S., Campbell, E.Q., Hobson, C.J., McPartland, J., Mood, A.M., Weinfeld, F. and York, R.L. (1966) *Equality of Educational Opportunity*, Washington DC., US Government Printing Office.

Conservative Party (1974) *Election Manifesto*, London.

—(1979) *Election Manifesto*, London.

Coons, J. and Sugarman, S. (1978) *Education by Choice: The Case for Family Control*, Berkeley, University of California Press.

Cox, C.B. and Dyson, A.E. (eds) (1971) *The Black Papers on Education*, London, Davis-Poynter.

Cox, C. and Marks, J. (1980) *Real Concern*, London, Centre for Policy Studies.

Cranston, R. (1985) *Legal Foundations of the Welfare State*, London, Weidenfeld and Nicholson.

Crompton, P. (1982) 'The Lothian Affair: a Battle of Principles' in D. McCrone (ed) *Scottish Government Yearbook 1983*, Edinburgh, Unit for the Study of Government in Scotland, 33–48.

Davis, K.C. (1971) *Discretionary Justice: A Preliminary Enquiry*, Urbana, University of Illinois Press.

Dennison, W.F. (1983) *Doing Better for Fewer: Education and Falling Rolls*, York, Longman (for the Schools Council).

—(1985) *Managing the Contracting School*, London, Heinemann.

Department of Education and Science (1967) *Children and their Primary Schools: a Report of the Central Advisory Council for Education*, London, HMSO (the Plowden Report).

—(1976) 'Admission of Children to Schools of their Parents' Choice', *Draft Circular*, London.

—(1977a) 'Falling Rolls and School Closures', *Circular 5/77*, London.

—(1977b) 'Admission of Children to Schools of their Parents' Choice', *Consultation Paper*, London.

Dixon, W.J. (ed) (1983) *BMDP Statistical Software*, Berkeley, University of California Press.

Donnison, D. (1982) *The Politics of Poverty*, Oxford, Martin Robertson.

Elliott, J., Bridges, D., Ebbutt, D., Gibson, R., and Nias, J. (1981a) *Case Studies in School Accountability*, Vols.1–3, Cambridge, Institute of Education.

—(1981b) *School Accountability: the SSRC School Accountability Project*, London, Grant McIntyre.

Farmer, J. (1974) *Tribunals and Government*, London, Weidenfeld and Nicholson.

Fletcher, A. and MacKay, J. (1978) *Scottish Education: Regaining a Lost Reputation*, Edinburgh, Scottish Conservative Party.

Flowerdew, R. and Aitken, M. (1982) 'A Method of Fitting the Gravity Model based on the Poisson Distribution', *Journal of Regional Science*, Vol.22, No.2, 191–202.

Forrest, R. and Murie, A. (1985) *An Unreasonable Act? Central-Local Government Conflict and the Housing Act 1986*, Bristol, University of Bristol School for Advanced Urban Studies (SAUS Study No.1).

Foster, P. (1983) *Access to Welfare: an Introduction to Welfare Rationing*, London and Basingstoke, Macmillan.

Fox, A. (1974) *Beyond Contract: Work, Power and Trust Relations*, London, Faber.

Friedman, M. (1962) *Capitalism and Freedom*, Chicago, University of Chicago Press.

Fuller, L. (1978) 'The Forms and Limits of Adjudication', *Harvard Law Review*, Vol.92, No.2, 353–409.

Galanter, M (1975) 'Why the 'Haves' Come Out Ahead: Speculations on the Limits of Legal Change', *Law and Society Review*, Vol.9, 95–160.

Galligan, D. (1986) *Discretionary Powers: a Legal Study of Official Discretion*, Oxford, Clarendon Press.

Garner, C. (1988) 'Educational Attainment in Glasgow: the Role of Neighbourhood Deprivation' in L. Bondi and M. Matthews (eds) *Education and Society: Studies in the Politics, Sociology and Geography of Education*, London and New York, Routledge, 226–56.

Glennerster, H. (1975) *Social Service Budgets and Social Policy*, London, Allen and Unwin.

—(1985) *Paying for Welfare*, Oxford, Basil Blackwell.

Goodin, R. (1986) 'Welfare, Rights and Discretion', *Oxford Journal of Legal Studies*, Vol.6, No.3, 232–61.

Gray, J., McPherson, A. and Raffe, D. (1983) *Reconstructions of Secondary Education: Theory, Myth and Practice since the War*, London, Routledge and Kegan Paul.

Halsey, A.H. (1972) *Educational Priority, Vol.1: EPA Problems and Policies*, London, HMSO.

Ham, C. and Hill, M. (1984) *The Policy Process in the Modern Capitalist State*, Brighton, Wheatsheaf.

Handler, J. (1978) *Social Movements and the Legal System*, New York, Academic Press.

—(1979) *Protecting the Social Service Client*, New York, Academic Press.

Hannon, V. (1983) 'Education : Some Forms of Legal Redress Outside the Courts', *British Journal of Educational Studies*, Vol.XXXI, No.3, 211–28.

Hargreaves, D. (1982) *The Challenge for the Comprehensive School*, London, Routledge and Kegan Paul.

Harlow, C. and Rawlings, R. (1984) *Law and Administration*, London, Weidenfeld and Nicholson.

Heald, D.A., Jones, C.A. and Lamont, D.W. (1981) 'The Conflict between the Scottish Office and Local Authorities over Local Government Expenditure' in H.M. Drucker and N. Drucker (eds) *Scottish Government Yearbook 1982*, Edinburgh, Paul Harris, 12–56.

Hewton, E. (1986) *Education in Recession: Crisis in County Hall and Classroom*, London, Allen and Unwin.

Hill, M. (1969) 'The Exercise of Discretion in the National Assistance Board', *Public Administration*, Vol.47, Spring, 75–90.

—(1972) *The Sociology of Public Administration*, London, Weidenfeld and Nicholson.

—(1976) *The State, Administration and the Individual*, Glasgow, Fontana/Collins.

—and Bramley, G. (1986) *Analysing Social Policy*, Oxford, Basil Blackwell.

Himsworth, C. (1980) 'School Attendance Orders and the Sheriff', *Journal of the Law Society of Scotland*, 25, November, 450–55.

—(1984) 'Scottish Local Authorities and the Sheriff', *Juridical Review*, June, 63–86.

Hirsch, F. (1977) *Social Limits to Growth*, London and Henley, Routledge and Kegan Paul.

Hirschman, A. (1970) *Exit, Voice and Loyalty: Responses to Decline in Firms, Organisations and States*, Cambridge, Harvard University Press.

Hohfeld, W. (1919) *Fundamental Legal Conceptions as Applied in Judicial Reasoning*, New Haven, Yale University Press.

Hoinville, G., Jowell, R. and Associates (1978) *Social Research Practice*, London, Heinemann.

Horowitz, D. (1977) *The Courts and Social Policy*, Washington DC., Brookings Institution.

Howe, L. (1985) 'The 'Deserving' and 'Undeserving' in an Urban Local Social Security Office', *Journal of Social Policy*, Vol.14, No.1, 49–72.

Jacoby, A. (ed) (1986) *The Measurement of Social Class*, London, Social Research Association.

Johnson, D. (1987) *Private Schools and State Schools*, Milton Keynes, Open University Press.

—and Ransom, E. (1983) *Family and School*, London, Croom Helm.

Jowell, J. (1973) 'The Legal Control of Administrative Discretion', *Public Law*, Autumn, 178–220.

Keating, M. and Midwinter, A. (1983) *The Government of Scotland*, Edinburgh, Mainstream.

Kellas, J. (1984) *The Scottish Political System*, Cambridge, Cambridge University Press (Third edition).

Kogan, M. (1978) *The Politics of Educational Change*, Glasgow, Fontana/Collins.

—(1986) *Education Accountability: an Analytic Overview*, London, Hutchinson.

Lewis, N. and Birkenshaw, P. (1979a) 'Taking Complaints Seriously: a Study in Local Government Practice' in M. Partington and J. Jowell (eds) *Welfare Law and Policy*, London, Frances Pinter, 130–53.

—(1979b) 'Local Authorities and the Resolution of Grievances – Some Second Thoughts', *Local Government Studies*, Vol.5, January, 7–21.

Lipsky, M. (1980) *Street-Level Bureaucracy: Dilemmas of the Individual in Public Services*, New York, Russell Sage.

McAuslan, P. (1983) 'Administrative Law, Collective Consumption and Judicial Policy', *Modern Law Review*, Vol.46, No.1, 1–20.

Macbeth, A., Strachan, D. and Macaulay, C. (1986) *Parental Choice of School* Glasgow, University of Glasgow Department of Education (unpublished report).

MacCormick, D.N. (1977) 'Rights in Legislation' in P. Hacker and J. Raz (eds) *Law, Morality and Society*, Oxford, Oxford University Press.

McCullagh, P. and Nelder, J. (1983) *Generalised Linear Models*, London, Chapman and Hall.

McFadyen, I. and McMillan, F. (1984) *The Management of Change at a Time of Falling School Rolls*, Edinburgh, Scottish Council for Research in Education.

McPherson, A. and Neave, G. (1976) *The Scottish Sixth: A Sociological Study of Sixth Year Studies and the Changing Relationship between School and University in Scotland*, Slough, National Foundation for Educational Research.

—and Raab, C. (1988) *Governing Education: a Sociology of Policy since 1945*, Edinburgh, Edinburgh University Press.

—and Willms, J.D. (1986) 'Certification, Class Conflict, Religion and Community: a Socio-Historical Explanation of the Effectiveness of Contemporary Schools' in A.C. Kerckhoff (ed) *Research in Sociology of Education and Socialisation*, Vol.6, Greenwich, Connecticut, JAI Press, 227–302.

—(1987) 'Equalisation and Improvement: Some Effects of Comprehensive Reorganisation in Scotland', *Sociology*, Vol.21, No.4, 509–39.

Marshall, T.H. (1963) 'Citizenship and Social Class' in *Sociology at the Crossroads and Other Essays*, London, Heinemann, 67–127.

Mashaw, J. (1983) *Bureaucratic Justice*, New Haven and London, Yale University Press.

Maynard, A. (1975) *Experiment with Choice in Education*, London, Institute of Economic Affairs.

Meredith, P. (1981) 'Executive Discretion and Choice of Secondary School', *Public Law*, Spring, 52–82.

—(1984) 'Falling School Rolls and Reorganisation of Schools', *Journal of Social Welfare Law*, July, 208–21.

Middleton, N. and Weitzman, S. (1977) *A Place for Everyone*, London, Gollancz.

Midwinter, E. (1980) *Education Choice Thoughts*, London, Advisory Centre for Education.

Ministry of Education (1950) 'Choice of Schools', *Manual of Guidance, (Schools No.1)*, London (August).

Nonet, P. (1969) *Administrative Justice*, New York, Russell Sage.

Parker, R. (1967) 'Social Administration and Scarcity: the Problem of Rationing', *Social Work*, Vol.XXIV, No.2, 9–14.

Parry, R. (1987) 'The Centralisation of the Scottish Office' in R. Rose (ed) *Ministers and Ministries: a Functional Analysis*, Oxford, Clarendon Press, 97–141.

Passmore, B. (1983) 'Long Hot Summer of Parental Discontent', *Times Educational Supplement*, 19 August.

Petch, A. (1986a) 'Parental Choice at Entry to Primary School', *Research Papers in Education*, Vol.1, No.1, 26–47.

—(1986b) 'Parents' Reasons for Choosing Secondary Schools' in A. Stillman (ed) *The Balancing Act of 1980: Parents, Politics and Education*, Slough, National Foundation for Educational Research, 28–35.

—(1987) 'Early to School: Under-age Admissions in Scotland', *The Scottish Child*, Vol.1, No.1, 11–13.

—(1988) 'Rezoning: an Exercise in Compromise' in L. Bondi and M. Matthews (eds) *Education and Society: Studies in the Politics, Sociology and Geography of Education*, London and New York, Routledge, 83–112.

Piven, F.F. and Cloward, R. (1972) *Regulating the Poor: the Functions of Public Welfare*, London, Tavistock.

Plant, R. (1988) *Citizenship, Rights and Socialism*, London, Fabian Society (Fabian Tract No.531).

Plewis, I., Gray, J., Fogelman, K., Mortimore, P. and Byford, D. (1981) *Publishing School Examination Results: a Discussion*, London, University of London Institute of Education (Bedford Way Papers No.5).

Prosser, T. (1977) 'Poverty, Ideology and Legality: Supplementary Benefit Appeal Tribunals and their Predecessors', *British Journal of Law and Society*, Vol.4, No.1, 39–60.

—(1981) 'The Politics of Discretion: Aspects of Discretionary Power in the Supplementary Benefits Scheme' in M. Adler and S Asquith (eds) *Discretion and Welfare*, London, Heinemann, 148–70.

—(1983) *Test Cases for the Poor: Legal Techniques in the Politics of Social Welfare*, London, Child Poverty Action Group (Poverty Pamphlet No.60).

Raab, G. and Adler, M. (1987) 'A Tale of Two Cities: the Impact of Parental Choice on Admission to Primary Schools', *Research Papers in Education*, Vol.2, No.3, 157–76; reprinted in L. Bondi and M. Matthews (eds) *Education and Society:*

Studies in the Politics, Sociology and Geography of Education, London and New York, Routledge, 113–47.

Reich, C. (1963) 'Midnight Welfare Searches and the Social Security Act', *Yale Law Journal*, Vol.72, No.7, 1347–60.

—(1964) 'The New Property', *Yale Law Journal*, Vol.73, No.5, 733–87.

—(1965) 'Individual Rights and Social Welfare: the Emerging Legal Issues', *Yale Law Journal*, Vol.74, No.7, 1245–57.

—(1966) 'The Law of the Planned Society', *Yale Law Journal*, Vol.75, 1227–70.

Ribbins, P.M. and Brown, R.J. (1979) 'Policy Making in English Local Government: the Case of Secondary School Reorganisation', *Public Administration*, Vol.57, No.2, 187–202.

Rutter, M., Maugham, B., Mortimore, P. and Ouston, J. (1979) *Fifteen Thousand Hours: Secondary Schools and their Effects on Children*, London, Open Books.

Saran, R. (1973) *Policy-Making in Secondary Education: a Case Study*, Oxford, Oxford University Press.

SASPAC (1983) *User Manual (Release 3.0)*, London, Local Authorities Management Services and Computer Committee.

Scheingold, S. (1974) *The Politics of Rights*, New Haven, Yale University Press.

Schelling, T. (1978) *Micromotives and Macrobehavior*, New York, Norton.

Scottish Conservative Party (1978) *Onward to Victory: a Statement of the Conservative Approach for Scotland*, Edinburgh.

—(1979) *Election Manifesto*, Edinburgh.

Scottish Consumer Council (1980) *A Charter for Parents: The SCC's Reply to the Government's Proposals*, Glasgow.

—(1981) *Education (Scotland) (No.2) Bill: Comments and Amendments prepared by the Scottish Consumer Council*, Glasgow.

Scottish Education Department (1980) 'Admission to School – A Charter for Parents', *Consultative Paper*, Edinburgh.

—(1981) 'Placing Requests, Information for Parents on Placing Requests, and Appeals', *Circular No.1074*, Edinburgh.

—(1984) 'Placing Requests: Under Age Children', *Circular No.1108*, Edinburgh.

—(1985) 'Placing Requests in Education Authority Schools', *Statistical Bulletin*, No.2/B6/1985, Edinburgh.

—(1986) 'Placing Requests in Education Authority Schools', *Statistical Bulletin*, No.5/B6/1986, Edinburgh.

—(1987a) 'Placing Requests in Education Authority Schools', *Statistical Bulletin*, No.9/B2/1987, Edinburgh.

—(1987b) 'Placing Requests in Education Authority Schools', *Statistical Bulletin*, No.9/B6/1987, Edinburgh.

Semple, W.D.C. (1980) 'Parental Choice: Administrative Problems' in *Choice, Compulsion and Cost*, Edinburgh, HMSO (Scottish Education Department Occasional Papers).

Sexton, S. (1975) 'Evolution by Choice' in C.B. Cox and A.E. Dyson (eds) *Black Papers: A Fight for Education*, London, Dent.

Simon, H.A. (1957) 'Bandwagon and Underdog Effects of Election Predictions' in *Models of Man*, New York, John Wiley, 79–88.

—(1965) *Administrative Behaviour*, New York, The Free Press.

Simon, W.H. (1983) 'Legality, Bureaucracy and Class in the Welfare System', *Yale Law Journal*, Vol.92, No.7, 1198–269.

—(1985) 'The Invention and Reinvention of Welfare Rights', *Maryland Law Review*, Vol.44, No.1, 1–44.

Smith, G. and May, D. (1980) 'The Artificial Debate between Rationalist and Incrementalist Models of Decision Making', *Policy and Politics*, Vol.8, No.2, 147–61.

Sosin, M (1986) 'Legal Rights and Welfare Change: 1960-1980' in S Danziger and D

Weinberg (eds) *Fighting Poverty: What Works and What Doesn't*, Cambridge, Harvard University Press, 260–86.

Stillman, A. and Maychell, K. (1986) *Choosing Schools: Parents, LEAS and the 1980 Education Act*, Windsor, NFER-Nelson.

St John-Stevas, N. (1977) *Better Schools for All*, London, Conservative Party.

Stone, J. and Taylor, F. (1977) 'Transfer to Secondary School – LEA Arrangements and the Information they give to Parents', *Where?*, No.131, September, 220–5.

Street, H. (1975) *Justice in the Welfare State*, London, Stevens and Stevens.

Titmuss, R. (1971) 'Welfare 'Rights' Law and Discretion', *Political Quarterly*, Vol.42, No.1, 113–32.

Tweedie, J. (1986a) 'Parental Choice of School: Legislating the Balance' in A. Stillman (ed) *The Balancing Act of 1980: Parents, Politics and Education*, Slough, National Foundation for Educational Research, 3–11.

—(1986b) 'Rights in Social Programmes: the Case of Parental Choice of School', *Public Law*, Autumn, 407–36.

—(1989a) 'Discretion to Use Rules: Individual Interests and Collective Welfare in School Admissions', *Law and Policy*, Vol.11 (forthcoming).

—(1989b) 'The Dilemma of Clients' Rights in Social Programs', *Law and Society Review*, Vol. 23 (forthcoming).

—and Adler, M. (1986) 'Parental Choice: Liberty or Licence?' *Journal of the Law Society of Scotland*, Vol.31, August, 305–10.

—Adler, M. and Petch, A. (1986) 'The Rights and Wrongs of Education Appeal Committees', unpublished paper prepared for the Scottish Education Department.

Walker, A. (1984) *Social Planning*, Oxford, Basil Blackwell/Martin Robertson.

Weale, A. (1983) *Political Theory and Social Policy*, London, Macmillan.

Welfare Rights Working Party (1975) *Which Way Welfare Rights?* London, Child Poverty Action Group.

Wellman, C. (1980) *Welfare Rights*, Totowa, N.J., Rowman and Littlefield.

West, E. (1970) *Education and the State*, London, Institute of Economic Affairs.

Whiteley, P. and Winyard, S. (1988) *Pressure for the Poor*, London, Methuen.

Wilbey, P and Crequer, N (1988) 'A Gothic Monstrosity of Law', *The Independent*, 28 July, 19.

Wilding, P. (1982) *Professional Power and Social Welfare*, London, Routledge and Kegan Paul.

Willms, J.D. (1986) 'Social Class Segregation and its Relationship to Pupils' Examination Results in Scotland', *American Sociological Review*, Vol.51, No.2, 224–41.

Wise, M. (1985) 'Sheriff Court Decisions under the Parents' Charter', *Journal of the Law Society of Scotland*, Vol.30, November, 439–42.

Woods, P. (1984) *Parents and School*, Cardiff, Welsh Consumer Council and Schools Council Committee for Wales.

Wyn-Thomas, B. (1985) 'Parents' Views on the Necessary Information' in A. Stillman (ed) *The Balancing Act of 1980: Parents, Politics and Education*, Slough, National Foundation for Educational Research, 23–7.

CASES CITED

Mrs A B or K v *Strathclyde Regional Council* (16 August 1982, unreported) Glasgow Sheriff Court

Black v *Strathclyde Regional Council* (27 August 1982, unreported) Kilmarnock Sheriff Court

APPENDIX A

Education Act 1980
1980 Chapter 20

Admission to schools

6.—(1) Every local education authority shall make arrangements for enabling the parent of a child in the area of the authority to express a preference as to the school at which he wishes education to be provided for his child in the exercise of the authority's functions and to give reasons for his preference.

(2) Subject to subsection (3) below, it shall be the duty of a local education authority and of the governors of a county or voluntary school to comply with any preference expressed in accordance with the arrangements.

(3) The duty imposed by subsection (2) above does not apply—

(*a*) if compliance with the preference would prejudice the provision of efficient education or the efficient use of resources;

(*b*) if the preferred school is an aided or special agreement school and compliance with the preference would be incompatible with any arrangements between the governors and the local education authority in respect of the admission of pupils to the school; or

(*c*) if the arrangements for admission to the preferred school are based wholly or partly on selection by reference to ability or aptitude and compliance with the preference would be incompatible with selection under the arrangements.

(4) Where the arrangements for the admission of pupils to a school maintained by a local education authority provide for applications for admission to be made to, or to a person acting on behalf of, the governors of the school, a parent who makes such an application shall be regarded for the purposes of subsection (2) above as having expressed a preference for that school in accordance with arrangements made under subsection (1) above.

(5) The duty imposed by subsection (2) above in relation to a preference expressed in accordance with arrangements made under subsection (1) above shall apply also in relation to—

(*a*) any application for the admission to a school maintained by a local education authority of a child who is not in the area of the authority; and

(*b*) any application made as mentioned in section 10(3) or 11(1) below;

and references in subsection (3) above to a preference and a preferred school shall be construed accordingly.

7.—(1) Every local education authority shall make arrangements for enabling the parent of a child to appeal against—

(*a*) any decision made by or on behalf of the authority as to the school at which education is to be provided for the child in the exercise of the authority's functions; and

(*b*) any decision made by or on behalf of the governors of a county or controlled school maintained by the authority refusing the child admission to such a school.

(2) The governors of every aided or special agreement school shall make arrangements for enabling the parent of a child to appeal against any decision made by or on behalf of the governors refusing the child admission to the school.

(3) Joint arrangements may to made under subsection (2) above by the governors of two or more aided or special agreement schools maintained by the same local education authority.

(4) Any appeal by virtue of this section shall be to an appeal committee constituted in accordance with Part I of Schedule 2 to this Act; and Part II of that Schedule shall have effect in relation to the procedure on any such appeal.

(5) The decision of an appeal committee on any such appeal shall be binding on the local education authority or governors by or on whose behalf the decision under appeal was made and, in the case of a decision made by or on behalf of a local education authority, on the governors of any county or controlled school at which the committee determines that a place should be offered to the child in question.

(6) In paragraph 6 of Schedule 1 to the Tribunals and Inquiries Act 1971 (tribunals under direct supervision of the Council on Tribunals) after "6", there shall be inserted "(*a*)" and at the end there shall be inserted—

"(*b*) appeal committees constituted in accordance with Part I of Schedule 2 to the Education Act 1980 (c. 20).",

and in section 13(1) of that Act for "6" there shall be substituted "6(*a*)".

(7) In section 25 of the Local Government Act 1974 (authorities subject to investigation by Local Commissioner) after subsection (4) there shall be inserted—

"(5) Any reference to an authority to which this Part of this Act applies also includes a reference to any appeal committee constituted in accordance with paragraph 1 of Schedule 2 to the Education Act 1980."

Information as to schools and admission arrangements.

8.—(1) Every local education authority shall, for each school year, publish particulars of—

(*a*) the arrangements for the admission of pupils to schools maintained by the authority, other than aided or special agreement schools;

(*b*) the authority's arrangements for the provision of education at schools maintained by another local education authority or not maintained by a local education authority; and

(*c*) the arrangements made by the authority under sections 6(1) and 7(1) above.

(2) The governors of every aided or special agreement school shall, for each school year, publish particulars of—

(*a*) the arrangements for the admission of pupils to the school; and

(*b*) the arrangements made by them under section 7(2) above.

(3) The particulars to be published under subsections (1)(*a*) and (2)(*a*) above shall include particulars of—

(*a*) the number of pupils that it is intended to admit in each school year to each school to which the arrangements relate, being pupils in the age group in which pupils are normally admitted or, if there is more than one such group, in each such group;

(*b*) the respective admission functions of the local education authority and the governors;

(*c*) the policy followed in deciding admissions;

(*d*) the arrangements made in respect of pupils not belonging to the area of the local education authority.

(4) The particulars to be published under subsection (1)(*b*) above shall include particulars of—

(*a*) the criteria for offering places at schools not maintained by a local education authority;

(*b*) the names of, and number of places at, any such schools in respect of which the authority have standing arrangements.

(5) Every local education authority shall, as respects each school maintained by them other than an aided or special agreement school, and the governors of every aided or special agreement school shall, as respects that school, publish—

(*a*) such information as may be required by regulations made by the Secretary of State; and

(*b*) such other information, if any, as the authority or governors think fit,

and every local education authority shall also publish such information as may be so required with respect to their policy and arrangements in respect of any matter relating to primary or secondary education in their area.

(6) The local education authority by whom an aided or special agreement school is maintained may, with the agreement of the governors of the school, publish on their behalf the particulars or information relating to the school referred to in subsection (2) or (5) above.

(7) References in this section to publication are references to publication at such time or times and in such manner as may be required by regulations made by the Secretary of State.

Nursery
schools and
special schools.

9.—(1) None of the provisions of sections 6, 7 and 8 above have effect in relation to nursery schools or to children who will not have attained the age of five years at the time of their proposed admission except that where the arrangements for the admission of pupils to a school maintained by a local education authority provide for the admission of children who will attain that age within six months after their admission those sections shall have effect in relation to the admission of such pupils to that school.

(2) None of the provisions of those sections other than sub-sections (5) and (7) of section 8 have effect in relation to special schools or children in need of special educational treatment.

SCHEDULE 2
School Admission Appeals
Part I
Constitution of Appeal Committees

1.—(1) An appeal pursuant to arrangements made by a local education authority under section 7(1) of this Act shall be to an appeal committee constituted in accordance with this paragraph.

(2) An appeal committee shall consist of three, five or seven members nominated by the authority from among persons appointed by the authority under this paragraph; and sufficient persons may be appointed to enable two or more appeal committees to sit at the same time.

(3) The persons appointed shall comprise—

(a) members of the authority or of any education committee of the authority; and

(b) persons who are not members of the authority or of any education committee of the authority but who have experience in education, are acquainted with the educational conditions in the area of the authority or are parents of registered pupils at a school;

but shall not include any person employed by the authority otherwise than as a teacher.

(4) The members of an appeal committee who are members of the authority or of any education committee of the authority shall not outnumber the others by more than one.

(5) A person who is a member of an education committee of the authority shall not be chairman of an appeal committee.

(6) A person shall not be a member of an appeal committee for the consideration of any appeal against a decision if he was among those who made the decision or took part in discussions as to whether the decision should be made.

(7) A person who is a teacher at a school shall not be a member of an appeal committee for the consideration of an appeal involving a question whether a child is to be admitted to that school.

2.—(1) An appeal pursuant to arrangements made by the governors of an aided or special agreement school under section 7(2) of this Act shall be to an appeal committee constituted in accordance with this paragraph.

(2) An appeal committee shall consist of three, five or seven

members nominated by the governors from among persons appointed by them under this paragraph; and sufficient persons may be appointed to enable two or more appeal committees to sit at the same time.

(3) The persons appointed—

    (a) may include one or more of the governors;

    (b) shall include persons appointed from a list drawn up by the local education authority by whom the school is maintained: and

    (c) shall not include any person employed by the authority otherwise than as a teacher.

(4) Half the members of an appeal committee (excluding the chairman) shall be nominated from among such persons as are mentioned in sub-paragraph (3)(b) above.

(5) None of the governors shall be chairman of an appeal committee.

(6) A person shall not be a member of an appeal committee for the econsideration of any appeal against a decision if he was among those who made the decision or took part in discussions as to whether the decision should be made.

(7) A person who is a teacher at a school shall not be a member of an appeal committee for the consideration of an appeal involving a question whether a child is to be admitted to that school.

3. An appeal pursuant to joint arrangements made by virtue of section 7(3) of this Act by the governors of two or more schools shall be to an appeal committee constituted as provided in paragraph 2 above, taking references to the governors as references to the governors of both or all the schools.

4. An appeal committee constituted in accordance with paragraph 2 or 3 above shall be included in the bodies to which sections 173(4) and 174 of the Local Government Act 1972 (allowances) apply.

Part II
procedure

5. An appeal shall be by notice in writing setting out the grounds on which it is made.

6. An appeal committee shall afford the appellant an opportunity of appearing and making oral representations and may allow the appellant to be accompanied by a friend or to be represented.

7. The matters to be taken into account by an appeal committee in considering an appeal shall include—

    (a) any preference expressed by the appellant in respect of the child as mentioned in section 6 of this Act; and

    (b) the arrangements for the admission of pupils published by the local education authority or the governors under section 8 of this Act.

8. In the event of disagreement between the members of an appeal committee the appeal under consideration shall be decided by a simple majority of the votes cast and in the case of an equality of votes the chairman of the committee shall have a second or casting vote.

9. The decision of an appeal committee and the grounds on which it is made shall be communicated by the committee in writing to—

 (a) the appellant and the local education authority; and

 (b) in the case of an appeal to an appeal committee constituted in accordance with paragraph 2 or 3 above, to the governors by or on whose behalf the decision appealed against was made.

10. Appeals pursuant to arrangements made under section 7 of this Act shall be heard in private except when otherwise directed by the authority or governors by whom the arrangements are made but, without prejudice to paragraph 6 above, a member of the local education authority may attend as an observer any hearing of an appeal by an appeal committee constituted in accordance with paragraph 1 above and a member of the Council on Tribunals may attend as an observer any meeting of any appeal committee at which an appeal is considered.

11. Subject to paragraphs 5 to 10 above, all matters relating to the procedure on appeals pursuant to arrangements made under section 7 of this Act, including the time within which they are to be brought, shall be determined by the authority or governors by whom the arrangements are made; and neither section 106 of the Local Government Act 1972 nor paragraph 44 of Schedule 12 to that Act (procedure of committees of local authorities) shall apply to an appeal committee constituted in accordance with paragraph 1 above.

APPENDIX B

Education (Scotland) Act 1981
Chapter 58

Placing in schools

1.—(1) After section 28 of the Education (Scotland) Act 1980 (in this Act referred to as "the principal Act") there shall be inserted the following sections—

"Duty to comply with parents' requests as to schools

28A.—(1) Where the parent of a child makes a written request to an education authority to place his child in the school specified in the request, being a school under their management, it shall be the duty of the authority, subject to subsections (2) and (3) below, to place the child accordingly.

Such a request so made is referred to this Act as a "placing request" and the school specified in it is referred to in the Act as the "specified school".

(2) Where a placing request relates to two or more schools under the management of the education authority to whom it was made, the duty imposed by subsection (1) above shall apply in relation to the first mentioned such school, which shall be treated for the purposes of this Act as the specified school.

(3) The duty imposed by subsection (1) above does not apply—

(*a*) if placing the child in the specified school would—

(i) make it necessary for the authority to take an additional teacher into employment;

(ii) give rise to significant expenditure on extending or otherwise altering the accommodation at or facilities provided in connection with the school;

(iii) be seriously detrimental to the continuity of the child's education; or

(iv) be likely to be seriously detrimental to order and discipline in the school or the educational well-being of the pupils there;

(*b*) if the education normally provided at the specified school is not suited to the age, ability or aptitude of the child;

(*c*) if the education authority have already required the child to discontinue his attendance at the specified school;

(*d*) if, where the specified school is a special school, the child does not have special educational needs requiring the education or special facilities normally provided at the school; or

(*e*) if the specified school is a single sex school (within the meaning given to that expression by section 26 of the Sex Discrimination Act 1975) and the child is not of the sex admitted or taken (under that section) to be admitted to the school,

but an education authority may place a child in the specified school notwithstanding paragraphs (*a*) to (*e*) above.

(4) An education authority shall inform a parent in writing of their decision on his placing request and, where they decide to refuse it, shall give him written reasons for their decision and inform him of his right to refer it under section 28C of this act to an appeal committee.

(5) The Secretary of State may, by regulations, make provision for deeming an education authority to have refused a placing request in the event of their not having informed the parent in writing of their decision on it in accordance with subsection (4) above within such period or before such date as may be prescribed in the regulations and different periods or dates may be so prescribed for different purposes.

Information as to placing in schools and other matters.

28B.—(1) Every education authority shall—

(a) publish or otherwise make available information as to—
(i) their arrangements for the placing of children in schools under their management;
(ii) such matters as may be prescribed by regulations;
(iii) such other matters as the authority consider necessary or expedient for the purposes of their functions under this Act;

(b) where a child falls, in accordance with those arrangements, to be placed in a school under their management—
(i) in a case where the authority propose to place the child in a particular school, inform his parent of the school; and
(ii) in every case, subject to subsection (4) below, inform the parent of the general effect of section 28A (1) and (2) of this Act and of his right to make a placing request;

(c) in making arrangements for the performance of their functions under this Act, formulate guidelines to be followed by them as respects placing in schools generally or, if they think it necessary, in any particular school in the event of there being more placing requests made in respect of certain schools or, as the case may be, that school or in respect of any stage or stages of school education provided there than there are places available;

(d) on a request to that effect made to them at any time by a parent of a child, supply the parent with any prescribed or determined information about any school under their management.

In paragraph (d) above, "prescribed or determined information" means information prescribed or determined under subsection (3)(c) below.

(2) An education authority shall, in performing the duties imposed on them by subsection (1) above, comply with any regulations made under subsection (3) below.

(3) The Secretary of State may by regulations prescribe or make provision for the determining of—

(a) the procedure in accordance with which education authorities are to perform the duties imposed on them by subsection (1) above and when they are to do so;

(b) how education authorities are to go about publishing or otherwise making available information under subsection (1) above or informing parents under that subsection;

(c) the kind of information which is to be so published or which is to comprise the information so made available or supplied to parents.

(4) The duty imposed by subsection (1)(b)(ii) above arises only when the existence of the child and the fact that he fails to be placed in a school under their management are known to the education authority.

Reference to appeal committee of refusal of placing request.

28C.—(1) Subject to subsections (2) and (3) below, a parent who has made a placing request may refer a decision of the education authority refusing his request to an appeal committee set up under section 28D of this Act.

(2) Subsection (1) above does not apply to a decision of an education authority in respect of the placing of a child in a nursery school or nursery class.

(3) Where a reference under this section has been made in respect of a child, no further such reference in respect of the child shall be competent during the period of 12 months beginning with the day on which the immediately preceding such reference was lodged.

(4) A reference under this section shall be lodged with the appeal committee within 28 days of the receipt by the parent of the decision of the education authority (which, if posted, shall, unless the contrary is proved, be presumed to have been received on the day after the date on which it was posted except that a decision posted on a Friday or Saturday shall, unless the contrary is proved, be presumed to have been received on the Monday next following), but the committee shall, on good cause being shown, have power to hear such a reference notwithstanding that it was not lodged within that time.

Appeal committees.

(1)28D.— Every education authority shall—

(a) set up and maintain such number of appeal committees; and

(b) make such other arrangements

as are necessary to enable references to be made under sections 28C, 28E(6), 28F(7), 28H and 63 of this Act and heard by the committees.

(2) An appeal committee set up under subsection (1) above shall be constituted in accordance with Schedule A1 to this Act.

(3) The Secretary of State may by regulations make provision for procedure in relation to references under section 28C of this Act and regulations made under this subsection may include provision—

(a) requiring the education authority to make information relevant to their decision available to the committee and to the parent referring that decision to the committee;

(b) deeming, for the purposes of this Act, an appeal committee to have confirmed the decision of an education authority on a placing request in the event of the committee's not having complied with section 28E(3) of this

Act within such period or before such date as may be prescribed in the regulations and different periods or dates may be so prescribed for different purposes;

(c) ancillary to or consequential upon provision made under paragraphs (a) and (b) above.

Appeal committees: supplementary provisions.

28E.—(1) An appeal committee may, on a reference under section 28C of this Act, confirm the education authority's decision if they are satisfied—

(a) that one or more of the grounds of refusal specified in section 28A(3) of this Act exists or exist; and

(b) that, in all the circumstances, it is appropriate to do so

but otherwise shall refuse to confirm the authority's decision and shall, where they so refuse, require the education authority to place the child to whom the reference relates in the specified school.

(2) Where, in considering a reference under section 28C of this Act of a decision to refuse a placing request where the specified school is a special school, an appeal committee refuse to confirm the decision, they shall have power, if the education authority have decided not to record the child to whom the reference relates, to require the education authority to reconsider their decision not to record him.

(3) An appeal committee shall notify their decision under this section and the reasons for it in writing to the parent who made the reference and to the education authority and, where they confirm the authority's decision, they shall inform the parent of his right of appeal to the sheriff under section 28F of this Act.

(4) Where, on a reference under section 28C of this Act, an appeal committee refuse to confirm an education authority's decision, the authority shall give effect to the placing request to which the reference relates.

(5) Where a decision of an appeal committee under this section is inconsistent with any decision of the education authority refusing a placing request to place another child at the same time and at the same stage of education and in the same school as that at and in which the child to whom the appeal committee's decision relates is to be placed, the education authority shall review their decision so to refuse and shall inform the parent of the other child in writing of their decision upon that review and the reasons for it.

(6) The decision of an education authority upon a review under subsection (5) above not to reverse their decision to refuse the placing request in respect of the other child may be referred to an appeal committee by the parent of the other child as if the decision upon the review were a decision refusing his placing request and the provisions of this Act relating to references of decisions upon placing requests and appeals therefrom (including those relating to appeal committees) shall apply accordingly.

(7) In paragraph 36 of Schedule 1 to the Tribunals and Inquiries Act 1971 (tribunals under direct supervision of the Scottish Committee of the Council on Tribunals) after "36" there shall be inserted "(a)" and at the end there shall be inserted—

"(b) appeal committees set up under section 28D of the Education (Scotland) Act 1980 (c. 44).".

(8) In section 23 of the Local Government (Scotland) Act 1975 (authorities subject to investigation by Local Commissioner), at the end of subsection (2), there shall be inserted the following paragraph—

"(f) any appeal committee set up under section 28D of the Education (Scotland) Act 1980.".

Appeal to sheriff from appeal committee.

28F.—(1) A parent who has made a reference under section 28C of this Act may appeal to the sheriff having jurisdiction where the specified school is situated against the decision of an appeal committee on that reference.

(2) The education authority may, but the appeal committee shall not, be a party to an appeal under this section.

(3) An appeal under this section—

(a) shall be made by way of summary application;

(b) shall be lodged with the sheriff clerk within 28 days from the date of receipt of the decision of the appeal committee (which, if posted, shall, unless the contrary is proved, be presumed to have been received on the day after the date on which it was posted, except that a decision posted on a Friday or Saturday shall, unless the contrary is proved, be presumed to have been received on the Monday next following); and

(c) shall be heard in chambers.

(4) On good cause being shown, the sheriff may hear an appeal under this section notwithstanding that it was not lodged within the time mentioned in subsection (3) above.

(5) The sheriff may on an appeal under this section confirm the education authority's decision if he is satisfied—

(a) that one or more of the grounds of refusal specified in section 28A(3) of this Act exists or exist; and

(b) that, in all the circumstances, it is appropriate to do so

but shall otherwise refuse to confirm their decision and shall, where he so refuses, require the authority to give effect to the placing request to which the appeal relates.

(6) Where the judgment of the sheriff on an appeal under this section is inconsistent with any decision of the education authority (whether confirmed by the appeal committee or not) refusing a placing request to place another child at the same time and at the same stage of education and in the same school as that at and in which the child to whom the judgment relates is to be placed, the education authority shall review their decision so to refuse and shall inform the parent of the other child of their decision upon that review and the reasons for it.

(7) The decision of an education authority upon a review under subsection (6) above not to reverse their decision to refuse the placing request in respect of the other child may be referred to an appeal committee by the parent of the other child as if the decision upon the review were a decision refusing his placing request and the provisions of this Act relating to references of decisions upon

placing requests and appeals therefrom (including those relating to appeal committees) shall apply accordingly.

(8) The sheriff may make such order as to the expenses of an appeal under this section as he thinks proper.

(9) The judgment of the sheriff on an appeal under this section shall be final.

SCHEDULE 1

(TO BE INSERTED IN THE PRINCIPAL ACT AS SCHEDULE A1)

APPEAL COMMITTEES

1. An appeal committee set up under section 28D(1) of this Act shall be constituted in accordance with this Schedule.

2. An appeal committee shall consist of 3, 5 or 7 members nominated by the authority from among persons appointed by the authority under this Schedule; and sufficient persons may be appointed to enable 2 or more appeal committees to sit at the same time.

3. The persons appointed shall comprise—

(a) members of the authority or of the education committee of the authority; and

(b) persons who are not members of the authority or of the education committee of the authority but are—
(i) parents of children of school age;
(ii) persons who in the opinion of the authority have experience in education; or
(iii) persons who in the opinion of the authority are acquainted with the educational conditions in the area of the authority;

but shall not include any person employed by the authority as director of education or as an educational adviser or, in the offices of such director or such adviser, as an assistant (in any capacity) to such director or, as the case may be, such an adviser.

4. The members of an appeal committee who are members of the authority or of the education committee of the authority shall not outnumber the other members of the appeal committee by more than one.

5. A person who is a member of the education committee of the authority shall not be chairman of an appeal committee.

6. A person shall not be a member of an appeal committee for the consideration of a reference of a decision if he was among those who made the decision or took part in or was present at discussions as to whether the decision should be made.

7. A person who is—

(a) a teacher at a relevant school (within the meaning of paragraph 8 below);

(b) a pupil at such a school;

(c) a parent of a pupil at such a school; or

(*d*) a member of a school council having functions in relation to such a school

shall not be a member of an appeal committee for consideration of a reference involving a question whether a child is to be placed in the specified school or excluded from the relevant school.

8. For the purposes of paragraph 7 above, "relevant school" means in relation to a reference to the appeal committee—

(*a*) the school which the child to whom the placing request relates attends;

(*b*) the specified school;

(*c*) the school which the education authority propose that the child to whom the placing request relates should attend;

(*d*) a school from which pupils are normally transferred to the school referred to in sub-paragraph (*b*) or (*c*) above; or

(*e*) the school from which the pupil has been excluded.

9. An appeal committee constituted in accordance with this Schedule shall be included in the bodies to which sections 45(4) and 46 of the Local Government (Scotland) Act 1973 (allowances) apply.

ABBREVIATIONS

ACC	Association of County Councils
AMA	Association of Metropolitan Authorities
CES	Centre for Educational Sociology, University of Edinburgh
COSLA	Convention of Scottish Local Authorities
CSYS	Certificate of Sixth Year Studies
DEO	Divisional Education Officer
DES	Department of Education and Science
DHSS	Department of Health and Social Security
EAC	Education Appeal Committee
EIS	Educational Institute of Scotland
ESRC	Economic and Social Research Council
ILEA	Inner London Education Authority
LEA	Local Education Authority
MP	Member of Parliament
PAL	Planned Admission Limit
PRC	Placing Request Committee
SASPAC	Small Area Statistics Package
SCC	Scottish Consumer Council
SCE	Scottish Certificate of Education
SED	Scottish Education Department
SPTC	Scottish Parent-Teacher Council
TES	Times Education Supplement
TESS	Times Education Supplement (Scotland)

INDEX

accountability, 2

Acts of Parliament

Education Act 1944, 6–10, 20, 28

Education Act 1980, 3,20, 28, 37–8, 49–52, 212+n, 213, 225

Education Reform Act 1988, 212–13, 220

Education (Scotland) Act 1945, 6–10, 20

Education (Scotland) Act 1962, 63, 73

Education (Scotland) Act 1981, 3, 20, 28, 39, 47–52, 58, 91–2, 137, 138, 139; effects *see under* placing requests (effects)

School Boards (Scotland) Act 1988, 212n

Self-Governing Schools etc. (Scotland) Act 1989, 212n

Adler, M., 2, 12, 22, 46n, 88, 159n, 160n, 174, 183, 202, 220n, 223

Adler, R., 5

administrative competence, 22, 106, 222

Admission to School: A Charter for Parents, 45–9, 63, 82

age

meaning of school age, 6+n, 73, 151, 152

under-age admissions, 47, 73–4, 85, 90–1, 139–40, 142–3; appeals over 51, 73–4, 87, 90, 139–40, 142–3, 150–4, 156–8, 162–3

number of requests for 168

Aitken, M., 176n

Alexander, D., 3

Alliance, Liberal/SDP, in Burns Region, 66, 68, 69

appeals, 21–2, 29n, 51, 84–5, 137–64

burden of proof in, 139, 140n, 163

committee composition/ membership, 36–8, 49, 65, 84, 88, 137–8, 145, 150, 155, 157

criteria for deciding, 60–1, 62, 137, 139, 146, 156, 157

effects, 22, 91, 92, 140, 141, 163–4, 222–3, 226

experience of, 141, 143–59

numbers, and numbers upheld, 32, 61, 62, 63, 141–3, 144–5, 150, 156, 157, 159, 161n

over under-age admissions *see under* age

parents' knowledge about, 112

procedures, 38, 138, 139, 145–54, 155–6, 158–9

requirement to review previous cases after, 47, 51, 138

to sheriff, 47, 50–1, 92, 137, 159–64, 223–4, 226; *see also* cases

under 1944/1945 Acts, 9, 15, 32, 40–1, 60–3, 81, 82

Arber, S., 104n

Argyle, M., 135

Asquith, S., 22

Atherton, Graham, 39n, 50n, 116

Baker, Kenneth, 212

Baldwin, R., 2, 6

banding, 14, 29

bandwagon effects, 123, 183, 185, 206, 217

Bankowski, Z., 21

Banting, K., 11

Bastiani, J., 114

Beales, A., 19n, 35n

Beckett, Margaret, 28n

Beith, Alan, 28n

Benn, C., 11, 16

Bennett, Andrew, 28n

Birkenshaw, P., 15, 29

Black Papers, 29

Blaug, M., 19n, 35n

Bondi, L., 12, 32, 88, 183

Borgatta, A., 170

Boyson, Rhodes, 19n, 28n, 35n, 35, 38

Bramley, G., 5

Briault, E., 12, 16

Bridges, D., 95, 134